CH00863238

# PAYING
## for the
# PAST

Geoff Green

There is a small island off the north west coast of Scotland, remote and uninhabited. This is Priest Island. In 1975 two men spent two hundred and sixty-two days there to escape the law.

# 1

# Their Day in Court

The courtroom is packed. My weary legs fold as I take my seat, and silence falls as the judge enters through a side door. Tension rises, quick as a blush, as he adjusts his garb and nods to start the proceedings.

The year is 1976 and I am about to witness the trial of two friends. Many say I should have been arrested with them, because I planned their escape.

But I did not plan their crime.

Despite the change in appearance following a year's deprivation—the gaunt faces, the straggly beards, the long hair—there is no mistaking them. Bellord would be longing to smell real coffee and dump his drab clothes. He needs to be with people again, enjoying good food and intelligent conversation, not in the dock of a criminal court. The judge asks if he has anything to say before being sentenced. Bellord adjusts his broken glasses and looks across at Jim Miller, the man who'd beguiled us all. Miller looks back with an encouraging smile as if to say, *you can do this*. Bellord hesitates, perhaps trying to recall something crucial that might explain their downfall. I thought his stammering was about to return, until he cleared his throat and in a clear educated voice began, 'Things seemed to go wrong when we started helping people...'

The infamous Lord Lucan disappeared in 1974. In 1975 Jim Miller and John Bellord disappeared in a similarly dramatic fashion. The timescale, less than a year between the two mysteries, allowed the media, public and others to speculate they might all be together, hiding in the same place. Yet their crimes were not related and they didn't know each other. So why make the connection? Because, allegedly, they had mutual friends, moved amongst the influential and wealthy and their departures were equally baffling and sudden. Their crimes were so different, yet both wrecked many lives. Lucan accused of murder, Miller and Bellord slipping into a catalogue of disasters from which they, and others, would never recover. In each case the police and Interpol responded to sightings across the globe: Europe, Australia, South Africa and the UK. They could not be traced. Psychics were, reluctantly, called in to help the police but in each case they failed. Lucan was never found. Miller and Bellord might have escaped detection too had it not been for the man who betrayed them as they had betrayed him. Their discovery and bringing to justice would not be quick and it would not be easy, the extent of their crimes only fully realised years after their escape.

My first interview with the police, following Miller and Bellord's failure to return from France, proved unexpectedly benign.

'Do you know anything about Miller and Bellord's disappearance?' asked the detective constable.

'No.' I'd been coached. *Only ever answer the question. Let them do all the work. Don't elaborate, don't be too enthusiastic with your lies, these guys can spot it. Remember body language.*

*Don't smile too much. Appear helpful but not too helpful. If asked for addresses or phone numbers, give them, without hesitation.*

'Where were you at the time they were in France?'

'Up north, working.'

'Doing what?' said the detective, tapping a pencil on his teeth and looking me straight in the eye. Neither of us blinked.

'Arranging a promotional tour for the company.' I left out Emperor Rosko's name, it was too easy to check. Might get away with it.

'Can you prove it?'

'I can give you an itinerary, petrol receipts and motorway stops.' *The M1 at least.* We'd printed a fake itinerary but it wouldn't stand scrutiny.

'I guess that puts them south and you north,' he said, not pressing for paperwork. 'How long have you known Miller?'

'Fifteen years.'

'Have you signed credit agreements?'

'Yes.'

'How many?

'Dozens.'

He raised an eyebrow.

'Any idea what happened to the money?' he continued, leaning closer.

His directness made me want to look away. 'What money?'

'The missing millions,' he said.

'Millions?' I repeated, my jaw ready to drop, 'I had no idea.'

'Really...? That's all for now but we'll need your home address and phone number,' he said, handing me his card. 'If you think of anything, call me—immediately.'

How interesting. I could have sworn I was an honest man. I could not believe the bare-faced manner in which I delivered each deception.

Margaret, Miller's secretary, and business manager John, were left holding the baby: the Sussex mansion where most of the crime had taken place. They rallied staff over the following weeks and we talked late into autumnal nights, melancholy, half pissed on Southern Comfort, the prescribed palliative for the duration it seemed. Occasionally there'd be a little music and a couple would get up and dance. Anything to get us through.

Apart from Marion, who'd known Miller for most of her adult life, no one challenged me about Jim and John's whereabouts. Obviously it came up, but only Marion actually said, 'you know where they are.'

# 2

# Miller

It was inevitable—at least, that's what I thought—that Miller and Bellord would return to Ullapool, once they'd finished their time in prison. They wouldn't have dared come back to the south of England, with an angry horde waiting. There were, I guess, still a hundred or more 'aggrieved', about to face legal proceedings, many in danger of losing everything. They'd be even more upset to learn that Miller and Bellord's sentence had been cut for good behavior, while the rest of us were still fighting the case.

I was certain, beyond any doubt, that Miller and Bellord had managed to get a friend or friends in Ullapool to help them escape from the Island and then protect them for some considerable time. Miller and Bellord could not have done it alone.

Take into account the early years they'd spent holidaying in the area and their proclivity for easy friendships and you have enough reason for them to consider a return to Ullapool. But had they gone back there, following their release in 1979, they'd have been surprised. They'd have stumbled straight into the middle of Operation Klondyke.

The Operation, nothing to do with Miller and Bellord, meant that the place was awash with plainclothes police ready to make the biggest drugs bust the UK has ever seen. Miller and Bellord might even have bumped into some of the officers that searched for them so fruitlessly in 1975. That might have been fun!

The journalist, Eugene Costello, who wrote White Gold, about that very drugs haul, observed: *'Throughout the 70s and 80s, the Highland village of Ullapool was a tough place to make a living. Renowned for its lawlessness—drinking and fighting offered the Friday-night entertainment—it was no place for the squeamish.'*

Ullapool was not exactly the idyllic place Miller and Bellord had fallen in love with earlier. But my story is not about drugs or Operation Klondyke, but it is about scams, blackmail, forgery, banks, bishops and ruined lives, in one of the most bizarre crimes of the century.

Most people who knew me and read the front page headlines, watched the media coverage and listened to the 'Chinese whispers' surrounding Miller and Bellord's arrest, would wonder how on earth I got caught up in such an affair.

Nothing is ever simple. Experiences and family life hardly prepare us for the future. It's always a mystery. But to understand how my past made me ripe for stepping outside the box and into a whole lot of trouble, I need to go back.

'Tell me about your early life. In your own words,' was Miller's stock line and the cue for my downfall. But one day he'd wish he'd never asked about my past and I'd wish I'd never told him. That's for sure.

*

Following protracted bouts of illness that left me feeble and physically underdeveloped, my education finished at fourteen. I slid to position thirty in a class of thirty one. Add to that my early life in a poor Welsh community and the loss of my mother and father at a young age and we may have the answer as to why I'd been psychologically and emotionally primed—groomed some might say—for my relationship with Jim Miller. A few of my friends were convinced he was predatory, gay possibly. The assumption not helped by his affected voice, odd gait and the fact that he lived with another guy, John Bellord. But I was not gay and he never assumed me to be. At least he never asked me about my sexual preferences and I didn't ask him about his.

Miller's hemiplegic gait was caused, so his mother admitted, long after their arrest, by polio. Jim Miller's account of his early misfortune was different. He had, so he'd said, fallen down a metal staircase. What did it matter? He limped with a high-stepping right heel. His right arm, folded and crooked, made him look limp-wristed and affected.

'Perhaps he's a father figure,' ventured my best pal Eddie when he'd heard of my newfound friend, questioning my over-enthusiastic account of meetings with Miller.

'After all, your old man was a bit of a bastard,' he snarled. 'He abused you didn't he?'

'Not really,' I mumbled, unable to recall telling Eddie about Dad. Jilly must have told him. My twin sister was inclined to confide too easily when she'd had a drink.

'I suppose if Dad did things like that now, people would call it abuse: the whacking, the belt, the drunken rages and locking himself in his room.'

'My old man wouldn't dare do that,' said Eddie, adopting a boxer's stance.

His theatrical response made me smile. 'Nowadays I expect we'd have got social services round. But it's what people did back then. Everybody's old man did it. If kids fell out of line or

dad got drunk, you got walloped. And if he slammed doors and
went quiet for a bit, it was no big deal.'

'What about mealtimes? Your sister said that was a bit
weird,' he said, unaware he'd named his source.

I'd be having a long conversation with my twin sister.
'Okay, so I never ate with my dad,' I sighed heavily, to let Eddie
know I was peeved. 'I can't ever remember sitting with him and
eating a meal.' Perhaps I was suffering from false memory
syndrome, it's all the rage now, isn't it? Ironically, one of the
first things I did after meeting Miller was to sit down at a table
and share a simple meal with him. That was about a year after
my father died.

'Bit sad, mate?' said Eddie, gazing into space as if
conjuring up images of my early life.

'Not really, it was what I'd got used to, I never questioned
it. No one questions what they think is normal, do they? Do
you?' I said. A child accepts his environment, however odd it
may appear to others.

'But he abused the girls'. I blurted. 'Now that was abuse,
even then.'

There were three girls in our family but my twin, Jilly,
arrived too late to be part of Dad's seedy practice. We were born
ten years after the others, he was past it then.

Eddie's face coloured, the scar on his cheek stood out like a
slash of chalk. 'Not Jilly?' His breath caught as he mentioned
her name, 'Tell me he didn't touch her,' he said.

Eddie'd always had a soft spot for Jilly. I often wondered if
they'd ever had it off. Perhaps he was horrified that he'd
sampled the spoils of my father's abuse.

'No. But he touched the other two, Babs and Dor,' I said.

'I thought I was your best mate,' he said with a flash of
anger. 'Why didn't you tell me?'

'What was the point?' I didn't want pity and I didn't want

to spend the rest of my time with Eddie having a post mortem on it. We fell uneasily silent.

'What did he do? Whack them. Fondle them?' asked Eddie.

'No, he raped them,' I said, suddenly loose-tongued.

Eddie wrung his hands, checked himself and stuck them in his pockets. 'You never can tell, can you?' he said, sighing deeply, 'I remember your old man tipping his hat to everyone in the street, he always looked so okay, so normal. A bit the worse for wear sometimes—coming out of the King's Arms—but always tidy, clean-shaven, clean-shirted.'

Eddie said this as if to soften the effect my father's crimes were now having on him.

'Always a real gent, my mum used to say,' he continued.

'Not my mum,' I said, 'she had to clean up after him.'

'Did your mum know—about what he did to the girls?'

'Maybe. We'll never know. One thing's for sure, it all stopped when Mum got hit by the motorbike. He went to pieces after that. I'd like to think he felt guilty for giving her such a life. But I doubt it. More likely he was depressed about losing his skivvy, the gentlewoman who cooked his meals, washed his socks and who seemed to have shut her eyes to the things that went on in our house. With all the drinking, he must have been impotent by then, couldn't get it up anymore. But it was too late, he'd already ruined the girls' lives. But I'm damned if he'll ruin mine,' I said, recalling the bittersweet moment when Dad went for me and I grappled him to the floor. Bitter, because I didn't want to hurt him and sweet, because it was the last time he ever raised a hand to me.

'Did your dad ever do anything kind for you?' asked Eddie.

'Course he did.'

'Like what?'

'He bought me a bike,' I said, without elaboration.

One day Dad came from the pub, pushing it. 'I got you this,

son,' he said.

I was over the moon. A week later he gave me an HP repayment card. He'd paid a two pound deposit and expected me to cough up the rest, ten shillings a month. I had to work forty hours a week in a greengrocer's to pay it off. But I had my bike.

'So he could do kind when he wanted to,' said Eddie, his expression softening.

'I guess so,' I said.

No doubt the shrinks would give me a suitable diagnosis for my condition, should I ever turn up for treatment: *Geoff Green suffered emotional deprivation in his early life due, in part, to prolonged absence of one or both parents and abuse of his sisters.*

'What happened to the biker who killed your mum, was he sentenced?' asked Eddie.

'No. The family didn't press charges. The guy was so devastated to hear she'd died, he almost had a breakdown over it. It was an accident. He was driving too close to the kerb. His wheel caught and he mounted the pavement as Mum was crossing.'

Eddie was a biker too. Yet I never worried about hopping on the back of his Norton and going too fast, faster than the bike that killed Mum.

'Dad and I should take some of the blame. We shouldn't have let her go shopping.'

'You can't stop a mum shopping, that's what they do,' said Eddie.

'This time it was different,' I said, picturing the scene clearly and painfully. 'I was building a model boat, the Golden Hind. I remember gluing a trillion matchsticks together. Mum asked if I'd pop across the road and get some spuds and greens for supper. She was up to her eyes in it and Dad was waiting, something he was never much good at.'

Eddie's eyes glazed over, probably wondering where on earth this was going.

'I was working on a tricky bit, the rigging, made out of thin black cotton and a devil to tighten and glue. 'Hang on, Mum— five minutes,' I shouted. Mum didn't wait and as she put her coat on to go, Dad opened his bedroom door.

'Get us a bottle while you're there, Abes.' Don't know why he called her Abes, her name was Amy, sometimes Flo or Floss. She huffed as Dad went back into his room. The front door slammed as she left. That was the last time we saw her alive.

A neighbour ran up three flights of stairs to give us the news that Mum had been knocked down. I had to tell my sisters, who'd gone to the cinema in Acton High Street. On my way out I saw the ambulance arrive. A crowd partly shielded her from my view but I could see between them. Mum was lying still and bloody, half on the pavement, potatoes and greens scattered across the road, scraps of vegetables limp in the gutter. Amongst the debris, completely intact, was Dad's bottle of booze. I felt sick, guilty and angry all at once. I ran up to the Granada cinema about a mile away. The manager flashed a message on the huge screen, interrupting the film. They could do that then, in a crisis. My sisters came out, pale and sobbing. They rushed toward me, grabbing my hand as we all ran home.'

I remember Dad's reaction to Mum dying. It hit him hard. And in his own way, he showed us how devastated he was by drinking more, something we didn't believe possible. That was his reaction to sadness or elation. Drink.

Eddie's smile had left him now. 'So could Miller be a replacement for the dad you never really had?'

'Maybe. I'm sure the psychiatrists would think so. I'd never thought of it like that. He's just an interesting guy who talks to me and seems to know what I'm thinking as if he's known me all my life.'

'Sounds mighty creepy to me. I'd hate the thought of someone knowing what I'm thinking and messing with my brain,' said Eddie, giving an exaggerated shudder.

'He's not exactly messing with my brain, is he?' I snapped, unsure why I was being so edgy. 'Yes, it worried me at first. I wanted to back off and not have anything to do with him, but it was only fear of the unknown, a fear of finding out too much about myself.'

'The unknown is scary. It's unknown for a reason. That's why normal people don't go there,' he said with the air of a seasoned philosopher. 'I can't for the life of me understand what made you go along with it.'

'Miller had the ability to express the things I couldn't, thoughts and dreams we usually keep secret. He was telling me the truth about me and what makes people tick. Sure, it's scary but I wanted to hear it. I think deep down, we all want it straight. But it's not always easy to listen to.'

'Then why bother? Life's tough enough without going down that endless road,' said Eddie.

'Dunno. Something clicked, like he'd turned something on in my mind that I couldn't turn off. It kept me awake, made me think. I'm hooked,' I smiled.

'You're fucking mad, mate,' said Eddie, summing up the situation.

'Maybe.' No change for the Green family there then. Looking back, his diagnosis was probably right.

Eddie was afraid of anything a bit too deep, didn't believe in all that psychology or religious stuff. Bullshit, he'd labelled it. That's why he was so easy to be with. What you saw was what you got, no frills, just a straightforward, uncomplicated pal. He was army through and through, a boxer, a hard man with a soft centre. The scar over his left eye was from a head blow that nearly blinded him. He laughed at the memory. It was his bravery medal and he was proud of it.

On our most memorable days, he'd get me to sit on the back of his Norton motorbike and do a ton along the Great West Road. No helmets then. 'And don't hold on,' he'd say, 'people will think you're a girl.' Then he'd whoop YEEHAW as we swerved past fast cars and long trucks. I'd got off feeling sand-blasted and shaken, but very much alive.

I showed Eddie a picture of Miller's house. He grunted, pretending no interest.

'I'd be asking myself some serious questions if I were you,' he whispered.

'Like what?'

'What would a rich, intelligent, professional bloke want with scumbags like us? We're council house, uneducated street kids. You can't possibly have anything in common. And what's he getting out of it? Think about it; old wealthy guy approaches young poor guy.

Why?'

# 3

# The Crooked Man

Not too long after that conversation, Eddie decided to make the army his career. He was moved around, did stints abroad and we lost touch. Throughout the coming years I'd have given anything to have had him around. I could have done with his straight talking and a bit of therapeutic sandblasting on the back of his Norton. No religion, no psychology, just living the moment.

I'd dismissed the idea that God might be a giant with a beard sitting on a cloud, pointing where we should be heading and zapping those who didn't keep in line. I needed an explanation that stood up to scrutiny but concluded that we all had the same black hole in our lives: something missing that we chose to fill with distractions.

Throughout life we get put on the spot: fill in forms, attend interviews, and get asked what religion we are. Some of us know we don't really have a religion but our courage fails us when confronted directly, so we put down C of E or Christian.

As children we are mesmerized by some of the believers we bump into. It's their utter conviction that enchants us. My uncle Will, for example, a round, kindly man with the polished red cheeks of a monk, always wore a beatific smile and a grey trilby.

His passions were laverbread and the Baptist Church. A Welshman who knew his bible inside out. He carried it everywhere and quoted passages at anyone who stood still long enough to listen. To everyone who knew him, he was saintly, but unbending in his belief that only Baptists were the true followers of God. That scared me. Anyone who was so certain of anything scared me. Uncle Will appeared tolerant of everyone but was, in fact, humouring those not of his belief. He smiled like an angel because, I guess, that's what he thought he was.

I was twenty one in 1962, married, and newly employed as a builder's labourer. My first job was to paint a pair of wrought-iron gates that guarded the stable block of a grand house. Honeywood House or The House as we called it, stood in Sussex countryside at the end of a long elm-lined drive with an entrance lodge. Vast lawns skirted a sunken rose garden and faded out toward lush downland. The House was magnificent, a twenty six bedroom country mansion previously owned by the wealthy, but odd, Lord Tredegar. Now it was a luxury nursing home from which Jim Miller and John Bellord also ran an alternative healing practice.

The very first day I was there, Miller crossed the courtyard from the main house in such haste, I thought I might be in trouble. I'd heard he was eccentric and his quick limping gait, crooked arm and immaculate appearance, unsettled me further. But his friendly smile soon dispelled all fears. He offered his hand, which I shook. He looked at me as a child would, direct, innocent. And as with a child's gaze, he appeared to see things an adult could never see. We entered a conversation that would influence the rest of my life. It would be the start of a deep and lasting friendship. But nothing lasts forever.

There were none of the niceties of polite introductions, the how do you do's, the what are you doing? And what a great day.

A wide mouth smile split his face, lips curling at the edges exaggerating the expression further. Oddly, it reminded me of the Joker in Batman, but not at all sinister.

He talked and asked totally unexpected questions. Considering it was our first meeting, I found it all very odd.

'I'm due to see the Bishop,' he started, indicating toward the House parking area before checking his watch.

'Do you believe in God or religion?' he enquired. 'Most people don't these days.'

He must have noted my wary look.

'Please don't take the question too seriously. I ask everyone, it's an interest of mine. I want to see how people react when they're put on the spot. So much more revealing, I always think.'

I wasn't annoyed that he'd caught me off guard but thought this might be the religious bit: the hook, the con, to get me to join some religious group or cult. I hesitated, not sure how to say what I really felt. We'd only just met, even my closest family and friends weren't aware of my ideas about spiritual stuff. I am uncomfortable with the word spiritual anyway. It conjures up visions of a philosophical snob with yet another belief system, bragging about their revelatory rite of passage as if they and their followers had solved the riddle of what we are all searching for.

He checked his watch again. 'Go ahead, tell me what you think. The Bishop's late.'

'It's not so much that I believe in anything particular so much as I believe in a bit of everything.'

He laughed. 'How interesting.'

'Right from when I was a kid reading fairy tales and later when I read books about spirituality and stuff I could see some truth in most of it. It's so confusing.'

Miller looked pleased. He took out his pipe and drew on it

slowly like he was sucking words and ideas out of the freshly lit tobacco.

'I only came to paint your gates...' I wanted to say. By then it was too late. He showed me the twenty-six bedroom house, the acres of ground, the stables, the Aston Martin and Rolls in the garage and the treatment rooms he used for his exclusive patients, before revealing he'd never been educated. He'd never been to school, because he'd spent his childhood and early adulthood in a wheelchair and on crutches. By sheer determination and desire, he learned to walk again and in the process, found his 'inner self'. His 'magnificent obsession', he called it. Something so powerful, he wanted to share the experience with others and, apparently, he wanted to share it with me right now. He wanted others to have what he had. 'When you discover that force deep inside,' he said, 'you can do anything and be afraid of nothing.'

Half an hour later the Bishop arrived.

I felt strange, as if waking from a half dream and, in the light of day, knew I had choices in my life. My initial enthusiasm was followed by a deep depression when I left the House that day. I couldn't sleep that night. I couldn't talk to my wife about my conversation with Miller, but somehow I knew that my life was about to change. That was the start of the rollercoaster years that would take us all headlong into incredible times and the insidious crime that followed.

# 4

# The House

So why tell the story now, decades later? Because things happened and life, *the thing that gets in the way of our plans*, as John Lennon so cleverly put it, led me back to the crime.

My brothers and sisters were gone, all dead and buried. Even twin sister Jilly, the strong one who always fought my corner, had died at fifty eight of a heart attack. A broken heart I think, from supporting a drug-addicted son who lived at home and made her life a misery. She kept that awful truth from me until just before she died.

Nothing would have kept my sister from her job. She was committed and driven to making that huge office run like clockwork. One day she didn't turn up. The police called at her flat and had to break down the door. She was lying peacefully in bed, arms folded across her chest, like the stone effigy of a lady in a cathedral, as if she'd been prepared for death.

Jilly's death was the hardest to bear. They say that about twins, don't they? That special bond that makes the relationship different from all others. Life seemed more fragile than ever, so temporary, so transient.

Now time was flying. My children and grandchildren were

growing up fast. The years with Carol, who was to become my second wife, rocketed by. A desire to meet Miller and Bellord again, haunted me. Perhaps Miller was a replacement father figure after all, some strict guiding patriarchal light. He'd be ninety now and I was approaching my seventieth. I wanted us to forgive each other, accept that we were all trying to be good men until our ambition overload muddied the waters of true purpose.

But while I was meditating, over weeks and months, the producer of a film company, Cineflix, rang me and wanted an interview for a documentary they were making about Miller and Bellord. I said yes and Amanda Sealy, the producer, came down to Sussex to interview me.

Over many months and after many production and post-production problems, I received a rough edit of the programme. I slotted the DVD into my computer. Familiar faces stared back at me from the screen: Norman Luck, the original crime reporter from the Daily Express who broke the story and gave it front page news, Detective Constable Dave Fickweiler of the Sussex Fraud Squad, Bob Cracknell, the psychic detective, and myself. The episode was presented by Hermione Norris of Spooks fame, a high profile TV show. Seeing this 'snapshot' of our adventure, prompted me to rewrite my story and take even more serious steps to find Miller. I wanted to know if we could ever forgive each other's betrayal.

The *gate painting moment*, I like to call it, happened while I was working for Harry Moore Builders. In between times I introduced Miller to my wife Tanya. We'd been together forever, since our teens. We met at the time I was singing with a skiffle group and a pop band in west London. Tanya didn't take to Jim Miller. She sensed what I couldn't, that I was in danger of drifting away from her. She was frightened of losing me to a passion that was taking me outside our cosy, conventional world and it really troubled her. The 'obsession' with Miller and his philosophy produced unease in our marriage that lasted until our divorce in 1980.

It sounds as if John Bellord had less of an impact on my life than Miller, but he was one of my heroes. His appearance, a cross between Trevor Howard and Kenneth More, coupled with a jaunty walk, gave him the air of a cinema hero. He came from a wealthy Catholic family who, as it turned out, didn't take to Miller either. They were particularly critical of the hold he seemed to exert over John Bellord, who eventually left his family and gave up a promising future in his father's engineering business. John Bellord was talented with a truly extraordinary intellect, a photographic memory and an astute business sense, and he was great fun. His communication and negotiating skills were enviable. And, as if that wasn't enough, he was an ace tennis player and an accomplished racing driver. He once took me up the M1 in the Aston Martin, at 180mph. There was no speed limit and no night traffic then.

So Miller, forever in the spotlight, could only fulfill his dreams through John Bellord's tireless support and extraordinary ability to take Miller's ideas and run with them.

Miller, always eager to talk about his childhood deprivation and the 'spiritual awakening' that helped him out of a wheelchair, saw his disability as an opportunity to meditate and access his 'true inner self'. But there was more to it than overcoming personal hardship as a means of growing into a more sensitive and enlightened human being. He helped others toward more fulfilling lives. He had a mission and nothing would stop him.

He attracted people from all walks of life: bishops, bankers, politicians, celebrities, the police, the sick, the criminal and us ordinary Joes who fitted somewhere in between. Most people would be scared of immersing themselves in this potpourri of humanity, fearful that they'd be attacked or robbed or done down in some way. Not Miller. He'd connect in a remarkable way, by observing their crimes and misdemeanors as nothing more than routine aberrant behavior, beings expressing themselves wrongly due to circumstance. Did anyone rob him or cheat him? Of course, and he expected it, but it didn't stop him gaining respect for the most part and a successful relationship with his fellow man or woman, sending them on their way with a positive and lasting experience.

His private patient list was growing, some were undoubtedly wealthy. He was an adept problem-solving psychologist and in constant demand. The rich gave generously, the less well-off paid nothing.

Miller would often spend a whole morning with a patient, encourage them to talk, find out what made them tick and discover what they really wanted from life. Then he'd devise the best treatment plan, heavily biased toward 'talking therapy'. He'd use other approaches from alternative and complementary therapies, some considered weird or downright whacky. 'There is a treatment for every patient', he used to say. 'And it was worth spending a little time fitting the patient to the therapy before starting a course of treatment.'

Diet, psychosomatics, iridology, radionics, meditation, homeopathy, vitamin supplements, and good old fashioned positive thinking. But he warned against the dangers of 'milking' the positive thinking bit. Appearing positive all the time disguises reality, he said. It gives people the impression that things are well when they are not or it can disguise lack of ability, particularly true if you have a position of power.

His inspirational story convinced patients that health and wealth were in their own hands. However, the cynics needed a little more convincing. But isn't it easy to believe something fresh and new? And if the new is delivered by an enigmatic, articulate and wealthy character, it seems doubly convincing. Like the kind of 'self-perpetuating' propaganda that new politicians or bosses use to stimulate others.

Miller postulated that those who worship money or power will do anything to get it. How then, does one go about alerting these materialistic cynics to their true inner selves, something, if they were religious, they already thought they had access to? The recipe for Miller's wakeup call was to show them that making money was simply a direction of energy and desire. Then tell them it is worth nothing without 'inner peace' or whatever name you care to give it. And once the penny dropped, people would gradually become more altruistic and philanthropic.

There were no powerful healthcare regulatory bodies then. You could be whatever you wanted to be: hypnotist, healer or medicine man. And that was, more or less, the way it's been since the dawn of time. But how anyone roots out the charlatan from the honest guy is anyone's guess. It's not what you believe, but that you believe, or so it seems. Your own brain and innate healing power does the rest.

Miller laboured the point over and over again, that the quirky ideas and beliefs of today often turn out to be tomorrow's science. 'Think of it', he would start, 'many of the things people didn't believe in, findings that were dismissed, ridiculed and rejected as science fiction, turned out to be true. That the earth was round, for example, that the telephone or television, 'would never catch on'. That DNA, a map of our genetic makeup, could ever be used to catch criminals or manipulate cells. Space travel? Impossible in a century that, earlier, decided that car and train travel was too fast and end in disaster. All were rejected as preposterous but all started off as an idea, an intuitive thought.'

I learnt fairy quickly that Miller was a natural born healer, if there was such a thing. And that his variety of therapies, were simply tools or stage props for the benefit of patients.

'Oh yes,' they would say, 'I had homeopathy, it was marvellous.' Or, 'He had this amazing new therapy, radionics: he takes a spot of blood and tunes you in on a machine.'

Or, he changes a diet here, teaches some psychosomatics there. All valid therapies in their own right, I'm sure. But I honestly believed that Miller had a unique healing power, and a power for influencing others in a mesmeric way.

The closest I can come to a snapshot of Miller as a flesh and blood character and his way of working is to picture Lionel Logue, the eccentric Australian speech therapist portrayed by Geoffrey Rush in the film *The King's Speech*, immaculately dressed, unqualified, quirky, dynamic, irreverent, reviled by the medical establishment and the establishment in general, but so effective in getting results. His therapy, like Miller's, took patience, and required dedication from his patients. Miller, like Logue, laid claim to an unorthodox treatment for stammering, he'd 'cured' John Bellord of the same affliction many years ago.

Gradually my interest in Miller's teachings, philosophy, psychology and self-belief, started to produce practical results. This was how it worked with virtually everyone he met. He got to us all. With my new found confidence, I started my own company and with my old friend, Albert Reynolds, created a building and shop-fitting company, 'Reynolds, Green, Builders and Shopfitters Ltd.' I then had more control of my time and, consequently, spent more of it with Miller and Bellord.

It was an exciting day when the directors of Reynolds, Green were summoned to a meeting with Miller and Bellord. We walked through the grand hall to their office, a spacious high-ceilinged room overlooking the sunken rose gardens and the downs beyond. The room flooded with daylight from all sides, courtesy of huge leaded glass windows, stretching from the low, wide window seats to the ornate ceiling cove.

Miller and Bellord greeted us warmly with friendly smiles and firm handshakes.

'Please take a seat,' said John Bellord, as he handed Miller some notes.

Miller studied them for a moment. 'We've got a lot of work for you. You might need more help,' he said.

Albert and I looked at each other and grinned. 'We can easily get more men,' I said, mentally running through our list of reliable tradesmen.

'I want a lot of alterations done on the House,' he started. 'I want the stable block converted to flats, so that some of the staff have a better place to live. I want the whole of the exterior paintwork done: repairs, a new sun lounge and more. Come with me,' he said, puffing hard on his pipe as he led us at a pace out of the House. 'The nursing home is doing well and everything needs to be right. A first impression helps fill it.'

We walked across the courtyard to look at one of the projects and heard raised voices from the open kitchen window. It was common knowledge, at least with those who knew the House, that Miller employed an excellent Chinese cook, Chong. He had an English wife, gambled his wages, threw utensils across the kitchen and drank too much. Miller also employed Chinese kitchen staff and had caravans installed in the grounds of the House, over on the west meadow, behind an unkempt high-walled garden. He fed and paid them. He also took on the odd reformed ex-con, or vagrant, to clean the House, help in the kitchen, or garden or act as auxiliary to the nurses. No matter what their past, he was out to change their world.

Miller showed us the stable blocks he wanted converted then took us to a place we'd never been, his personal accommodation. The tiny studio flat set between two out-buildings, surprised us. The very male studio, smelling of tobacco and old leather, was tasteful but modest. Whitewashed walls, a couple of red hide chairs, a Chesterfield, a large glass-topped coffee table and a York stone fireplace, above which hung an old original landscape painting. And that was about it. The kitchen, more like a galley, was modest but functional. The place was immaculate. I learnt later, that Miller and Bellord did their own cleaning.

'Small, isn't it?' he smiled, 'It's everything we need.'

I was impressed. He lived so modestly yet owned a mansion to spread himself out in. His philosophy was becoming more credible by the day. The trappings, so it seems, were a means to a philanthropic end, employing and helping people rather than the accumulation of wealth.

It was an education to observe Miller and Bellord working together, Bellord the intellectual, Miller the impulsive, intuitive philosopher.

Miller asked me to call at his flat the next day and pick up the keys to the barn. At eight a.m. he was up, ready and formally dressed. His dark hair, a few streaks of grey at the side, neatly slicked back. He wore a dark pinstripe suit that looked Saville Row but was in fact Marks and Spencer (I'd seen his jacket on a chair in the office the day before). And a shirt so startlingly white, it must have been bleached.

Back at the House we discussed further projects for Reynolds, Green. Miller pressed tobacco into his briar, clicked a lighter with his crooked fingers and puffed away. He stood for a moment, watching the smoke rise, then looked at me. 'Never be too harsh on those of us who need our little crutches to get through life,' he laughed, waving his pipe. 'Do you know what this is?'

*A pipe?* I thought sarcastically.

'It's a grown-up's dummy,' he said, roaring with laughter.

It was something he did often: give psychological explanations for what or why people did things. What tricks and props they used to get through life. It brought things down to earth, made everyone seem flawed and human and reassured us that we were all in the same boat, even the enigmatic, incredible Jim Miller.

He was quick to point out what sheep we all were, easily influenced by advertising and propaganda. How a strong persuasive character can make a weaker one do things against their will. As if on cue, a nurse interrupted us. She was signing off, on her way home and handed Jim a set of notes. She wore a grey dress.

'I thought you hated grey,' said Miller.

'Everyone is wearing it now,' she said, smoothing down her dress before leaving.

Some dude in a fashion house in another country had got this girl to wear a colour she'd hated.

# 5

# The Eccentrics

There were strict instructions on how to proceed with the alterations, but no plans. In all the time we worked at the House, planning permission was never applied for. Flats for the Chinese staff were to be built on two floors. The upper floor, built around a newly constructed minstrels' gallery, would overlook a huge Chinese mural depicting scenes of life in China. Miller wanted them to feel at home.

We were congratulated on our efforts and invited to a party at the House. Informal dress, nothing fussy. Tanya and I arrived at seven. The Chinese chef had produced a scrumptious buffet for over a hundred people. We felt out of it. Miller crossed quickly through the crowd to greet us.

We knew some of the staff. Matron Joan Sparrow, secretary Margaret Cutler, chauffeur Johnny Farnton and Harry, the new chauffeur for the Roller. Harry, an ex-con we learnt later, had somehow managed to acquire an official Rolls Royce cap and badge. Roy Plomley of Desert Island Discs fame was there, bishops, racing drivers, detective inspector so and so, heads of finance companies, bank managers, singers from the Royal Opera House, Robin Richmond from the BBC, plus the man who delivered the groceries, the gardeners, nurses, cleaners. All introduced as if they moved in the same circles.

It was extraordinary. Miller spent as much time with us 'poor' people as he did with the wealthy and famous. He really did seem to think of us as his flock, each needing help or guidance. Even now, I don't think this camaraderie was some grand design for what happened over the years to come. But I do believe that the ease with which Miller attracted people from such diverse backgrounds, the good, the bad and the ugly, meant that eventually, something was bound to go wrong.

Matron Joan had the gift of generating light, easily felt by those around her. She was in at the start of Miller's project, perpetuating his magnificent obsession. She gave up everything, including her job. Joan sold up and donated all her worldly wealth to help finance Miller's work. Over time she politely questioned some of Miller's ideas and found herself excluded from his close circle. It was all history by the time I joined 'the club', so I would never quite know the full story. Looking back it seems as though Joan might have been too dogged with her questioning.

Despite the cooling relationship, there were moments of materialistic generosity toward Joan. Not long after my introduction to Miller, he suggested replacing Joan's old banger of a Saab, with which she was perfectly comfortable, with something better. To see the petite matron cruise up the House drive in a new Mercedes Sports seemed as out of place as if Mother Teresa was driving it. She was so self-conscious and embarrassed to be seen by the staff and patients that Miller conceded defeat and opted for a more conservative motor.

Other things were going on. A brick stable, fairly close to the main house, had been converted into a small chapel for residents and staff of the nursing home. The Bishop, the same one who visited Miller the day we first met, performed a blessing and declared the chapel 'fit for use'. A gable-end wall was knocked through to take a sizeable stained glass window. Because it faced east, the morning sun shone through, lighting up the speaker with an ecclesiastical glow. Miller and Bellord became lay preachers.

Miller commandeered a vagrant helper to act as altar boy and insisted on him wearing a surplice and cassock. Malcolm, an ex-Borstal lad who worked in the kitchen, fancied taking part in a church service. Malcolm was how I imagined Dickens's Bill Sykes: someone who, even clean-shaven, appeared dark-jowled, with a boxer's nose, thick, black unkempt hair and heavy brows. Before his 'inauguration' while some of us were having coffee in the staff room, Malcolm, in his church regalia, flopped into the nearest chair and propped his feet on a coffee table. The sudden movement caused his purple cassock to part, revealing a huge Bowie knife strapped to his calf. He smiled at our look of horror. 'Wherever I go, so does my baby. I've been caught out before,' he laughed, patting the weapon affectionately. No one challenged him and no one told Miller.

These capricious characters would sometimes steal from the House or get into trouble with the law. Miller saw them as struggling human beings, not criminals. 'Those ill or in hospital have been wrongly repressed, those in prison have been wrongly expressed,' he'd say, *ad infinitum.*

Reynolds, Green could have set up home here, we had so much work. Nearly all our tradesmen were being kept busy as Miller dreamt up more and more projects. He would often take me aside to talk about psychosomatics. The way the mind affects health was of particular interest but he warned about the 'unhealthy' pursuit of health, when people exercise, diet and attempt to reach perfect fitness by physical and regimental means. Fitness alone does not necessarily mean good health. It was easy for me to miss the point.

I didn't know a great deal about the House or its history. Miller gave us a tour of the grounds, the sixteen acres and gaggle of out-buildings. The north side of the House faced an extensive well-cared for lawn which ended abruptly at dense forest. Just outside that interface, stood an underground building known as the ice house. It had been used, Miller said, for a wine cellar, but filled in by previous builders and the heavy oak door wedged shut. Grains of soft dust, lime and cement, leaked out from between the door and frame, leaving a thick powdery line. It was the first time since my association with the House that I'd felt anything other than warmth and friendliness. It gave off a cold chill and others had noticed it too. Okay so it was an ice house for cooling wine, but how was it possible to feel this chill after it had been completely filled in, and on a summer's day while standing two yards away?

We continued our tour. He showed us the summer house, where the chef stored vegetables, and were told not to keep our paint in it. The summer house was eccentric, if that can be said of a building. Made from half split, burnished logs, the walls incorporated a series of detailed leaded lights depicting garden birds. Each window portrayed a different scene, an intricate work of art, lavish considering it was a glorified garden shed. And if one believes houses have souls and that memories can be passed down through their walls, then this was indeed a remarkable place.

Lord Evan Tredegar, an immensely rich aristocrat, poet and painter, had previously owned the House. Tredegar was also a pilot, gourmet, parliamentary candidate, diplomatic attaché, journalist, a major in the military and in the employ of the secret service, MI8 (Military Communication Interception). Evan Tredegar was known as the ultimate fixer, he knew everybody and was chamberlain to the Pope, an advisor on art to the Royal Family and rumoured to be Queen Mary's favourite bohemian.

Tredegar, who also knew the Nazi Rudolph Hess, was occasionally referred to as, 'The High Priest of Black Mass' because of his occult connections and association with Aleister Crowley, The Beast. He also knew Dylan Thomas, Walter Sickert, Augustus John, Gore Vidal, HG Wells, Aldous Huxley, Terrence Rattigan, Noel Coward and the Sitwells.

Both Evan and his mother Katherine loved birds, but she was obsessed and spent much of her time making birds' nests, using the materials her avian friends would use. She once made a nest big enough to sit in! As far as we know, it was Katherine who commissioned the building of the delicate summer house. It still stands, watertight and cosy as a bird's nest, now storing vegetables in the grounds of the House.

I didn't know about the Tredegars when I first met Miller in 1963. Had I done so I might have thought history was repeating itself and that houses are capable of reincarnation; because Miller also appeared to know everyone, threw grand parties and made life more fun for us all. He seemed every bit as eccentric as Tredegar himself.

There were times, before I met Miller, when I was sure my life was going the way it was supposed to. I was married to the woman I loved, had my newly born son Mark and was looking forward to more kids. There was a future out there for me in the building trade. I'd learned more skills and started my own business. We had good friends and an active social life but rather too much partying and dancing for my liking. Tanya loved that and I wanted her to be happy. But once Miller started talking about the endless possibilities awaiting the eager soul, that life could be anything you wanted it to be, I knew I'd been kidding myself. From here on I would be living two lives, like a dividing human cell, both parts having the same genetic information but destined for different tasks.

Miller, Bellord and I were in the office. I'd been invited to a demonstration of radionics. Miller took a blood sample from me, placed the slide on a pad and scanned it electronically.

I was waiting for something to happen, a mild electric shock or wave of some sort of energy.

'Best to explain this simply,' he started, buttoning up his crisp white coat. 'Each person has a vibration. Think of it as something like the precise frequency of a radio station. That vibration is peculiar to each individual and it shows up electronically on this diagnostic machine.'

*How?* I may have looked sceptical but I was fascinated.

'When that person is ill or out of balance in some way, that shows up too, like static on a badly-tuned radio station. But we can tune them back in.'

*Yeah?*

'We have to believe in something extraordinary to make any sense of it: that we are all operating in a universe that is so intrinsically linked and so subtle that science has yet to discover, and may never discover, its physics or chemistry.'

Metaphysics, the theoretical philosophy as the ultimate science of being and knowing, interested me. Two words stand out for the sceptics, speculation and theoretical, because metaphysics is based on another's experience and thinking. Einstein and Stephen Hawking show how extraordinary things are being discovered daily. Not just extraordinary things, unbelievable things, and in no time at all, we take them for granted.

'Not having discovered something does not mean it isn't there,' added Miller. 'It may be centuries before we understand stuff fully at this level. But be encouraged,' he said, aware of my doubts, 'Radionics wasn't thought up by some crank, some crazy weirdo. It was developed by an eminent doctor, Albert Abrams, who believed in the subtle balance of the human body as reflected in our blood. He was a wealthy man who spent a great deal of his life pursuing research, without funding. He was a master of observation, a tireless experimenter and truth-seeker. His fundamental discovery was that, under certain conditions, the human nervous system will react to the energy-field of external elements such as persons with disease conditions, samples of disease tissue etc. All this stuff follows the principles of physics,' he declared.

It was too much to swallow. He proceeded to tell me about a recent patient, an elderly lady from a wealthy family. This story turned up again in a BBC documentary about Miller in 1980. The woman's illness appeared undiagnosable and untreatable. The family were at their wits' end. Her young nephew had heard about Miller and his remarkable healing practice. Without the rest of the family knowing, the nephew managed to obtain a pin-prick of blood and sent it to Miller who 'tuned' her in over the next few days. The family witnessed a remarkable recovery. Doctors could not explain what had happened, except to assume she'd had a remission. 'There could be no other explanation,' they'd concluded.

Well, who knows?

Miller's successes were frequent and dramatic. If he was a catalyst for something extraordinary in people's lives, that was good enough for me. And, so it seems, good enough for those who flocked to him and parted with their money. If this went on now, Derren Brown, the celebrity illusionist and 'guru buster', might have done a programme on it and blown the whole thing as a theatrical con. But would he? Once he'd shot the footage and edited the results, I think he may have had to stop it going on air (in Derren's programme, *Miracles for Sale*, he exposed greedy faith healers who set out to make money and fool people) because, as far as I know, Miller never took money from the poor, rather, he gave it. I was convinced, particularly in retrospect, that all he did was tap into people's minds and lives in order to heal and help. The array of healing therapies Miller practiced and used were simply a hook on which to hang true healing power. He was, I think, something akin to a human placebo.

Miller asked me what I thought of his practices, his ideas.

'I don't understand them, but I am interested,' I admitted, my mind swaying between belief and a laughable scepticism.

'You shouldn't expect to understand too much. All difficult ideas have to be taught and learned before one begins to comprehend. Every day I learn something new, every hour probably. Not just for patients, about myself too. That's what life is about, learning and not being afraid of things we don't understand.

I'm convinced there are good, genuine people out there, thinking outside the box 'beyond science' and helping people in extraordinary ways. But who are they? Probably they are the subtle healers who do what they do without fanfare or without seeking wealth or power.

I mentioned bishops, the chapel and lay preaching but not Miller's take on religion. He took what he believed to be the core of truth in each, but rejected the parts twisted by men seeking power for their own gain. Propaganda. That interesting word and practice goes back centuries, born out of the need for the Church to obtain power, mostly by deception, a persuasive mix of admission or omission. Spin, as it's called today.

Miller was acutely aware of the religious and spiritual propaganda that pervades religion, but his heart was, 'with Jesus'. He believed in the man, his teachings, the sacrifices he made and the reason he walked the earth. It seemed that the bishops knew about Miller's eclectic beliefs and distrust of 'organised religion'. The bishops didn't appear threatened, but then Miller was never antagonistic. Maybe that is why they were drawn to him. There was something, innocent, naive, but so basically honest and true that they could well believe their own narrow path might be a poor imitation of Miller's.

Although he was an Anglican lay preacher, Miller wasn't a true Anglican nor did he belong to any religious denomination, he had plenty to say and the pulpit suited him. And the only way into a pulpit was to adopt a religion. He never prepared a sermon. Whilst the service was going on, he would look around the congregation, absorb the atmosphere, and home in on one or two members of the congregation who drew his attention. Then he'd climb the pulpit steps, take an unhurried look around and start his sermon. It could be about anything but it always struck a chord. He was a master of the spontaneous and the particular.

# 6

# Meditation and Money

Body language. Miller was big on that too.

'See that man leaning against the wall?'

'Yeah,' I said, as the figure moved off at an unhurried pace.

'Anything wrong with him?'

'Bit scruffy?'

'He's given up, had enough of life. He's young yet his shoulders are sagging. He can't hold himself up. He moves like someone three times his age, with little energy, worn down by the life he's living. The old canvas bag he's clutching is greasy and frayed but there are no workman's tools in it, only a bundle of papers sticking out. He's an academic. And if you get close enough to see his eyes, I'll take bets, they will be dull and his speech mono-tonal.'

'Maybe he's just finished a tough night shift, or had a row with his wife. Or got a hangover,' I said, in the poor chap's defence.

Miller tilted his head and smiled lopsidedly at my reasoning. 'Check it out if you want. Ask him the time or something; then you'll see it too. I dare you.'

I didn't. Perhaps I should have done. But I knew Miller was

right because after staring at the guy for a few seconds, I swear, I could feel his despair.

Miller proceeded to tell me extraordinary things about how body language reflects how and where you are in your life. How it can make you virtually invisible or turn people's heads when you enter a room. This was hard to swallow, Lord of the Rings stuff, but Miller had something of the Gandalf about him.

Miller proved the 'disappearing act' to be true on a number of occasions over the years. He'd been in a room full of people, yet I'd no idea he was there. He'd change his posture, lower his head a little, walk slowly and sit quietly in a corner. Most of the time he'd energise a room with his entrance, his fast-walking limp, head high, intelligent eyes sweeping the room, people would turn toward him. And that made others invisible.

This extraordinary uneducated man admitted to only reading a few books in his time. But he did cite Jack London's *White Fang*, about a dog and the triumph of good over evil, as a read worth the effort.

Peter and the Wolves, the pop group I sang with, were invited to perform at the House. The band were all younger than me, all at university. Anyone studying at university for a degree was a god. As with the powerful and wealthy, guys who'd had a university education intimidated me. I felt inferior, often struck dumb by the depth and anguish of my inferiority.

We were all nervous about the reception our music would get—mainly Beatles and rock with some rhythm and blues and a few ballads—performed in front of bishops and bankers. Surely they'd want opera or the classics. Though Miller was keen, it didn't mean everyone else would be. To make it as light as possible we put in as many ballads as we could muster. They all seemed to enjoy it, a little foot tapping here and there and a burst of enthusiastic applause at the end. Or were they being polite?

Miller was a bit taken aback by the volume but you can't hold back enthusiastic young musicians.

Expensive cars were a constant in their lives. There was a pecking order: the Mercedes, a solid, reliable car but not too flashy, for seeing the bank manager and local businessmen. The Rolls Royce and chauffeur for the big guns: heads of finance companies, conservative millionaire business men. The Ferraris and Aston Martins for like-minded souls, men who loved speed, cars and even more money: the Brands Hatch, Silverstone and Goodwood gang.

Little Harry, the Rolls driver, loved cars too. He'd polish and tend to the Roller like it was a baby needing constant care. Even waiting for Miller and Bellord to cross the courtyard from the House, he'd flick a lambswool pad over invisible dust on the bonnet, or polish a wing mirror he'd tended to only moments earlier. Harry was a nervous guy, acutely aware of his dodgy past and no doubt grateful for his turn of fortune. Whenever Miller and Bellord approached he'd snap smartly to attention, raising himself to his full five feet two. His hunched shoulders, quick darting eyes and birdlike features reminded me of a baby vulture.

Miller and Bellord didn't just own and drive cars, they fine-tuned them. They were brilliant mechanical problem-solvers and had turned some of the outbuildings into luxury garages. The tasteful conversions were fitted out with pits and ramps and held half a dozen cars. They had the latest state of the art diagnostic equipment and their own petrol pump fed from an underground tank, filled up by Shell when required.

But Miller also had enemies; the orthodox, the sceptics who called him a quack, the allopathic medical establishment who must have felt threatened that some upstart was suddenly making their patients better. Rephrase that, some unqualified upstart was making their patients better. Others thought he was a gay egotist seeking reputation and money. Miller didn't care and dismissed them all for their narrow, fearful attitude toward his 'search for truth' and pioneering health care.

Did it really matter what form the cure took, whether it was medicine, radionics, a plant, mind medicine, love or simply an idea shared? If it connected in some way (we'll never quite know how) and the patient got better, that surely, is it.

Miller demonstrated the power of thought in a number of ways. Psychosomatics and meditation were high on his list. He could lower his blood pressure by meditating and entering a deep state of relaxation. I thought it a great trick and was completely cynical—until I learnt how to do it. Psychologically it was a reversal of the 'white coat syndrome' where blood pressure goes up when visiting the GP. If it works in that situation, common sense tells us it must work in reverse, all it needs is a little training, a little mental application.

Miller felt passionately about karma, metaphysics and cause and effect. His explanations were simple. Life goes on and we have lessons to learn. And like being at school, if we fail to grasp something, we have to work through the problem until we solve it. Reincarnation, an explanation for why we are all in different stages of evolution and suffer differently because we need to come back and finish what we started, seemed equally difficult to understand. But it had some attraction because the concept did not require an association with religion.

As a child, I'd always struggled with Christianity and found it hard to contemplate Jesus Christ as a catalyst for such chaos. Catholics hating Protestants, Methodists getting 'uppy' about their little corner, the Anglicans even more superior, the anti-Semitism, the shunning of those outside a particular church and the subsequent withdrawal of support. To a child it was crazy and enough to put you off religion. In later life I was still not swayed. To witness theologians fighting over finer points of the Bible, Catholics and Protestants still at it, Islam getting a big foot in the door, and confounding things further by interpreting the Koran in different ways, some neither peaceful nor tolerant, was, to say the least, damaging to their cause. Agnostics and atheists were also claiming 'truth' and replacing it with the secular and scientific.

But, religion aside, don't we all have our rituals, superstitions or intractable belief in something that gets us through, however eccentric?

We certainly seem to.

*I was waiting for my wife Carol outside the 'Apple' store. A young girl, dressed to attract attention, walked through the entrance to the back of the shop, said a few words to the assistant who looked baffled, and walked back through the entrance. She stood for a moment, breathing deeply, facing the glass shop front. I thought she was about to head-butt her own reflection. Instead, and with great deliberation, she made a sign of the cross before resting her forehead against the glass. Maybe she was cooling her head but it looked too ritualistic for that. Then she turned ninety degrees, rattled phlegm around her throat and spat fiercely into the corner before walking on. It was obviously an important ritual to her. I'd have loved to have known her story, to have known her.*

I have often been asked how the organ scam actually came about, how it developed and how it worked. Much of it remains a mystery, particularly the bishop's blackmail link, but with the blessing of hindsight and loose tongues...

*Miller and Bellord's success depended largely on their ability to persuade banks and finance companies to hand over money. Amongst other factors, they were convinced by M&Bs*

*prosperity: an assumed wealth, not actual, as it turned out.*

*Miller and Bellord were good at this: expert, believable, emotionally intelligent, psychologically cute. Miller fronted it. Using the same charismatic approach to persuade nominees to part with their signatures came easily too. Their, help the church, story was also believable, and the potential sponsors - friends, colleagues and acquaintances: far easier to deal with than financiers - had been won over some time ago.*

*It worked. They told people they were selling organs to churches - institutions that were reluctant to sign hire purchase agreements - so could they help out, by completing hire purchase forms, signing as nominees? Miller and Bellord would act as guarantors: Miller, totally convincing, articulate, cleverer than bankers (it seemed), certain about the future. Bellord, something of the aristocrat about him: beautifully spoken, educated. Good team. Small risk.*

*Large sums were raised, along with a huge loan, borrowed against The House. As far as the nominees were concerned, Miller convinced each individual that they were part of something intimate: a few trusted people. Later, it was revealed that there were a substantial number of us involved - dozens certainly - maybe hundreds.*

*One can accept a story, that a few churches are being helped by charitable friends, because the request came from Miller who had the ability to make you feel the most important person in the world, once he'd got you alone. We all felt charitable and special. Brownie points given. Charity request donation box ticked. And we received a fee...*

Miller and Bellord installed an electronic church organ in the House chapel. A visiting churchman, so impressed with the sound quality which until recently had proved a poor imitation of the traditional pipe organ, wanted one. Sold. Miller bought another and sold that on too. This was the beginning of Southern Organs, a company set up to buy and sell electronic organs for churches and the entertainment industry.

Big companies like Yamaha and Hammond were aiming to perfect the electronic piano and keyboards and synthesizers, favoured by pop groups and bands. John Bellord with his quick brain soon learnt to play the organ to a half decent standard. His playing came across relaxed and confident. Miller had a liking for the instrument too but could only play one piece. He'd learnt it by ear and preferred the large church organ. All the better to blast out Bach's Toccata and Fugue in D, as loudly as possible. That piece of music, which was also on the soundtrack to the brutal futuristic film Rollerball, has kept cropping up in my life ever since.

Miller established the first shop in Southwick, West Sussex. It was a grand affair, opened by the Bishop of Guildford, George Reindorp. Tea and buns with the charismatic bishop in the little coffee shop in Southwick Square was an event. He wore his regalia and the café staff were duly astonished and deferential. He was a great joker and kept us amused. He'd missed his vocation as a standup comic. He never mentioned religion.

It would take something a bit more trendy than the sound I heard, to make such a business flourish. To me the basic instrument was old fashioned and boring.

Miller installed a teaching lab and employed talented musicians to give lessons. He wanted to make the organ and electronic instruments appealing to an untapped population of musicians searching for new sounds in a developing industry. Over the next few years Miller's organ empire grew. He opened ten shops in the south east and bought the conveniently named Miller Organs, from the prestigious Hammond Organ company. Miller Organs were the church division of the Hammond Organ business. They must have been losing money otherwise why would they sell it?

Not long after Southern Organs came into being, Miller asked if I wanted to earn a bit of extra money by sponsoring a church organ. For a moment I experienced a subliminal flash of concern and perhaps, for the first time, doubted his integrity. Miller must have spotted my reaction. 'No pressure of course, but it is a good and safe opportunity.'

My questions came thick and fast. 'What's involved? Why me?' Why can't you sponsor the church organs, or get the bishops to choose someone wealthy from their flock?'

'We have been sponsoring them,' he said, drawing the words out for emphasis, accentuating the machine gun tempo of my questions. 'The banks and finance companies have been accommodating and falling over themselves to do business with us.'

'Can't see how I can help. You must know my credit rating won't stand that sort of transaction.'

'No problem, you have us behind you now,' he smiled, 'the banks and finance companies know all about it. They're happy as long as John and I guarantee the deal.' He waited for my response, but was met with silence. He continued with convincing enthusiasm. 'You've met these finance people yourself. They want to help. We have to sign as guarantors in each case; it ensures absolute protection for anyone who wants to sponsor an organ.'

'Anyone? How many sponsors are there?'

'Only a few close friends; those we trust and who trust us.'

'I still can't see why the church can't find sponsors?'

'Of course they can, but they are touchy about hire purchase. Sounds daft, such a wealthy institution unable to buy an organ, but then it's not exactly a priority. Once they hear such a beautiful sound made electronically and indistinguishable from a hugely expensive pipe organ, they are keen to move it up the list of church 'must haves'. So we offer a way to do a deal.'

'How do you get your money back?'

'From donations and legacies given by generous congregations, over a period of time. Once the agreement is paid off, we can repeat the process.'

'Why don't they wait until they have the money in the first place?'

'I'm afraid that's where hard-nosed business comes into the equation,' said Miller, leaning back in his seat and lighting his pipe. 'Southern Organs want to make a profit and be successful. It's a golden opportunity. The scheme allows us to do a lot of business quickly. The finance companies are willing to climb on board and the banks are eating out of our hands.'

He laboured the fact. 'Nothing could go wrong for the sponsors or nominees because John and I always act as guarantors. Can't you see? It's all about us and our credibility.'

I guess we've all, at some point, acted as guarantor for sons or daughters, to help them finance their car or raise a mortgage, and wondered if it would end up being our debt.

I was prudent enough to look up the meaning, in law, of these terms that got bandied about so casually:

Nominee: *A person or company whose name is given as having title to stock, real estate etc. but who is not the actual owner.*

Sponsor: *A person who vouches for or is responsible for a person or thing. But does not own it.*

Guarantor: *A guarantor guarantees whatever he or she puts their name to. Ultimately the guarantor will be pursued for any outstanding debt, e.g. if the sponsor/nominee defaults the guarantor is liable.*

On signing the HP agreement, the guarantor signs a letter and receives a copy of the agreement with all signatures.

My conclusion? We're all making a fast profit too, but safe

in Miller's hands. Whatever the outcome, the buck stopped with him.

Few realised, until much later on, that Miller's guarantor scam stretched to other money-making projects: mortgages, loans, investments, including punters' investments in Miller's companies: Southern Organs, National Organs, Miller Organs plus a host of other money-making tricks, all on the back if his unassailable reputation and charisma.

But the organ transactions weren't just a simple one to one scam. Miller knew and dealt with heads of many finance companies and banks. Any sponsored organ could be proven to be legitimate stock, with a traceable serial number, delivery note and invoice from the manufacturer. It would sit in a stockroom looking innocent, ready to be dispatched. Several companies financed the same organ, each unaware (apparently) that it was also on the books of a competitor. But in reality, or so it seems, they simply closed their eyes and put their faith in Jim's juggling act. Math: Cost of organ five thousand pounds, multiplied by eight finance company agreements = forty thousand pounds. What could possibly go wrong?

In the 1970's an electronic church organ cost anything from five thousand pounds upward: a fortune. The fee paid to me for sponsoring an organ was fifty pounds. At the time it was an average week's wage. I signed, and then worried. Miller held all the payment books and made every single monthly deposit. Not a penny actually went through a sponsor's bank or building society account. Didn't this prove that the 'money' men knew exactly what was going on? And, if not, wasn't it decidedly odd that banks and finance companies allowed several agreements to be guaranteed by the same two people? How many agreements were there? If it was just a few, that wouldn't be a problem and Jim had assured me I was one of a close knit group of friends.

Albert and I delivered a church organ to Guildford, and a

few other places. This reassured me that these expensive electronic organs were actually being bought by churches. We didn't usually get too involved in the transport system used by Southern Organs but were occasionally called upon to help out.

Later, the shops stocked hi-fi and television sets too. Miller created a huge leisure centre in Tunbridge Wells selling all of the above, and an even more sophisticated teaching studio alongside cameras and film making equipment. Dennis Streeter, an old friend, passionate about photography and the developing technology of the music and television world, was to become a director of the group. Miller bought a factory in Storrington as the production centre for making the Miller church organs. Then Miller and Bellord formed a new company, National Organs, and imported organs from Japan. The Japanese contingent, slick polite businessmen in expensive suits, came over and set up substantial export deals. Miller got on particularly well with the Japanese. He respected their culture and was impressed by their courtesy. Quite a bit of bowing, greeting and nodding went on. Miller was good at culture.

Reynolds, Green did all the shop fitting and building work. It was remarkable how it slotted together, this massive jigsaw that, from where I was standing, looked unlikely to be completed. Miller had regular meetings with heads of banks and finance companies to negotiate favourable hire purchase deals. The office at the House was buzzing and the banks and finance companies were queuing up to give Miller credit.

It became a money-raising scheme that would create huge wealth and move the two philanthropists into the world of the criminal and fraudster. There was no turning back. The gravy train was traveling too fast to stop,

The casual observer might have been excused for thinking that Miller and Bellord had gone materialistic in pursuing such a course. They'd be wrong. Everyone involved was exposed to

Miller's work, his ideals, beliefs and practices. That exposure was bespoke; tailored to fit the individual, some of whom might be put off by the full range of his beliefs and practices.

My 'lessons' became more important by the day. I was sceptical about many things. After all, I kept reminding myself, I was a poor, uneducated miner's son who'd never seen life any differently than in the context of earning a crust. Miller assured me this scepticism was healthy. His teachings made me more aware of the world and its inhabitants. Inevitably life started to change. It wasn't all good and not at all easy.

It was probably a summer's day when he went deeper still into the spiritual stuff. It was certainly sunny and mild. I remember feeling relaxed when Miller called me over for one of our routine sessions.

He lit his pipe, pressed the smouldering tobacco with his finger and inhaled deeply. We both watched the smoke rise and a shaft of light cut through it. We sat silently for a moment, Miller enjoying the peace and me waiting for him to speak.

Do you have any trouble concentrating?'

'Don't think so. Why?'

'You need to be able do it well if you are to succeed in anything.' He walked over to the mantelpiece and lit a candle. 'We want you to succeed. John and I think you have something special and we're all on the same wavelength.'

*Really*, I thought, a bit puffed up by this remark, which may have been Miller's intention. With the candle flickering away in broad daylight and Miller poised, his pipe held still, the solemn expression, I felt a prayer, or something, coming.

'Bear with me,' he said, as I fidgeted in the chair. 'This is about concentration, about seeing things in great detail, then remembering that detail accurately.'

I blinked several times, tried to conjure up interest, and waited for him to continue.

'Look at the candle, its shape, its size, the way the flame makes the wax edges translucent, the shape of the flame, the twist of smoke rising, the hot edge of the wick glowing, the blueness at the flame's centre, and the faint smell of burning wax. The only thing on your mind should be that candle. Stop when you think you have it all. Don't concentrate on anything else,' he said.

'I stared and concentrated, my eyes flitting toward other things: the stone of the fireplace, the ticking clock, the frame of the landscape painting, then the landscape itself. Then back to thinking about physical labour and what I was working on at the House. Yes, I should be working.

'Only the candle. Leave everything else out. Concentrate. Hold that candle in your mind. Got it?

'I think so,' I said, the image flicking in and out as I tried to draw it back to my mind's eye.

'Remember the image and close your eyes. See how long you can hold it: just the candle, nothing else. As soon as something else comes into the picture, open your eyes. Be totally honest. Don't keep them closed to impress me, it won't work.'

I wasn't about to try and fool him and opened my eyes quickly as other things came into the picture. Not just things on the mantle, everything.

He laughed. 'That's how good your concentration is,' he said.

I was annoyed with myself and not a little surprised at how badly I'd done. I could feel a lecture or should I say lesson coming on.

'If you can concentrate fully, the world is yours. You can see your life's projects through to the end no matter how tough. You will be more patient, more effective at problem solving and discover a world you never knew existed.'

*By fixing the image of a candle in your mind?* I thought.

'Practice, practice, practice. Be honest while you are learning, open your eyes as soon as the image spreads or includes other things.' He paused, pressed his eyelids firmly as if to transfer the image straight to my brain. He knew I wasn't getting it.

'And here's something else that will help. Something you may find easier because it's the other end of the scale. It's about letting go of images, not holding on to them. Meditation.'

This sounded more like my cup of tea. 'You mean thinking?' I asked.

'More or less. There's a lot of mystery surrounding meditation. It has many forms, often based heavily on concentration, which most people, including you, find difficult. Here's one method that may suit you.' He drew on his pipe, found it had gone out and tapped the burnt ash into the grate.

'Close your eyes as you did before and let thoughts drift into your mind. Without effort, let them come. Easy, eh? Now the harder bit. Let the thoughts go. Don't hold the things that come into your consciousness or worry about them or develop them in any way. Let them go. You will get a stream of thoughts that wander all over the place from one subject to another. Don't worry. The system is working. Then you'll find letting go becomes easier and problems start to crystalise and then give you ideas for resolution. Because you will find that the important things, the ones you need to prioritise, will make themselves felt more acutely. Like filtering tea leaves to allow you the full taste of the real drink, the bit that matters.'

'Sounds impossible. How long does all this take to learn properly?' I asked, not wanting to spend a lifetime sitting in a cave meditating on a candle.

'Not long to get results, but a lifetime's work, as is concentration. It's like honing a knife edge that gets sharper and more effective with effort and time.'

'Try it again now. The candle first, then the meditation. Aim for ten to fifteen seconds for the candle to start with but don't be surprised if you don't last that long. Meditation is timeless. Do it daily, treat it as a discipline you would not miss, like brushing your teeth, several times a day if you can. We'll do a few sessions together with John. He had to learn too.'

John Bellord getting into meditation made it all the more desirable.

# 7

# The Motor Racing Manager

Miller had other acolytes, maybe many. He'd got in with the police, built a skid pan for their new patrol cars and helped with driving skills. And, no doubt, discussed psychology, philosophy and self-confidence. At least one guy left the force to join Miller and eventually became manager of one of the shops.

I believe I was part of the inner circle of interested philosophers: John Bellord, Johnny Farnton, Miller and myself. There was an inner, inner circle, Miller and Bellord only and an inner, inner, inner sanctum: Jim Miller alone, powerful and mysterious. I strongly believe that even John Bellord was denied access to what Miller was planning all of the time. But like the rest of us, he had his own secrets.

Long before Southern Organs came into being, Miller employed Margaret, an attractive, tall blonde, as his secretary. She was immaculate and efficient, his office champion. When Southern Organs started up and running a nursing home became only part of her brief, she took on her extended role with ease. To this day, Margaret has remained one of my dearest and most loyal friends. It never occurred to me during those incredible years, that one day our friendship would be tested to the limit.

The organ business seemed to be going well. Reynolds, Green had finished refurbishing the latest shop and fitting out the Storrington factory, including new offices for Miller Organs and National Organs on site. But Miller wanted more. He wanted increased sales and more churches buying top of the range organs. They were expensive, but less than the cost of maintaining an old pipe organ. A new set of pipes was prohibitive.

'We're going to hire a hall and put on a concert,' declared Miller.

No big deal. He'd put on a number of small concerts in towns where he'd sold organs. All were well attended and produced extra sales.

'Where?' I asked, expecting somewhere like Brighton.

Bellord smiled lopsidedly and closed his eyes briefly, a sign that Jim Miller had something not altogether sane up his sleeve.

'The Albert Hall,' he said, chuckling, obviously pleased with the idea. 'It's their centenary. Can you believe the Albert Hall is a hundred years old? And we are going to put on the best organ concert the world has ever seen.'

I didn't know much about the organ business but disliked pipe organ music.

'Geoff, John and you, Johnny, we're going to London. I've booked an appointment to see the manager and discuss business. We'll take the Rolls, for fun,' he said.

One of the most surreal things I have ever experienced was to pull up outside the Albert Hall in a chauffeured Rolls Royce, walk into that remarkable building and be given a welcome tour fit for royalty. Once inside, you could feel the energy. The greatest artists, orchestras and performers in the world have been gracing its stage for a hundred years. Sinatra played here, Yehudi Menuhin, Bob Dylan, The Beatles, Jimi Hendrix, Liza Minnelli. The Queen, the Dalai Lama, Winston Churchill and

Nelson Mandela gave great speeches here.

The manager, for whom nothing was too much trouble, walked us through every level of that grand place. The circles, the boxes, the stalls, backstage, the offices and the maze of corridors. Finally, we stood in front of the biggest piped organ in the UK. The Beast, someone called it. The ten thousand 'speaking pipes' seemed to disappear into the vast space above. It was to be the centre piece, the star, in the greatest organ concert of the century. We were treated with such respect, as if we were looking to buy the place from an eager estate agent. I expected Miller to say, 'We'll take it'.

No doubt the Royal Albert Hall would be pleased to see the great 'Beast' played so well, and to do that we needed the greatest living organists. Reputed to be the greatest classical organist was Marcel Dupré, now frail, but willing to cross the Channel from Paris. We believe it was his last great concert. He died later that year. Nicolas Kynaston, resident organist at Westminster Abbey agreed to play, as did Reginald Foort, an English musician now living in the US, the only man to get a number one hit, *In a Monastery Garden*, with the theatre organ.

The compère of this great concert would be the new director of music for the Southern Organs group of companies, Robin Richmond, who ran a popular radio show for the BBC, *The Organist Entertains*. The centenary concert introduction would be delivered by George Reindorp, the Bishop of Guildford. I never knew how Miller organised the next bit. The Queen's Household Cavalry would trumpet away to announce the beginning of the Albert Hall Centenary Organ Festival. All we had to do now was advertise the concert, then print and sell five and a half thousand tickets.

John Bellord began to wonder at the economics of bringing Reginald Foort from the United States for a single concert. He shared his doubts with Miller who suggested a national tour of

the provinces. Foort would play all the theatres that still had
Wurlitzers and pit organs. It would be a good way of extending
Reginald Foort's stay and making more money.

By putting in his usual one hundred-percent energy and
commitment, the concert and tour were a sellout. Though,
looking back, one could never be sure how many tickets were
simply given away to swell the audiences or impress specially
invited guests.

Throughout the rise of the 'organ empire', Jim Miller took a
particular liking for Bognor Regis and its quaint seafront theatre.
Just across the road some new flats were going up and Miller
fancied one as a holiday retreat for himself and his staff. He
bought a whole block, then dragged the four of us round to the
local furniture store and pointed at furniture and fittings with the
mouthpiece end of his pipe.

'Four of those, four of those, four of those...' said Miller.

The salesman will never forget the day he made more profit
than he'd done in a year.

There is no doubt in my mind that much of what Miller did
was close to magic, the stuff performed by illusionists. Get to
know your quarry, watch for body language, pick up on
subliminal clues about their past that would look clever when
you revealed certain facts later on. Facts they would have
forgotten they'd revealed because the whole approach was so
cleverly orchestrated. It was about being observant, sensitive,
and fearless. Add to that a strong voice, empathy and a real
desire to help and it was an approach that could not fail. And, so
it seems, his philosophy works particularly well where money is
involved.

It was unclear how the next stage of Miller's life came
about. Certainly his love of fast cars made it a possibility. He
was about to enter the world of motor racing. It started with a
minor championship, Formula Ford. But his introduction to John

and Angel Webb, the husband and wife team who ran Motor Circuit Developments, ensured his interest would grow and his planned sponsorship programme reach epidemic proportions. Angela Webb disarmed me. A natural head-turning blonde, beautiful, discreet with her tasteful expensive jewelry, classic clothes, ready smile and perfect teeth. I was smitten. Her husband, John Webb, a small, dapper man with steely eyes and a warm, firm handshake must have been too. The successful, wealthy pair had struck it off nicely with Miller.

John Webb couldn't have failed to be impressed with Miller and Bellord's passion for cars. And their knack for sorting out complex mechanical problems was legend. As with patients, they'd spend a long time listening, first to the engine, noting the response on acceleration then listening to it ticking over before and after a run. They'd lift the bonnet, touch this and that, feel its heart and pulse before coming up with a diagnosis, then a solution. Always a solution. It seemed like Miller used the same 'tuning in' approach for everything.

'Ever thought about a career change? asked Miller, his eyes alight with some new plan.

'Not really,' I said, caught off guard. Not true, everyone dreams about changing their lives from time to time. But what else could I possibly do that would generate enough income to support my family?

I'd have loved to do something else, but wasn't qualified to do much, at least nothing that would have brought in the cash like our building business. I must have had twenty jobs in my life, some interesting, some less so, but none had been big earners. Apart from my success in the building trade, they were simply life experiences.

'I want someone to organise the motor racing programme,' he said, pausing for effect. 'I want you to be my Southern Organs Motor Racing Promotions Manager,' he continued, lighting his pipe in silence. 'Good pay, fast car, more time to study philosophy and 'our work'.'

'Me?' I laughed, self-consciously, 'I know nothing about cars or motor racing. You'd be better off with a top man, someone who knows the business inside out. It would be a disaster to hire me for that post.'

'That's where you're wrong, believe me. I don't want an enthusiast and I'll tell you why.

It's a cut-throat business and drivers will do anything to get a sponsor. There are hundreds, possibly thousands of young hopefuls trying to get a drive. Motor Circuit Developments and such organisations are crying out for wealthy men to step in and put money into championships. What do you think would happen if I employed an enthusiast?'

'You'd probably end up with someone who could actually do the job,' I said. He ignored my sarcasm.

'I'll tell you what would happen. I'd get someone who is so keen to help the drivers and racing contacts that he will take Sid Miller to the cleaners and I'd be broke within a week.'

He rarely mentioned his real first name, but 'Sid Miller' was often used amongst the racing fraternity and press.

'But I know absolutely nothing, truly. I've never even been to a motor race. Don't know the front end of a racing car from the back end,' I said, palms damp from a mixture of anxiety and excitement.

He looked at me as a parent looks at a child that hasn't quite understood something he's been told a thousand times.

'Good, that's why I want you in. You'll act under instruction from me and have the interests of Southern Organs at heart. You won't cheat me or try and fix lucrative deals with your best mates and I know you'll do everything you can to learn about the business. I want you to write press releases, organise track advertising, mix with the drivers and mechanics, meet the circuit bosses and arrange hospitality suites for race days, including the high profile presence of our products: especially electronic pianos and synthesisers. There are a lot of wealthy people in motor racing and I want Southern Organs to get a slice of the pie.'

'How can I possibly take on such a post? I have absolutely no idea how to go about it.' Was he really expecting me to go on this trip to fairyland? It sounded exciting but, Hells' bells, I'm a builder!

'John and I will teach you everything you need to know. We'll introduce you to everyone and we're here if you have a problem. Think big. Remember, you can do anything. Do you believe I'd even dream of asking if I didn't think you were capable?'

'Does John Bellord feel the same about employing me?'

'We've known you for years and we trust you completely. You're interested in our work, you're reliable and we both like you. We're confident that, with our help, you can do it.'

'What about my business? I'll be letting Albert and all my customers down. It will be tricky explaining it to my wife Tanya; she's a bit uncertain of things as it is.'

'I'd be happy to talk to Tanya, let her know how much better off you'd be. How much better off she'd be too.'

Courage failed me. I couldn't tell Miller about her lack of enthusiasm for my association with him. Lack of enthusiasm was putting it mildly!

'Your business is doing well, you have a lot of good tradesmen and I think you'll be surprised at how Albert will take the news.'

'It's taken us both a lot of hard work to get to where we are now, the banks are happy and we're both settled in our nice comfortable homes. Plus, there is absolutely no way Albert could afford to buy me out.'

'We won't ask him to.'

'What do you mean? I can't give it away.'

'If you have faith in me and where we are going, give him the business.'

Typical Miller, always generous and weighing up the right thing to do. 'Don't expect others to follow your dreams. It's all down to you, so if you want to do something crazy, make sure no one else suffers.'

'By the way,' he added, 'the pursuit of nice and comfortable is not the best way to spend your life.'

I knew he was right.

But they did suffer. Tanya became anxious at me giving up everything I'd built up, everything I'd worked for. Surely the racing job would be a flash in the pan. Mother-in-law, Madge, was horrified and always resented the grip Miller had over me. She may have been right, she liked safe and comfortable. But I was on a roll, greedy for knowledge and adventure and full of optimism for all that Miller was doing. He had a golden touch and surely that was worth being linked to. My fortunes seemed to be changing too. So I said yes, and with the confidence of a man who knows nothing, took on the job of Racing Promotions Manager for Southern Organs International Racing. The Great Pretender.

Albert was magnanimous about my choice but must have thought me crazy. I think he was uncertain, as many people were, about Miller and his grand design. For, me it was turning into the time of my life. And as Miller advised on so many occasions, 'please don't take life too seriously.'

What's the worst that can happen? I couldn't imagine much past: lost job, marriage breakdown, hostile mother-in-law, unhappy kids. He certainly lived by the not too serious philosophy. His financial dealings, like playing Monopoly, were more like fun than business.

John Howell, someone Jim knew from years back, appeared on the scene. John was a big guy, British Kendo champion, spoke Japanese (handy for the import business) and thought the world of Miller and, importantly, was interested in his work. He had a prestigious job with Decca Communications and a good pension. Miller persuaded him to give it all up and help manage the Southern Organs and National Organs Companies. Looked like there might be another anxious wife on the scene. John worked from the House for much of the time, and we became friends. Our friendship would be tested too, but as with Margaret, he stuck by me despite my betrayal.

The canary yellow sports car, a Jensen Healey, was mine, so I could visit the racing circuits with the air of someone at ease with fast cars. It was nice and a pleasure to drive but after all, it was just a car. I had use of a Range Rover too and a modest Ford Escort for family outings.

Of course I was nervous, who wouldn't be? I was leaving my comfort zone and the building trade which had provided a home and a good living for me and my family. The next few weeks and months I read all the motoring magazines, traveled around the circuits and met the managers, drivers and motoring media. It was a steep learning curve.

Although everyone I met was friendly and helpful, in the scheme of things, I was pretty low down in the pecking order.

At first, Miller and Bellord accompanied me most of the time. What with the driver, Johnny Farnton, wearing sunglasses and all of us dressed in immaculate suits, white shirts and sober ties, we must have looked like the mini mafia. The racing fraternity would have seen us as an odd foursome.

Then I was set loose. I had a private meeting with John Webb of MCD at Brands Hatch. I looked and felt the business. I was driving a flash car to Brands Hatch, had money and kudos and hobnobbed with successful characters. I was letting it get to me. And why not, I was a young man who'd been given a golden opportunity to change his life.

How were we going to get to the circuits quickly? Miller was a busy man, still running the Nursing Home and his healing practice, still looking after the sick, the needy and the criminal. Still running the Southern Organs Empire. I visualised John Bellord pressing his forehead as Miller announced, 'We'll use a helicopter', and wondering when Jim was going to stop spending.

Someone once asked if I was scared of Miller. I guess I was, but not in the way people thought. I was scared of his ability to make people reflect and analyse their own short comings. It can lead to a whole lot of trouble, permeate relationships, destroy them even. Because most had not been privy to Miller's 'teachings' the world at large would have no idea what powerful forces were being released, the outburst of energy and completely new way of looking at things. It was scary but uplifting too. I didn't believe anyone could truly read minds but it seemed damn close some of the time. My real concerns were more to do with process of self-discovery, and all that entails, rather than Miller's power per se.

Something else about Miller kept all of us on our toes. His spontaneity occasionally bordered on the reckless. I can remember a particular summer's day, it was seasonably warm and the four of us were togged up in suits and ties for an important meeting some drive away. I can't remember exactly what the meeting was about, something to do with Southern Organs at a guess, but I do remember the feeling I always got when big preparations were underway: the need to go to the toilet just after you'd been or the odd bead of sweat between the shoulder blades.

We were driving the wrong way. This was definitely not the way we'd planned.

'I've decided not to go to the meeting. We need a treat so we're off to the cinema. Any objections?' said Miller.

*None. You're the boss, Jim.* We all shook our heads.

Steve McQueen starring in *Le Mans* was a film about the legendary twenty four hour race. There didn't appear to be a plot, hardly any dialogue, no one spoke at all for the first thirty five minutes, but there was a whole lot of racing going on. Some of the film was taken from original footage of the 1970 Le Mans. Miller bought huge ice creams. We were like kids bunking off school for the day. I think Miller's interest in the film was, most likely, the battle between the Porsche and Ferrari team. Miller was definitely a Ferrari man. Porsche won. Sitting in a cinema while a group of businessmen, assembled somewhere for an important meeting, waiting for us to turn up, seemed incredibly selfish. Jim could do selfish and I could never be sure whether it was tactical, to shake everyone up, or rudeness. For my part, I could not enjoy the film. I was feeling far too guilty.

I never did hear how he explained it away. He must have lied.

# 8

# Air Racing

I wasn't, by any means, privy to everything going on behind the scenes. From gossip, that unreliable yet often useful source of information, I got the feeling that Miller was not quite processing the amount of business he'd planned. So what does one do when the banks and finance companies get precious about their credit? First you have to deal with the cash flow, negotiate better interest rates if you can. Then, to make absolutely sure you still hold the reins, create your own finance company!

Miller joined forces with a couple of bankers in the south east to form his own finance company, Eastbourne Finance. The Monaco brothers, his new partners, were known affectionately as Tweedledum and Tweedledee on account of their squat roundness. I was convinced that all of Eastbourne Finance's business came from the Southern Organs group. If true, they were in Miller's pocket and would be reliant on him for everything.

Eastbourne Finance no longer exists. But Eastbourne Financial Services does. Nine of their bosses and staff have been arrested for running a mortgage scam over many years.

Mother-in-law, Madge, had been suspicious of Miller from the start. 'Wouldn't trust him as far as I could throw him,' she'd said. That wariness was based on the opinion of her 'spook', some weird imagined entity that she swore warned her when something portentous loomed. She'd be the first to sniff at anyone else's beliefs but 'spook' was, to her, infallible.

Her feeling of mistrust persisted, until she was invited to the House and exposed to Miller's charm. She succumbed to investing a thousand pounds, a substantial sum in 1970, in Southern Organs. Miller offered to pay her interest monthly, in cash. She was yet to learn that 'spook' (if he/she/it was responsible for her change of heart) on this occasion, had failed her and would continue to be a source of misinformation for years to come. Why would anyone give someone a grand without a rock solid guarantee? Because he was Jim Miller, mesmeriser extraordinaire. She simply had his word and a hurriedly written contract.

We couldn't be in two places at once and what with the championship season about to take off, Miller and Bellord, along with Robin Hood Garage, set out to design and build a towable demonstration caravan. It would be taken to racing venues around the country as a way of promoting Southern Organs and their products.

The long vehicle would be luxurious, with a curtained draped interior, chandeliers, spotlights, carpets and extension verandahs at each end, where punters could be entertained. Inside the mobile showroom would be a range of organs, keyboards, synthesizers and advertising material. The unit would be manned by one of the shop managers and two attractive hostesses with Southern and National Organs logos printed on their silk sashes.

Hospitality suites at racing venues were available wherever

we went, but not all of the time. We were confident of success but to be sure, we needed to spread the word more frequently, at more venues and in a more flexible mobile fashion.

I received a letter from Sterling Finance congratulating me for paying off 'my organ' quickly and stating they would be happy to offer more finance in the future. When I told Miller he said, 'Hang on to that letter, it will help your credit rating. Would you like to sponsor another?' he asked, without much hesitation.

Of course, the money would come in handy and, after all, he was the guarantor. Were alarm bells ringing? Yes, but not too loudly. My life is full of alarm bells. If I took notice of them all I'd never leave the house. Besides, I wanted the money.

Sister Joseph, who worked at the House, had twin sons who built and flew planes and were members of the BFA, the British Flying Association. She introduced her sons to Miller. He expressed an interest in meeting the BFA boss, Fred Marsh, who was looking for someone to put up the money for next year's flying programme. Never missing an opportunity to sponsor something, Miller decided to venture into Formula One air racing. This must have been the forerunner of the now famous Red Bull and American Formula One Air Racing, described as the 'world's most extreme sport'.

Formula One Air racing did have some popular appeal in Europe and Miller wanted to be the first to bring it to the UK. He put up a five thousand pound prize, to be paid out at the end of the season, and sponsored heats at Biggin Hill, Sywell and some of the motor racing circuits. Health and safety issues seemed minimal then.

The planes were owned, hand built and flown by their proud pilots. The planes started from a grid, like racing cars, and had to complete a number of circuits against the clock. Pylons defined the parameters of the circuit for the low flying aircraft. Penalties were given for flying too low, too dangerously or too close to the crowd. It was thrilling stuff and teams from the continent competed against the Brits.

More than any other sponsorship deal, this was closest to my heart. These guys were passionate about their planes, their babies, built from scratch. Every nut and bolt, every last sprayed and polished surface was lovingly finished. Then they had to test fly them. Then race them.

\*

'Are you having an affair?' asked Miller at one of our still available and still robust 'life lessons'. 'John and I think you've changed. Something's happened in your life, bit of an odd glow about you. Do you want to talk about it?'

'Of course things have happened,' I chuckled nervously. 'My new career, new car, plus all this stuff I've been learning about over the last few years.' I was chewing the edge of my fingernail and examining the result. Miller would have picked up on the body language. His eyes, with that innocent childlike stare that always threw me, had an expression that preceded revelation or some blockbuster piece of knowledge he'd managed to pluck out of the ether.

'You don't love her,' he said.

Now that is something he couldn't possibly know. *He's fishing, implying he's had some psychic revelation. Or someone's talked.* He didn't wait for my defence.

'The stuff we've learnt together over the years,' he started, emphasizing 'stuff', 'was bound to change your life,' he said with exaggerated softness, as if he were talking to an errant schoolboy. 'People don't usually last the course, it's too scary. As well as making you aware of self and others, it liberates people in extraordinary ways. You have more power, more influence and more confidence. It can be like a child let loose in a sweet shop and it can release a vigorous, promiscuous sexuality too. Gradually you learn to handle it, or you can end up losing everything you love. I believe you to be at that most dangerous stage; a man with newly realised confidence.'

'My marriage isn't working anyway. I've known my wife since we were in our teens, we got married too young. We'd had no other real sexual experiences, apart from some hot snogging with teenage crushes. We were virgins.'

'So, under the circumstances, you wouldn't mind if your wife experimented too: took a lover and risked her marriage?'

He lit his pipe, drew heavily on it and blew a long stream of blue smoke toward the ceiling. We watched it rise and thin out as if some obscure reasoning was manifesting within. Maybe I was meant to work something out. Then he gave me his psychotherapist's look, a penetrating studied expression of superior knowledge.

'Bring your new girlfriend over I'd like to meet her. While she's here, I'll prove to you that you are, most definitely, not in love with her.'

I was never going to do that and never did. My brief affair with Rachel was over fairly quickly. But Jim was wrong about the love bit. Thirty five years on, if I ever bump into any of the women I'd had affairs with, I still loved them. So it was true and lasting love after all. I fell in love often, and suffered a broken heart along the way, sometimes from girls I'd never even kissed.

Portsmouth Football Club was going through a bit of a lull. Their boss, Ian St John, talked to Miller about team motivation and Miller offered his services. I have to admit to a huge thrill walking into the hospitality suite at Fratton Park and seeing the startling green floodlit pitch. I'd never been to a football match, at least, not a professional one, and it was truly energising. You could feel the crowd's adrenaline and for the first time I appreciated the term 'football fever' and why people get so worked up about the game. It's no good watching it on telly, you really have to be there to appreciate the live theatre of it all.

'We're going to help this club,' he announced.

As far as I knew, neither Jim Miller nor John Bellord had the slightest interest in football.

'I'm taking on the role of team sports psychologist. We're going to motivate these lads and help them improve their game.'

I guess he could do that. Of course he could.

'And Geoff, in addition to the motivational stuff, we're going to use radionics.'

We? It wasn't that I didn't believe it worked, it was a concern about how others would view it. These guys were hard-bitten professional sportsmen, used to physios and tough talking coaches grinding on about warm ups, stretches and the killer instinct.

They'd think it was gobbledygook and walk out.

'We won't explain the whole process. They won't be ready for that. By the way, you'll be the one collecting blood samples from the team. You know how to do it, you've had enough practice. Just make sure you write the name of every player, date of birth, time you take the sample and number each slide.'

On the given day some, but not all, of the team walked into the clinic. I wore a white coat and felt shaky. The team was intrigued and I was adequately professional, it seemed. They assumed we were doing routine blood tests. Miller put the samples on his radionics machine and one at a time we 'tuned them in'. In the meantime, Miller gave pep talks to the team about self-belief, competitive but controlled aggression and most importantly, the inside truth about winning. 'Games,' he would say, 'like most things in life, are won mentally, not physically.' Sure you have to be super fit,' he said, 'but in the end it's the attitude that clinches the victory.'

He illustrated this theory with examples of how super-fit sportsmen win one day and lose the next with no apparent change in fitness level or competition. The only thing that changes, he suggests, is their mental and emotional attitude, their state of mind. The bit that makes you win. He would transpose this philosophy into everyday life. It's the state of mind that takes you where you want to go and gets you anything you want to achieve.

Throughout my association with Miller, friends and colleagues asked about sex. Were Miller and Bellord really just a couple of gays grooming others? Grooming yes, but not for sex. Perhaps they'd had a transient gay relationship when they'd first met, as young men. Not so easy to 'come out' in those days, same sex relationships would have been unlawful.

Can homosexuality be switched off? Are you once gay always gay? I have known people shift from being heterosexual to bisexual to gay. Anyway, there was never talk of ex-wives or girlfriends, though we did hear a rumour that Bellord had once been close to marriage. Unfortunately, the fact that he lived with Miller and did everything as a team, put them squarely in the gay bracket for most. Personally I think they were asexual, as other such spiritually-aware people can be. Miller made it obvious that he admired the traditional family. He liked kids and was mischievous when they were around, full of practical jokes and treats.

I don't think Miller was attractive to women but Bellord certainly was. In all the time I'd known them, they never sought and, as far as I knew, never had gay friends. All the guys in the shops and factory and all the racing drivers were all strongly heterosexual with families, girlfriends and kids. I don't think Miller or Bellord really desired or needed sex. I could, of course, have been wrong.

Roughly once a month, managers of the shops would meet at the House for a company meeting. They were and had to be, hard-nosed businessmen, practical, confident and enthusiastic. The meeting was a relatively casual affair, everyone scattered round in easy chairs, coffee served, banter interspersed with serious discussion and disclosure of the latest sales figures, advertising ideas and what was happening on the racing front. Some managers were very concerned about the cost of our racing programme and feared that Miller might be gambling away profits on his latest toys. Only hard work and belief in Miller and his passion and philosophy kept the ball rolling.

During such a meeting Dave Haskell, sitting opposite the large windows that looked out toward the woodland and the ice house, suddenly went pale and seemed to be lost for words. It was unlike him. We thought he might be about to have a heart attack or faint and pitch headlong onto the floor.

Miller walked over to check on him. 'Are you okay, David?'

David loosened his tie. 'I'm okay now,' he said, his colour returning.

'Don't try and get up, we'll get you checked out. I think we'll stop the meeting here,' said Miller, timing David's pulse against the seconds on his watch. 'See you all next month.'

David's 'turn' may have, inadvertently, spared Jim some serious questions about money and motor racing.

All the managers left, apart from Dave. A concerned Jim Miller, after checking him out, asked what had happened.

'I couldn't say while all the guys were here, I'd have felt a right idiot.'

Miller waited.

'I saw ghosts at the end of the lawn. Monks with cowls: looked like they were floating across the grass.' He pointed toward the neatly trimmed lawn broaching a gravel path close to the ice house.

There's a micro climate around that spot, probably caused by the chill of the subterranean air of the ice house hitting the warmer air of the woodland as it meets the grass. Shapes can appear in the misty residue.

Miller wanted to check further. 'Do you mean you think you saw ghosts?'

'I actually saw them. I looked hard. I don't believe in ghosts but there was absolutely no doubt. It took them a few seconds to cover the end of the lawn, then they disappeared.'

Miller smiled. 'Lots of people have seen them. It's part of the House history. You are lucky to have seen the monks.'

David did not appear to think he was lucky at all. The experience had obviously shaken him and the fact he'd seen something he didn't believe in must have shaken him further. No more was said. David, as far as I know, was not one of Jim's acolytes and was treated with due caution regarding things metaphysical.

Miller rarely mentioned the history of the House, but others, including some of the night staff, reported seeing these ghostly figures. It was decades later, when computers and search engines became part of daily life that I was able to research the history of the House and the Tredegars. Evan Morgan, Lord Tredegar, had been involved in a private occult society in London called the 'Black Hand'. It had thirteen members and Evan was known as the 'Black Monk'.

Johnny Farnton and I loaded the demo caravan up with organs and equipment, put the generator and petrol in the back of the Range Rover and left for the M1 and our route up north. It would be our first long trip with the new set-up. The organ shop staff were due to follow and we were meeting Miller and Bellord at the racing circuit. It was a clear day so I put my foot down and coasted along at sixty.

The caravan seemed stable, despite its awkward load, and there was little traffic. Although we were doing sixty on a slight downhill gradient, a large haulage truck decided to overtake. We could feel the suction effect on the steering as the lorry edged close to pass us. I touched the brakes and changed down a gear to ease our speed. We heard a mighty crack. I felt a judder and sensed something metallic buckling behind the Range Rover. The newly designed 'A' frame of the demo vehicle had failed. It buckled, and severed the braking system between it and the Range Rover. The steering was useless, gone completely. The weight of the demo caravan, now slewing sideways, caught up with the Range Rover, pushing it along in parallel as if attempting to overtake us. Without brakes or steering, the Range Rover managed a weird pirouette before flipping onto its roof.

The generator, petrol, and all our clothes were thrown out through the exploding windows and onto the motorway. The roof was crushed downward with all the Range Rover's weight on top of it. Amazingly nothing hit us as we slewed sideways, the demo vehicle pushing us toward the safety barrier.

Johnny, face bloody, slid out upside down through the windscreen. I pulled myself out the same way. The doors were crushed and immovable. Johnny was not really hurt but the amount of blood must have put the wind up him. An ambulance came but after a quick check in Accident and Emergency at the local hospital, we were allowed to go. It really was a miracle. I was completely unscathed and all Johnny had was a couple of scratches.

We called Miller at the circuit. He sounded relieved but Johnny and I knew he would be furious because he believed that most accidents were avoidable. Accidents, he said, were caused by lack of awareness or concentration, not being tuned into what was happening around you. He recited the caveat again and again: that one should never concentrate a hundred percent on any single thing. Ten percent should be taking in or be aware of the peripheral stuff so's one can respond quickly to the unexpected. I thought of the candle sitting on his mantelpiece and how crap I'd been at the exercise.

# 9

# Storm Approaching

We needed some young blood to market and sell the electronic synthesisers and keyboards. We needed to drag Southern Organs into the twentieth century. A few suggestions came up. One involved the disc jockey Emperor Rosko, Mike Pasternak, son of film producer Boris Pasternak.

'Why him?' asked Miller.

'Couple of reasons for a start: one, he has a huge following as a broadcaster and DJ and two, he follows the Radio 1 car racing championship around the MCD circuits, touring the country.'

'What do you think he can do for us?' asked Miller, cutting short my list of accolades.

'How about we tie up one of his tours with demos of synthesizers and keyboards? Managers of groups and bands can follow his tour and we could advertise our stuff and increase sales in the younger market.'

'You mentioned Radio 1 motor racing,' he said, obviously warming to the idea.

'Rosko's interest in motor racing would be a great link to it all. He might even be interested in driving for Southern Organs.

He joined the pirate Radio Caroline which gave him loads and loads of publicity. He's famous.'

'Never heard of him.'

The fact that Jim Miller hadn't heard of him was not unexpected and proved, unequivocally, that Emperor Rosko was popular with the young.

'He's on Radio 1 daily with Dave Lee Travis,' I added, trying to hold back a smile, knowing damn well that Miller wouldn't have heard of him either. 'He doesn't live that far away. We could run it by him and see what happens?'

Throughout the year Southern Organs got involved with a catalogue of racing programmes and celebrities. One of our most successful race days was the 'Lords and Commons' event at Brands Hatch. Members of the House of Lords and the Commons raced saloon cars against each other. The prize was a pretty decent organ. The publicity was great because all the media photos showed our organ prize being played by a lord or politician. It was good use of the racing budget and it paid off handsomely.

Divina Galica, downhill ski champion, wanted to further her career by getting into motor racing and Jim would be her ticket. There would be loads of publicity for Davina and Southern Organs.

My days were kept busy sending press releases to motoring magazines, newspapers, radio and television. Monthly updating of all the drivers' profiles and championships needed constant scrutiny. Plus all the exciting stuff happening in between needed writing up and reporting. Race track advertising required strategic thinking and tough negotiations to get the best deal for our races. Between us we dealt with invitations and entertaining at the trackside hospitality suites. This presented the perfect opportunity for drivers, celebrities and sponsors to meet.

Miller and Bellord became friends with ex Formula One

champion, John Surtees. We met at the Surtees' home on occasion and Jim negotiated a Formula One drive for Dave Morgan, an up and coming driver. The drive was arranged for the 1975 British Grand Prix at Silverstone. Southern Organs' Touring Car championship would be there too, plus the Radio 1 crowd. We aimed to print a special edition newspaper full of ads, info, profiles and articles.

Rosko knew Alvin Stardust. 'How about we get Alvin to present the trophy for our race?' I said to Miller and Bellord, a little too over-enthusiastically.

'Alvin who? I was thinking along the lines of the Duke of Kent. I know someone who knows him,' said Jim.

The Duke of Kent presenting our championship trophy? *Not if we can help it, Jim.*


Despite everything that was going on we still had time for lessons: healing, metaphysics and more.

'We need space too. If we have no space in our lives, we're lost,' my mentor would say.

*Yeah, yeah, Jim, so you've told us all, a trillion times.*

I was becoming more distant from my wife. Miller's advice was always, let go. My reply was, I couldn't.

'We don't own people,' he smiled.

'What about kids?'

'We have a certain responsibility to them, but far less than you think. Of course it's incumbent on us to teach them independence, look after them when they are young, teach the little people everything we know in terms of morals, good manners, etc. Then we have to let them go. As soon as possible. That is what all teaching is about, including mine. The sign of a good teacher is when they say, 'I've taught you all I can you are ready to move on'.'

This was hard to swallow. It felt as if Jim and John would

forever be a part of my life.

'There will be moments in your life,' he continued, 'when you are ready, and another teacher will come, not always in the form you'd expect. I will add a bit of advice. Don't try to teach others, learn from them.

The responsibility for what your children do next, however terrifying, will then be down to them. When they leave the nest, parenthood will either have left a good impression or get thrown out the window. Your example, however, will remain with them all their lives.'

'Shouldn't we be advising them all the way through?' I queried.

'Only if they ask. Once you let them go, the relationship should be a true one, not some misplaced and interfering duty that controls their lives.'

'That's hard.'

'Who said anything about easy? We don't always know what's best,' he said, standing to indicate we must move as we had an appointment with Alvin Stardust. 'You have to let your wife go. I don't mean leave her, I mean let her free...it needs to start in the mind, you are suffocating her with your demand for love.'

*But really, Jim, what the hell would you know? You don't have a wife and kids, you haven't even got a girlfriend. Emotions run high. You seem to control yours so well. Perhaps it's easier when you don't get into the marriage and sex stuff.*

'Do you think I might be oversexed, needing these affairs?' I blurted.

'I'd be very surprised if you were,' he said, clenching his teeth around an empty pipe to disguise a developing smirk.

*You really cannot read my bloody mind, Jim Miller. You couldn't possibly know.*

'You might feel starved but, I can assure you, it's not of

sex. Your need is for love really, and although it might seem confusing, it is so totally different. If you were deprived of food or drink you would experience a similar craving and be unable to think of anything else. It's deprivation of sex with love, not an unnatural sex drive, that is your problem. You are completely normal.'

*Can I have that in writing?*

Alvin, a good man, struggling like the rest of us, needed Jim's advice. Fame appears to make things even more complicated than ordinary life. He had issues, emotional ones plus practical problems with record companies and professional credibility. He met Jim over at the flat a few times and no doubt got his confidence boosted and his problems put into perspective. He'd never been to a Formula One race and admitted it was a long-held ambition. Miller's offer struck the right chord. Alvin would be helicoptered in to Silverstone. He'd avoid the fans, have lunch with us in the hospitality tent, watch the race and finally, present the Southern Organs Touring Car trophy to the winner.

There was more. Jim met up with John Surtees and other Formula One impresarios. They were wined and dined in the usual way but behind the scenes, a deal was clinched. Although I was Racing Promotions Manager I was not privy to some of the deals until they'd been done. Miller arranged the Formula One drive for Dave Morgan alongside teammate John Watson, together they would form the Surtees team for the 1975 British Grand Prix at Silverstone. Dave's single drive was to cost Jim Miller a stack of cash.

Bellord must have been exasperated. He managed the accounts and knew only too well what a strain this new venture would have on the books. Even the constantly optimistic Jim Miller must have trembled slightly at the thought of what he was doing. So we printed the Southern Organs British Grand Prix newspaper, booked Alvin Stardust to present our trophy and got Dave Morgan his first Grand Prix drive.

Like most glamorous professions, the reality is ninety five percent getting ready for the event and five percent limelight. With motor racing, the driver enjoys the whole package. For girlfriends and wives who have to sit around during this preparation and watch their guys constantly consulting with teams, tinkering with cars and running the gamut of mood swings that go with the territory, the experience is often boredom punctuated with high excitement. For a young woman or girl to say she is going out with a racing driver bestows a certain glamour on her life. In reality, she is secondary to the car and ever will it be thus. To be around when an engine blows or when a car fails to qualify, or loses a lead, because the wrong tyres were chosen when the weather looked uncertain, can be hell. But the long tension-packed wait followed by the thrill of the drive was, apparently, worth it.

# 10

# Thank You, Fraser Darling

Johnny Farnton had been troublesome in the past, but with Miller's guidance we were certain he'd learnt his lessons. That is, until the police called at the House. Johnny, foolishly and nothing to do with needing money, had suffered a bout of light-fingeredness in a local store. He was spotted and so terrified that Miller might get to hear of it, decided to escape arrest by jumping through a plate glass window. Johnny survived but was lucky not to have died. When he arrived back at work, following medical care, he was contrite and beside himself with rage at his own stupidity. Miller always handled these crises well. He knew that Johnny would be punishing himself harder than anything he could say or do. That was Miller's wisdom. The person who let you down then feels so much more guilt.

Part of the way through my role as Southern Organs Racing promotions manager, it struck me that racing drivers were probably being asked to sponsor church organs too, a sort of quid pro quo. These guys were hungry enough for a drive, some desperate. They were sitting ducks for such a deal and some would have signed anything.

Following a heap of letters from hire purchase companies congratulating me on my excellent record, Miller asked if any of my close friends would like to earn some extra cash. I introduced him to a few. Miller spun his tale and got them on board. By now it seemed so unexceptional and he never failed to labour the fact that the banks and finance companies were all in on it. We didn't doubt him for a minute. After all, they were invited to his parties and left free to mingle and chat. It was all so jolly. The banks and finance companies were making a stack and no one was suffering. Miller borrowed the money, paid the HP agreement off quickly, took out more agreements and did the same over and over again. I was convinced the system was working perfectly because of the letters dropping through doors announcing clearance of debts and, in the process, an offer of even more credit.

*The.... Credit Group Limited*

*Dear Mr. Green,*

*My attention has been drawn to the excellent manner in which your account has been conducted and I would like to thank you for entrusting us with your financial arrangements.*

*We are aware that the present economic situation has caused unforeseen difficulties in the balancing of personal budgets and we, therefore, feel that it is an ideal time to bring to your notice our low cost revolving credit scheme...*

If things went wrong, the finger would ultimately point at Miller and Bellord, the guarantors, sitting in a mansion surrounded by a profitable empire.

It doesn't get much bigger than the British Grand Prix at Silverstone. Jackie Stewart and Murray Walker were the commentators. Jackie described it as one of the finest Formula One races he'd ever seen, with men competing more against the elements than each other. We'd arranged press passes, finalised the trackside advertising with *Aerosigns,* and our team of helpers were about to distribute tens of thousands of free copies of the Southern Organs Grand Prix racing newspaper.

Alvin Stardust was already on his way in by helicopter. Dave Morgan was tinkering in the pits with teammate John Watson. John Surtees hovered, hoping his team would do well and that the weather would stay dry. We all met up in the hospitality tent for lunch. Jim and John, their faces glowing with excitement were, as ever, togged up in immaculate suits and shirts. Alvin Stardust arrived in head to toe black leather gear, enough rings to stock a jewellers plus the biggest, sleekest, quiff in the world. He looked great: enigmatic, charismatic and our honored guest who would present our trophy in front of thousands. Alvin was a most disarming guy, gentle, shy almost. It was quite extraordinary that the same guy could stand up in front of huge crowds and rock like the devil.

The marquee filled with a cacophony of sound as the excited race crowd drank, ate, raised excited voices and generally built up a head of steam for the great afternoon.

On the grid David Morgan, not surprisingly, was way down the line up. Tom Pryce was on pole, Emerson Fittipaldi, Niki Lauda, James Hunt behind, all on slicks, dry weather tyres. We were on the edge of our seats. The bookies did not expect Dave to win, but if he could put on a good show it might put him in the running for a team place somewhere. I doubt if even Miller could or would put up the huge sums of money demanded by Formula One to further Dave's career. But the now is what's important and he was giving Dave the chance of a lifetime.

Cloud threatened with just a splash of rain at first, not enough to pull the drivers in for a tyre change. A strong wind blew up and dried the track quickly. We breathed a sigh of relief. A few laps later it chucked it down, rain and hail. Fittipaldi, who went on to win the race, had already decided on a tyre change. It was the right decision at exactly the right time. A new chicane had been built at Woodcote Corner and the consensus was this might have been a real problem, particularly on the first lap with cars bunched together and no chance for tyres to warm up. But the first laps were okay and the cars settled into the race. Then came more torrential rain, only much worse. Cars slid on their dry weather tyres, crashing, piling up to form the beginnings of a substantial and expensive scrap yard. Dave Morgan, team mate John Watson, Jody Scheckter and James Hunt were amongst them.

The cost to team Surtees must have been substantial. For Miller, it was portentous and in a bigger sense than we could have imagined. Miller believed in 'signs', events that had an effect on a bigger picture, caused not by chance but by lack of forethought, preparation or something less tangible than the physical reality. The race ended in carnage and was cut short. Luckily no one was killed, but only six cars finished the race with Fittipaldi declared the winner whilst he waited, exhausted, in the pits.

Every now and then, with all the changes in my life happening so quickly, I felt I was going crazy, like most people at some point in their lives. My episode of feeling 'out of it' could be a genetic thing as my whole family had tasted psychiatric care or experienced a breakdown. Mum suffered with 'nerves' and got no help from anyone, least of all her six children. My eldest sister, Dor, had a 'breakdown' as did my middle sister, Babs, who experienced several breakdowns with years of extensive therapy and medication. I could understand why, both had been raped by their own father and Babs's daughter abused by her stepfather. Babs's downward spiral came, I guess, not specifically from the act of learning about the abuse, but because she'd kept it to herself. She was in denial, ignoring what was going on inside the family home, frightened and silent, complicit even. The long term effect eroded her spirit and decimated her life. Surely her brain could not help but malfunction from the sheer neuropathic overload.

One day, Babs's two children from her second marriage did something I could never forget or forgive. Babs collapsed with a fatal stroke and they cremated her without telling me. I found out from niece Pam, at the last minute. She'd been kept in the dark too. I raced to the crematorium in London, sixty miles from where I lived, only to find the service was over. I asked if I could see the urn containing her ashes so I could give some ritual blessing to her remains, but they'd been taken too. I left a message in the book of remembrance, the words illuminated by the chapel calligrapher to give it the special goodbye I'd been so cruelly denied.

Dad spent time in Shenley Mental Hospital. I remember the steel-framed beds arranged in straight rows with hardly a book space between them. The air of piss, dirt and decay pervaded everything. The tough-looking carers and green, gloss painted walls, stained beige and streaky brown from attempts to scrub them down was so depressing. Everyone smoked, including the staff, adding a constant, surreal cloud to the already cloying atmosphere.

Dear brother Don in the US was in therapy for years, and seemed no better at the end of it than when he'd started. To be fair, they were trying to sort out a man who'd given in to alcohol and drugs.

Jilly hadn't been abused by Dad, yet she'd cracked like the rest. It was revealed, all too late, that she'd been knocked about and robbed again and again by her son to feed his drug habit. So

Jilly ended up in psychiatric care too. How particularly sad it was to visit your twin, the other half of you, in such a depressing and desperate place. Could we blame our parents for passing on a dodgy legacy: rogue genes that spread like a forest fire through our innocence?

It was no big deal when the first letter dropped through the door of an organ sponsor asking if the finance company could view the product described in the HP agreement. Miller treated it lightly, quickly dismissing it as an error on the part of the company who probably hadn't realised Miller's name writ large as guarantor. Perhaps it was a new enthusiastic administrator yet to learn what the set up was. He made some calls.

I am not politically minded and only sit up and take note when things political affect me dramatically and personally. There were stirrings in the office, talk of big economic changes on the horizon and Miller, who didn't read newspapers because they were 'full of propaganda and prone to bias', started discussing the politics of the day in some earnest. Margaret Thatcher had succeeded Edward Heath in April 1975. Income tax was raised two per cent and VAT, although already high on petrol, leapt to a whopping twenty five percent and extended to cover a wide range of luxury goods, including all the products sold by Southern Organs.

It looked as if UK trade was about to go pear-shaped. Harold Wilson warned that the British economy faced, 'possible wholesale domestic liquidation'. Lord Balogh, economist and energy minister at the time, predicted that the continuing balance of payments deficit could provoke a 'violent withdrawal' of short term money if people took fright. And they did.

Miller didn't panic, he had friends in high places and was on first name terms with the band of brothers who held the reins of investment and banking. But if they flipped, it could prove to be a real problem.

We are used to a little unrest when politicians make dramatic statements through the media. For Miller and Bellord, there was much at stake and too many people involved who'd bent the rules and made illicit profit. All were complicit and so far no one had suffered financially, everyone got paid. It seemed like the perfect scam.

When I received my first letter from one of the HP companies' lawyers, I scrutinised each paragraph hoping to spot an encouraging word or two, something like: *'after making a stack of money out of you we feel it only reasonable, during these difficult times, that we meet to discuss matters.'*

*Too late now, Jim, you were a good teacher.* I can read body language pretty well, pick up atmosphere and mood and run a fairly accurate mental post mortem on the man in the office chair, the one with the washed out look and a few more lines around the eyes and mouth. Add to that a discernable slump of the shoulders, an unlit pipe (unheard of this time of the day) and no morning joke. Of course it didn't last. By lunchtime the first peal of laughter resonated as he answered the phone, then the call for coffee, the straightening of shoulders—and a damn good puff of the freshly lit pipe, sending up an unusually massive cloud of blue smoke toward the corniced ceiling.

Despite the economic changes Miller didn't reduce his staff, shut down any of the shops, reduce production at the factory or cancel his racing sponsorship. He simply called more meetings to discuss best ways forward to 'see us through' this temporary setback. The racing programme should have been the first cutback and my job should have been the first to go, but he kept his cool and his promises. His problem solving strategy was to talk to the guys with the money, the guys who'd made a packet for doing virtually nothing. They would now be asked to help out by giving Jim time to adapt to the changing financial

and economic climate. We all knew he'd find some way round
the impending crisis and we were all behind him.

Directors attended the House more frequently: Alan Chase,
Dennis Streeter, the Monacos, John Bellord and John Howell.
Miller chaired. They were all successful men, many citing Miller
as the catalyst for their good fortune. The bankers and investors,
however, stopped visiting and took to writing, at least their
lawyers did. They'd had an attack of ethics, something they were
not prone to, and started nitpicking the small print in the credit
agreements. Their letters were concise, impersonal and
threatening.

I was spending less time in the office. There was too much
going on that didn't concern me, the profit and losses at the
shops, how the Miller organ factory was doing and whether sales
of Japanese products across the UK were on the up and adding
sufficiently to the coffers.

John Bellord was looking more tired by the day, trying to
balance the books. Miller carried on as normal; still practical
joking, chatty, businesslike but a little more strained. Margaret
Cutler and John Howell were fielding phone calls, stalling,
buying time while Jim Miller considered his position. It was
untenable.

I spotted Miller walking toward the House, crooked arm
gripping his pipe, left arm swinging like a pendulum with an air
of hurrying purpose. I slowed my pace but followed him in. He
smiled as I entered but said nothing as we walked toward the
office. He flopped, sighing, into his leather chair and took on his
classic pose: head straight, clear blue eyes staring at nothing in
particular, index finger and thumb of one hand gripping a lighter
which he spun gently round. He was now relaxed, focused, in
meditation and problem-solving mode. The rhythmic rotation
was hypnotic. Something big was brewing.

We could see it coming. Knew it had been coming for some

time. We'd ignored too many signs and had too much faith in Jim Miller and his extraordinary capacity for problem solving. He was only human, after all.

If the walls of their cosy flat could speak, they would spout metaphysics and the power of cause and effect. But walls cannot speak, or they might have saved Miller and Bellord from what lay head.

Desert Island Discs. What appeal a desert island would have now. We had long conversations about what could be done, without revealing the full extent of what was going on, we discussed options. John Bellord wanted to face up to the crisis and let the law sort it out. Miller, who could not bear to think of everyone turning against him, wanted to disappear for a while. If only he could have time to meditate, think things through and return refreshed. He was too tired to think straight.

They loved Scotland, particularly the area around Ullapool where they'd spent many happy times. It would be their perfect choice for a retreat. The argument against it was that everyone knew of their passion for the north west. It didn't take long to realise that somewhere so obvious could never be safe. There were no easily accessible uninhabited islands in the UK.

We all have robust pals, leaders of the pack who we follow until one day some life crisis renders them vulnerable and impotent. Suddenly we have the stage and are surprised at how naturally we take over. Such a moment happened with us, with Miller and Bellord and me. In a smoke-filled room on a depressingly hot summer's day we talked of a plan, then agonised over it before deciding a couple of months in hiding was the best option. The desert island image stayed with us and like so many things over the last few years, if enough thought, desire and energy emanated from us, things would happen.

I had a couple of days off. Miller and Bellord wanted to take the weekend to talk their plan through and meditate on it.

Not only the plan, but the consequences it would have on those left behind and what practical steps they could take to ensure Southern Organs carried on in some shape or form. I didn't need to be included in that practical stuff, not yet. They were never going to reveal the full extent of what was going on to me. Eventually I would find out, but not from Miller or Bellord.

I told Tanya I needed a bit of time out. She knew things weren't right, the kids noticed too. But kids know how to handle crisis, they play. We Greens are a secretive lot when it comes to airing problems. We don't.

One of my passions is reading, so what better way to relax and put the impending crisis on hold, than to be amongst books? I spent a morning in Brighton, browsing book shops in the Lanes, when an old volume caught my eye. It's fair to say that I was still sceptical about some of Miller's ideas and thinking and that an inanimate object, such as a book could make its presence felt if you were, 'tuned in' to a particular wavelength. The volume that virtually jumped off the shelf was, Island Years, by Dr Frank Fraser Darling, ecologist, ornithologist, farmer and conservationist. This book, written a year before I was born, became the blueprint for our plan.

Darling describes his years living on a group of islands off the north west coast of Scotland. There are hundreds, at least forty, off the coast of Ullapool alone. Darling chronicled a chunk of this time spent on Iona, but the Island that made my heart race, a seminal moment, was Priest Island. Darling had spent a year there. It is the southernmost island of a group known as The Summer Isles. Priest is uninhabited with several fresh water lochs and is close, but not too close, to the mainland.

I did a bit more research. The Summer Isles are popular but seasonal tours of these islands do not include Priest. That's because the unpredictable swell of the sea around it can be tricky and it is too far out to make the extra trip economical. The

Island's history, including isolation of a disgraced priest and banishment of a sheep stealing outlaw, seemed ironic. Darling also describes a small stone bothy at the heart of the island which might provide a little shelter for the new outlaws.

My return to the House on Monday morning was a relief. Miller and Bellord looked more relaxed. Perhaps they'd come up with a new idea of where they might go or managed to sort some deal out with the money men.

'You must have some idea of how much trouble we're in. We've done what we can over the weekend to sort things out but haven't been that successful. We're going to let a lot of people down. John and I are so tired and worn out with it all. We have to get away for a while and gather our energy to enable us to face everyone. The greedy banks have been scared off by the new economic changes and the subsequent decline in business. They are going after the organ sponsors for return of the organ or the money owing on the agreement.'

'I don't have an organ, Jim,' I said, convinced this might be a good thing. They couldn't take back an organ that wasn't there, could they? That would prove they, the money men, were negligent in the first place. Who would give someone money for a product that didn't exist? Now the banks and finance companies began to desert Miller even faster than they'd been drawn to him in the first place. Social gatherings were bereft of many who were only too eager to be seen at the House not so long ago.

'If we disappear for a while it will help. We are the guarantors and in with the banks and finance companies up to our necks, as they are with us. Of course, we are small fry in the big scheme of things but they have suddenly decided to look virtuous. They will pull the plug on Southern Organs deals. The sponsors, of course, will be unable to pay, so they will come after us, the guarantors. If we are missing they'll be stumped and they know it. Give us two or three months away from it all, by which time it will all have died down and we will be able to face everyone again.' His face softened into a weary smile. I detected a hint of pleading in his voice, like he was not totally convinced I believed him, or that he even believed it himself.

Any enthusiasm for my Priest Island plan was not apparent. I showed them a map of the Summer Isles with Priest stuck way out on the periphery, and had already been thinking about how we could do the trip.

'It looks a bit of a long way out,' said Miller, glancing toward John Bellord for comment.

'It's deceptive because of the scale,' said Bellord, as he took the map.

I explained about the source of fresh water and the possibility of fishing for a bit of extra food. I told them about the bothy and the isolation and pointed to the shoreline closest to the Island. 'I worked out that point is about four miles from Priest and the surrounding countryside is virtually unpopulated, apart from a few farmhouses.'

'How would we get there, fly?' said Miller smiling, 'Get Captain Barratt to take us by helicopter?' The hint of sarcasm was not lost on me.

'We'd buy a dinghy. On a good day, even if we only make a few knots, we should get there in less than an hour,' I said, noting a definite interest from Miller as he moved toward the map. He took it, feeling the paper between his fingers, taking its pulse to see if it felt good and looked good before nodding in half approval.

'It's worth thinking about. We haven't come up with anything better,' said Bellord.

'I'm a bit worried about the whole thing. We've no experience with boats or the sea, have you?' asked Miller.

'A little,' I said, 'when I was younger, I sailed a Mirror

dinghy with a friend of mine.' I decided not to mention the fact that it had only been one sail and in calm waters off a sandy beach.

They didn't seem impressed, but neither did they question me further. It would have been pointless. Time was running out and no other remotely viable plan came up.

# 11

# The Quartermaster

As far as I remember, Miller and Bellord expressed no desire to read Darling's account. Had they done so, they would have discovered the bits I'd left out.

I was so confident of the Priest Island plan, compounded by the book 'jumping' into my hand at the right time, a good sign for sure, that I didn't want them going wobbly on me. Besides, I wasn't about to let unhelpful facts get in the way of a good plan.

So what did I leave out? I made little of the fact that Darling watched from the shores of Scoraig and Dundonnel for many months, waiting for the right conditions, before setting off for Priest Island. He worked to a strict daily routine, weighing the conditions, predicting the likely weather, watching tides and using his telescope to look more closely at the sea beyond Little Loch Broom. Darling's boat, which had to accommodate his wife, child, goats, chickens and sufficient stores and tools to enable them to stay for a year or more, would have had a much tougher time. Nevertheless his thoroughness and early attempts ended in near disaster, he'd had to turn back.

Our plan had distinct advantages. Because of the compactness of our craft, we could chose a launch site anywhere along the coast and get as close as possible to Priest. Our nippy rubber dinghy, the one I'd had my eye on, with a twenty plus horsepower engine, would get us across to the island within the hour. Our window of opportunity regarding conditions and tide would be flexible.

I took on the role of quartermaster. Together we drew up lists of stores, enough to last two or three months, then I went shopping. Top of the list was a dinghy large enough to hold the three of us plus some equipment and stores, plus a second smaller dinghy to enable Miller and Bellord to fish and explore the island coast on calmer days. In an emergency they might, if the weather was kind, even make it back to Little Loch Broom.

The smaller craft would also serve to carry extra provisions for a longer stay, in case their planned return was delayed. One item was not negotiable, a chemical toilet. Miller insisted and waived any attempts to dissuade him. We'd have to accept that the Elsan toilet, plus the necessary chemicals, would take up an inordinate amount of room in the dinghy.

'What's your plan for laying a false trail? It'll have to be watertight,' I said, no pun intended.

'We'll tell the staff we're going on two weeks' holiday. That will give us a bit of a breathing space, until the police get called in.'

The police were a more recent addition to Miller's prediction of what would follow. Once people realised they weren't coming back, things would hot up.

'Where's the fake holiday going to be?'

'We'll use the helicopter to fly us to France. As it's the first holiday we've had for years, a little farewell party is in order.' Even now he was thinking of parties, but with some sadness. 'I want to say goodbye before we leave, they deserve that. It may be some time before we see everyone again. And when we do, they will no longer be our friends.'

I picked up on the fact he'd said, '...they will no longer be our friends.' It struck me, for the first time, they may not be mine either.

'The farewell party will reassure everyone that we are actually leaving for France. They'll watch us take off from the front lawn and Captain Barratt will be the perfect witness. He will be the one who drops us in Calais.'

'Then what?'

'We'll send some postcards from France and arrive back in the UK on the ferry at Dover. You will pick us up with the boats and stores packed in the trailer and drive us to Scotland.'

It sounded so simple, and in a sense it was, but simple doesn't always mean easy.

I'd no experience of tackling sea and tide, never driven an engine-powered dinghy and had little idea of how to pitch a camp or choose the right tents for extreme conditions. Over the next couple of months I paid many moonlight visits to Miller and Bellord's flat. I bought stores a little at a time, packaging and labeling everything and storing it all in a disused garage. A Cortina estate was to be our getaway vehicle. Miller thought such a common vehicle would be less noticeable. He was in denial because it turned out to be the same canary yellow as my Jensen.

I would need an alibi for the three days I expected to be gone. Not a problem. I was often away at the race circuits for a couple of days at a time and we'd already discussed setting up venues for Emperor Rosko's promotional tour for the company. We decided my cover would be a trip up north to organise it. The plan was slowly coming together: the holiday, farewell party, postcards, their return on the Dover Ferry, all tied in with my almost foolproof alibi.

The toughest part would be facing my family on my return from Scotland, especially Tanya, the kids and mother-in-law.

Father in law would be fine, dear gentle Frank who wouldn't judge or criticise anyone. Much of his leisure time was spent pottering around with his little Ford 'Angular'. He must have been sixty when he decided to learn to drive and buy a car. Totally unexpectedly, he passed his driving test first time and surprised everyone.

He was nervous as hell once he was let out on his own, especially when Madge sat next to him for her inaugural outing. He almost got to our place, about half a mile away, without hitting anything, but not quite. The windscreen misted up and he was anxious about driving his wife. *Crunch, screech, scrape.* All down the side of a parked car. Fortunately, only minor damage was done to the car, but irreparable damage was done to Madge's confidence in Frank's driving. But that didn't stop him lavishing love and care on the 'Angular'. He knew nothing about motors but he checked oil and tyres daily, whether he used the car or not, and polished it to perfection. Frank was everyone's mate, including mine.

We nearly got rumbled, quite early on in our plans. Marion and Johnny Farnton lived in a cottage fairly close to Miller's flat. Marion came out one night and asked me what I was doing at the House so late and what was I carrying? I mumbled something unconvincing about getting stuff ready for the Rosko tour, busy, busy, not enough time in the day. Now, she would be particularly vigilant.

My relationship with Marion was one of polite tolerance. We rubbed along because we were part of the Miller and Bellord gang, but I never felt she ever quite took to me, maybe because I was late on the scene. Johnny and Marion had known Miller for many years. I think there might have been a bit of jealousy, because I was spending more time with Miller and Bellord than her and Johnny. *Just wait. When she finds out what we've been up to, she'll explode and I'll get both barrels.*

Rubber boats are more buoyant and less prone to sinking than wooden ones, should they fill with water, unless one had the misfortune to hit something sharp, a rock or some hidden object. In addition they can be deflated, rolled up and stored in a relatively tight space and fitted into a small trailer. I bought two dinghies, an Avon S220, the one I'd first had my eye on, weighing a hundred kilos, four metres long and two across the beam with a twenty horsepower Chrysler engine (looking back it should have been fifty, but what did I know?) Then I chose a second craft, destined to stay on the Island. A two metre long Avon Redstart weighing in at sixteen kilos, with a two and a half horse power engine. This smaller craft was not a parsimonious choice. It needed to be small enough for one man to carry, launch and operate whilst being capable of getting the two men back to shore, should unforeseen circumstances arise. We wouldn't know that 'til we saw how the big dinghy handles.

We thought of a thousand things that might go wrong but which we'd hoped never would. The worst of our fears focused on the unpredictability of the sea and tides. I knew from Darling's account, weather can change in a moment and the waters beyond the mouth of the loch could be deceptive.

Miller and Bellord had an alibi that would hold up for two weeks. Mine would only last three days, four at most. Perhaps we'd get to Priest Island but the weather would prevent my journey back. Suppose we'd been rumbled and were already being hunted, or Marion had decided on a bit of detective work following our moonlit encounter? What if we were spotted at the Dover terminal, or when we stopped for petrol? And what if others were already on the island? Darling may have started a trend when he wrote Island Years praising its solitude and beauty. There may be whole families squatting on it. And who, if anyone, owns it? We hadn't got permission to land, or stay. Questions rattled around my head.

My time away would be brief, but what about when I returned home from the journey? I knew I'd have to lie to everyone and keep it up for some time. But when Miller and Bellord reappeared in a couple of months or so and sorted things out, surely I'd be forgiven. Might even be seen as a loyal friend who'd gone the extra mile.

Our list was virtually complete. The inflatables, stashed in a covered trailer, were kept in my garage at home. The neighbours were used to me and my building business: the storing of trailers, ladders and the paraphernalia of the trade. The stockpile of equipment and food for the trip were packed in the yellow Cortina estate in one of the House garages. The garage, close to their flat a short way down the main drive, was off to one side in a small courtyard surrounded by greenery. It couldn't be seen from the House or the drive unless someone was particularly nosey and strayed off the main track.

I was the youngest and physically strongest. Once I'd left the island I would be on my own in seas we'd yet to face. In case I had to get into the water, maybe to pull the boat in for the final yard or two, or for some other emergency, we'd added a long rope in addition to the painter already attached to the dinghy's nose. I'd insisted on a wet suit and flippers to enable me to stay longer in cold water and swim further, if I had to. Flares for the two were critical and probably the only means they would have for contacting the shore or a passing fishing boat when they were ready to give themselves up. Given Miller and Bellord's take on life, that wouldn't be long. In fact it wouldn't surprise me if their stay was a brief one. They'd be itching to sort things out!

As anticipated, the Elsan chemical toilet took up more than its fair share of car space. Rice and food were packed, wrapped then double wrapped. Some dried food and cans of protein, fish and ham were included in an attempt to ensure a balanced meal, albeit heavily preserved in chemicals that neither Miller nor Bellord would normally have touched. Foil-wrapped Oxo cubes were a good concentrate suitable for hot drinks and maybe the odd treat as gravy. No point taking fruit or vegetables in their raw state, they'd rot in days. We'd rely on the lochs for fresh water and surely the seal population wouldn't mind sharing a few fish.

By way of explanation, Miller wrote letters to his company directors, Dennis Streeter, Alan Chase and the Monacos. I would deliver them once their fortnight's 'holiday' was over. They did not discuss their contents for one simple reason, if the men opened the letters in front of me, Miller and Bellord wanted my response to be totally convincing.

# 12

# Escape to Priest Island

*When we embark on these ploys we certainly do not seek adventure, for to our minds adventure often means incompetence somewhere or carelessness at some earlier time.* Dr Frank Fraser Darling - Island Years.

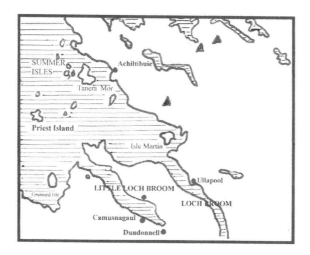

September 10th 1975, the day of my departure and their escape. Only death or war could have changed that date. Things were hotting up. If the banks called the police in to investigate now, we wouldn't be going anywhere. Miller and Bellord would be under close surveillance. Amazingly, their ability to juggle, persuade and paper over the cracks of what was happening held good.

The House staff were genuinely keen to see the two men take a break. I couldn't say the same for the shop and factory staff. And had the racing drivers caught scent of their trip I think we might have had a riot on our hands, since the end of the season was imminent. Championship prizes and sponsorship deals were due to be paid and next year's programmes discussed. There would be no more racing sponsorship, no more deals at all.

That morning I drove to the House in the Jensen. The thirty mile drive through the rolling Sussex countryside, the clear bright morning and light traffic eased my tension, despite the nature of my business. I hadn't slept well but didn't feel tired. In fact, I felt very much alive.

The Catholic Church at West Grinstead is a pretty church, apart from its new ungainly steeple, looking mean and temporary with its reduced girth and thin metal cladding. I had passed it on my way to the House for many years. I remember the old traditionally built steeple, robust and easy on the eye. Perhaps, I thought cynically, the church had decided to cut back on maintaining the fabric of the building to buy an organ.

There is only one way to approach the House by road and that is up the beech-lined drive toward the front of it. Before you reach it and on the left along a short gravelled drive, stands the garage complex and Miller's flat. Straight ahead, in a sizeable courtyard, is the imposing house fronted with high gables and a striking Italian door. The door is said to be one of a pair, the other destined for Chequers, the Prime Minister's residence. From windows either side of the entrance, it is possible to see visitors approaching the House by car. We knew this and that is why the leaving party was being held in the main hall. Unless someone decided to wander across the courtyard at the wrong moment, I'd not be seen. Miller and Bellord would be keeping an eye out for straying guests.

The Jensen spun a cloud of dust as I turned off the narrow road into the drive of the House. I remember many such small details vividly because my senses were now so acute, I swear I could hear the House guests from here, two hundred yards away from behind closed doors, where we needed them. I didn't want any sharp-eyed amateur 'tec roaming around seeing things they shouldn't.

The crunching of my car tyres on the gravelled approach stopped with an odd silence as I entered the cobbled courtyard to the garages. My task at this point was simple. Park the Jensen, drive the loaded Cortina out, put the Jensen in, lock the doors and drive away. The helicopter would be here soon and I needed to be gone. I thought I'd checked everything, one car out, one car in, padlock doors then drive off. But I couldn't. I'd left the keys of the Cortina on the passenger seat of the Jensen, which I'd locked inside the garage. The padlock had been left undone especially for me. The plan was already showing cracks. The helicopter was due and I should be on the M20.

I ran across to the entrance hall of the House. The place was heaving with staff and well-wishers drinking champagne and making merry. This may have seemed over the top for two guys planning a couple of weeks in France. Not really. Everyone knew the strain Miller and Bellord had been under. They hadn't had a break in years and we all wished them well and wanted them to come back refreshed and ready to save their empire. It was only a hundred yard dash, yet my run felt Olympian. Heart pumped, face flushed, breathing laboured. I tapped the shoulder of the nearest person. 'Could you pass a message to Jim? I need to see him,' I said rather breathlessly, deciding against adding, urgently, 'I'll wait here.'

I'd only seen Miller this furious once before, when the banks started to close in and one of the drivers decided to whine on about his car and sponsorship money. Miller was on the edge that day and he blew. Ever heard a drunken sailor on a night out with his mate? No contest. The scene was about to be repeated. One thing saved me. He couldn't let it happen now, not with all these people, not with all our plans. 'Wait outside', he said, before walking calmly across to the office. The search for the spare garage keys must have been frenetic. He slipped me the spare key. He'd calmed down. 'I think I've covered the situation, I told people there'd been a few hitches with your planned trip up north and you had to tie a few things up with me before you left.'

Would that wash? It wouldn't convince Marion for a start and there were a few other sharp eyes that would find it odd. Most would have expected my journey to have started yesterday. And what odd timing. If I was around, why wasn't I at the farewell party? Too late to worry now, I had to drive home to pick up the trailer and get to Dover. I drove slowly in the hope that anyone watching would see all was calm. As I left the tree-lined drive for the open road, Captain Barratt's Bell Jet Ranger hovered overhead.

The drive to Dover was uneventful, at least in terms of traffic. To say it was uneventful from a mental point of view would be lying. I spent most of the time convincing myself of the wisdom of our plan. After all, I was aiding and abetting lawbreakers. But the bigger picture was what mattered. I needed to ensure that Miller and Bellord had enough time to find perspective and come back with a resolution. To do it, they needed time away from the developing storm. What about my family, the friends I introduced to Miller, my job, my home, my life? I'd told so many lies to protect them. Sure I was sorry, anxious and worried how I might be viewed if it came out I'd helped them. Someone had to. Look what they'd done for hundreds of people over decades and now they needed help. The risk to everything I had was high but what else could I do? My conscience was driving me. I had no choice.

I'd rather be two hours early than a minute late. This obsession allowed me plenty of time to rearrange the load in the Cortina. It was cramped but I was surprised at how a little rearranging made a more comfortable space for my two passengers. Parking along the promenade gave me a good view of the ferry terminal.

The weather was good but time dragged. It could have been the opportunity for further reflection on my betrayal of family and friends. But with our adventure imminent all I could think of was the journey and Priest Island, and of course, whether they would actually get to Dover in the first place. Suppose the police had already started looking for them? Perhaps they'd been picked up on the ferry. I glanced at my watch, they were horribly late. Maybe they'd decided to stay in France or were already on their way to a distant land, South America or some other place outlaws might choose to escape justice. The bishops, the money, the fraud and my erratic search for meaning to life had no real place in my thoughts now. I was truly living in the moment, something Miller encouraged.

The sky was overcast now and a sea mist started to drift toward the prom. I was certain the hands on my watch were stuck. I put it to my ear, it was still ticking. I peered toward the terminal. A few people milled around, some holiday makers queued at kiosks and stalls.

Two men strode purposefully along the prom toward me, one limping, his overcoat collar turned up. Both wore dark glasses, seemingly oblivious to the darkening sky. The Mafia?

No, Miller and Bellord. We were relieved to see each other, but no embrace. I wedged their bit of hand luggage, a briefcase and hold all, between the packed contents of the estate. Once in the car, the sun appeared and we pulled away from the seafront and out toward the motorway.

'The helicopter arrived as you left,' said Miller, without mentioning the lost key incident. He knew as well as me what a close call it was. What an idiot I'd been, what an omen it might prove to be.

'How was the goodbye?' I asked, itching to know.

'Everyone came out to wave us off. It was quite emotional,' said Miller. John Bellord nodded agreement. 'But such a relief. We can't tell you.'

Stepping into that helicopter after years of struggle must have been one hell of a moment. Then to observe the people who trusted them, peering up from below the soaring helicopter, smiling and waving, comforted by the knowledge that Miller and Bellord were having a break with no idea of what was about to happen...They would not be seeing these two men for some time.

'So everything went well?'

Miller had been overcome, cried even (unheard of) and Bellord, acting as Trevor Howard or Kenneth More would have done, kept a stiff upper lip and remained dry eyed.

'Once we reached Calais,' continued Miller, 'We bought postcards, sat in a cafe, wrote brief messages on them and posted them on our way back to the Calais ferry.'

I looked in the rear view mirror. Both men, calm and silent, looked straight ahead.

'Any problems, anyone suspicious on the ferry? Did Captain Barratt say anything much?' I asked.

'He thought nothing of it. He's used to ferrying us around. Besides, he's not a local man. Doubt if he knows anything. He acted normal. I would be able to tell, wouldn't I?' he said, in clipped nervy sentences.

'Once in France, we took great pains to ensure we were noticed; chatted to the cafe owners, ate a meal, made a great thing about buying postcards and stamps and asked for directions.'

And if Jim was in 'notice me' mode, there must have been many witnesses to their arrival in Calais.

Their return on the ferry was different. They had to be invisible. Okay, Jim, now was the time to show the world you can do that too. Their sail back to Dover had been uneventful. Apart from the need to acquire the mentality and stealth of fugitives, suspecting everyone, they'd acted the relaxed but silent travellers. It would have been extraordinary bad luck if anyone remembered two casually dressed middle aged men taking a ride on the lunchtime Ferry to Dover.

It was going to be a long day. Now we had to drive the eight hundred and sixty miles to Ullapool.

We all admitted to a feeling of intense relief and calm. Odd, given that we were a long way from realising our plan. Yet what had been achieved so far was not insignificant. Driving along the M20 through Kent and heading for the M1 was a time for letting go and looking forward to the peace and isolation that would rejuvenate and resolve. I was convinced this was the beginning of a solution. Not that running away in itself solves anything, but time, space and reflection do. Surely an uncluttered life on the island could only sharpen their perspective and prepare them for a clear-headed plan.

Newport Pagnall service station on the M1 was our first stop since leaving Dover. It allowed Miller and Bellord a quick break, but no dallying around the shop and restaurant area. It was common sense to keep them out of the way, not paranoia. But his awkward limp would be a real give away once the police were informed. For now, no one knew where the hell they were.

Or did they? I topped up with petrol, filled flasks with coffee, bought water and sandwiches and decided to phone Tanya. The opportunity to phone again may not happen. She sounded relaxed and not in the least suspicious. She asked about my trip, organising the Emperor Rosko programme up north.

'Any messages?'

'Yes. Marion from the House rang. She asked where you were.'

'What did you say?'

'Told her what you told me. That you were up north, organising that Rosko thing.'

'Marion already knew that, everyone does. Besides, it's none of her business,' I said sharply, my hands clammy on the grimy phone.

'She doesn't believe that's what you're doing,' said Tanya, with no obvious sign that she didn't believe me.

'Where does she think I am?' I changed the phone to my slightly drier hand.

'She thinks you're in France with Miller and Bellord.'

I smiled. Marion was clever but not that clever. Good, at least she believed they were in France.

'Is that what you think?'

'No, I believe you. You'll be back in a few days. They've gone for a fortnight. So why lie about it and pretend you're somewhere else?'

'Thanks, Tan. I think I'd better call her.'

I had to quash Marion's detective work right now. Hopefully it wouldn't be too hard. I rang her number with a reverse charge call, not out of meanness but to help compound my alibi nicely.

'Hi, Marion,' I said cheerily, to a frosty silence. 'Tanya said you thought I was with Jim and John in France.'

'Are you?'

'Of course not. You can see I'm ringing from a Daventry exchange. I'm trying to arrange the Rosko tour.' I'd almost convinced myself.

She didn't sound convinced, but had nothing else to go on. Marion is suspicious by nature, or to be fair, just sharper generally. She'd been compelled to take the call, note I was ringing from a Daventry exchange and have to direct her suspicious mind somewhere else. Daventry was exactly right. It was up north, and many miles from where she thought Jim and John were or should be.

I returned to a very alert pair of very hungry men. I told them about Marion's call; a piece of news they didn't need. It would haunt us, that call. Not that she knew where we were but she was on the trail, and who knows where it might lead. Marion was always a dog with a bone and she'd worry 'til she'd got every last shred of meat off it.

The drive followed a series of names on a map, a measure of time and distance, stepping stones to Priest Island. I drove a steady sixty to seventy mph up the M1, onto the M6, Carlisle, Inverness and the north west.

Thoughts of our escape from the House faded with each mile. Getting to Ullapool and finding the best launch site for the dinghies was all that mattered now. Research of the area had been impossible and I knew that would prove to be a big mistake, but what could I have done? I hadn't been to Scotland, never mind the area we were headed for. Jim and John had been to Ullapool several times but never with the need to discover a launch site for some future escape.

It's easy to forget castles, towns and buildings in the far north west. It's all about mountains, lochs, moors, heather, coast and vast empty spaces, one of the great wildernesses of Europe. We were approaching the village of Garve. The landscape was becoming more rugged and barren by the mile as we drove along the edge of the Loch that had lent its name to the small community. The population, fed by a single track railway line, boasted little: a station, shop, post office, hotel and a clutter of cottages. The continuing good road led on for half a mile before dividing, left toward Gairloch, Torridon and Kyle and right for the more direct route to Ullapool.

The A385 directed us up in a sweeping climb. The view passing the Corry Bridge over the braes of Ullapool, took my breath away. Jim and John had experienced it before, but to me it was magical. The panorama of Loch Broom, one of the great sea lochs of the north west, cleaved the mainland. A pepper of buildings trailed toward Ullapool Point. The distant outlines of the Summer Isles came into view, sharpening as we got closer. We were so close to our destination now, hardly a dozen miles from Priest Island.

The sea-like liquid silk, the mountains sharp as a shadow show, the colours of the landscape vivid. The intoxicating air stung our eyes with its sudden coolness. I could see exactly why Miller and Bellord had been captivated. I'd be surprised to learn of anyone coming here and not falling in love with the place.

The planned launch of the dinghies relied on finding a suitably secluded spot, away from prying eyes without being too difficult for trailer access.

Parking in Mill Street, a few hundred yards from the fishing pier, we filled up with petrol, including the spare fuel cans for the two boats. It would be our last fill up before leaving for the Island. There was a risk Miller and Bellord had to take, and that meant putting aside their fear of being spotted. Stiff, with aching muscles, they got out of the car and stretched like waking cats. It was quiet and peaceful with only a few locals going about their business. No one seemed bothered about a car with a trailer. Surely it wasn't uncommon in an area that welcomed campers and fishermen.

Sandwiches from the small cafe satisfied our doubtful hunger, a few bites and we were full, too excited to eat more.

I walked with John Bellord down to the chandlers, the Captain's Cabin, on the corner of New and Shore Street. This building was, and probably still is, the local meeting place. It dates from 1798 and was built as the great store of the village and known locally as The Corner of the Store.

The one inch ordnance survey map and tide charts we bought were of little help. We couldn't work out the tide chart but we did get some idea of scale and detail which, until now, we'd not had the chance to establish. Perhaps with a bit of time and John Bellord's sharp brain we'd work it out, but time was not on our side.

On a hunch we made for Achiltibuie, a tiny community scattered around Badentarbat Bay. From Achiltibuie westward we could see the Summer Isles nestling in that part of the east Atlantic known as the Minch. Aeons ago glacier disruption split the mainland and in the process, moved the same Torridonian stone that formed the majestic peaks of the north west, to form these Islands.

From a distance they looked inviting, as far away things often do. The reality is different. Apart from the largest, Tanera More, these islands are barren, isolated and uninhabited. And we were counting on it. From Achiltibuie it looked to be a straight, quick hop from island to island until we got to Priest but there were too many people around. Three strangers pushing two inflatable dinghies loaded to the gunwales off the coast and out of season? Given the potential witnesses, the risk was too high.

We faced two immediate problems; one, the locals, the other, rocks. Some of these islands were little more than rocks themselves. Steep, aloof and jagged enough to tear a dinghy on contact. We had yet to learn just how rocky this coast was and decided not to leave from here.

In fact, the whole stretch of Loch Broom confounded us. Too many dwellings overlooked it, a little smoke from a chimney here, a man outside his house chopping logs there. We were gradually moving further and further away from the Island. We checked our information again. Either the cliffs and rocks were too treacherous, making it impossible to carry and launch the dinghies, or the drivable roads and tracks did not allow us close enough to water. The substantial load we'd packed made even the briefest hike impossible.

Precious hours had already been wasted. We eroded more time by contemplating launches from a more southerly point; Gruinard Bay or Greenstone Point. From Gruinard Bay, Priest was visible, a straight run without taxing our navigation skills or using up precious fuel. The road also ran close to the beach. As we drove nearer, caravans came into view. All inhabited with much hustle and bustle as people went about their business. Perhaps we were being paranoid. It looked like the perfect sheltered spot from which any local might launch a dinghy. But three strangers and a trailer?

Caravan people seem particularly vigilant, or perhaps bad weather was coming. A lot of opening and closing of doors, stepping outside, rocking the caravan to test stability and generally fussing around, was evident. They checked gas and water levels, they sat on tiny stools and chatted. This vigorous routine coupled with a half decent memory might be our undoing. 'Yes,' they'd say,' *we saw the three men, one with a limp, two dinghies piled high. Took straight off from the beach and headed toward Priest Island.'* Someone would point and wave a finger. *'Got my scope out, didn't see them land though, too rough, they must have gone round the other side for somewhere to get ashore. They'd be lucky. None of us have landed there yet.'*

Our hunt, both north and south, proved fruitless. Not a

single place where respectable criminals could safely unpack and launch their getaway boats. We'd either have to compromise, take a chance, or go home and face the music.

The Destitution Road, constructed in 1847 to provide work for the stricken crofting population of the west coast during the famine years, wound ahead. We'd taken the route to Dundonnel and Little Loch Broom. Past the Forest of Fannich we left trees for high moorland scarred with black gullies and the remains of the ancient Forest of Caledon. Fraser Darling's Brae House overlooked this Loch. It was from this very place he planned his adventure to Priest with his wife Bobby. To my mind, Little Loch Broom was prettier than Loch Broom and was, I imagine, how Loch Broom must have looked a century earlier without its spread of houses, shops and hotels.

A small parking patch appeared on the road ahead. It overlooked the Loch at Camusnagaul. We parked and noted with increasing excitement, the not too steep rocky slope that extended roughly down from our parked Cortina to the shoreline. It was by no means perfect, but it was the best deal so far. The proposed launch site was more or less at the head of the Loch, making our sea journey much longer. But the light was fading and we'd driven nearly a thousand miles. Were we likely to find anything better? Not a single vehicle passed us during the next couple of hours and few houses dotted the landscape. Plus, we'd lost a whole day.

Now we were three times further from Priest than we'd anticipated. In the cosiness of home, with a child's school ruler to gauge distance, I'd reckoned it to be no more than four miles, give or take. Now it was closer to twelve. Could fuel for the boats be a problem? Four miles would have only taken an hour or so. But twelve sounded quite a trip, half the width of the English Channel at Dover.

The grey darkening of a cloudy September evening in the

north west appeared suddenly threatening. Miller, who seemed to have lost all common sense, wanted to leave for the Island straight away. I could understand his impatience but he must have worked it out, we'd reach the Island in darkness. The thought chilled me. If we couldn't land, it would be a very long night bobbing about off shore waiting for dawn. If we ever saw dawn.

Thankfully Bellord agreed with me and wanted to wait for morning. We'd got used to trusting Miller's judgment and were within a whisker of trusting it now. But tired as we were, we must have sensed the blip in his judgment. We were exhausted and likely to make mistakes. This was a unique situation, a level playing field, none of us had enough knowledge of sea and sail to pull rank. The blind were leading the blind.

No one wanted to lose a precious twenty four hours, especially me. I was due back and unable to get to a phone for at least another day. What would Tanya think? What would Marion think? Would the police be alerted early because of that critical delay? Not for Miller and Bellord, but for me. *Racing manager disappears on trip up north.* They'd find out pretty quick there wasn't a Rosko tour. What towns and venues would I be visiting? Where was I staying? Nobody would know because our plan never factored in a day's delay.

Jim sat behind me while John spread the map over the steering wheel and dashboard.

'If we're here,' he said, sticking his finger on a kink in the coastal road, Camusnagaul we assumed, though we'd not spotted a sign announcing it, 'we should be able to look straight up the Loch and see Priest Island.'

We looked up simultaneously. Light was fading but we should have seen something, at least a vague shape. Nothing. Nothing between the rugged landscape shaping the mouth of the Loch and the black horizon of a dark sea. We'd parked the

Cortina off a slight curve in the road, maybe that was the problem. Not to worry, we should be able to see it clearly from the launching rock. But not until morning. *If we do see it, our suspect navigation 'skills' will be redundant. Point the boat at the Island, rev the engine and we'll be there in no time.* Being positive sometimes means lying to yourself.

'Suppose the weather gets rough while we're out there and we end up in the drink?' asked Miller, in an untypically negative tone.

'Hang on to the ropes at the side of the dinghy at all times. Don't let go until we reach the Island. If we get ditched then we might have to swim a few yards.'

I'd picked upon the brief silence.

'We can't swim,' he said, without elaboration. 'I thought you knew.'

At first I panicked but the question was, did it really matter? They'd not have a chance anyway. My wet suit and flippers would help me in the short term, protect me from the icy waters of the Minch, at least for a while. Any attempt by Miller and Bellord to swim would have ended in disaster, they would not have survived. If the boat capsized in heavy seas, the chance of getting back into the boat would be slim. It would drift away and maybe end up stuck between rocks on Priest Island. Or float engineless to another land. The cold would have killed them in minutes.

We looked at the slate grey loch below us, hardly impressing the shore with its gently pulsing lap. The land rose steeply on the opposite side, the sun-drenched green turning a lichen dark as the evening shadow moved blanket-like, swiftly covering the brow.

Another hour or so and it would be dark. It would take at least that long to get everything down to the flat grey rock at the water's edge, and given Darling's experience and helpful diary, we'd been warned that a calm loch here would not necessarily indicate a calm sea out in the Minch. Without binoculars we had no way of seeing beyond the mouth of Little Loch Broom.

A childlike innocence permeated our plan. A situation that might have been written for Enid Blyton's Famous Five (or Infamous three or even the Three Stooges).

We were naive to say the least and not following the script. Drive to Ullapool, launch reliable boat, starts first pull, off pretty deserted beach. Putter along on a calm sea wondering why we'd worried in the first place. Island straight ahead, a stone's throw from our launch site. Land in small cove on inviting and completely uninhabited island, pitch tents, find fresh water loch, drink tea, return to nice warm car, drive home. Sit on the secret for a couple of months then, hey presto!

Putting on the wet suit would be difficult. It could wait till morning. The night was bitter, rivulets of condensation ran down the windows and doors. Our breath came in plumes of fine steam. This would be our hotel for the night. And night came all too suddenly.

No one slept, at least not for more than minutes at a time. The coldness gnawed our bones, slowly refrigerating us on the edge of a loch in the middle of a wilderness.

Although the night had descended quickly, the morning appeared slowly, a faint light that seemed to trick the eye each time we stirred. Then the sun came up behind us and lit the water along its length, but we still couldn't see Priest Island. Wherever that damn pile of rock was, we'd have to launch from here, we couldn't be that far out.

# 13

# Rough Sea

I'd never seen Miller and Bellord looking crumpled and unshaven before. Odd how it made them appear so vulnerable, so ordinary yet so vagrant.

The haggard three stepped out of the car, stiff, aching but suddenly alert when a cold blast swept down the loch from the west.

'Let's go,' said Miller, hugging himself, exhaling breathy clouds into the still morning air.

'I'll do a recce first, take a few things with me and see how tricky it is. If it's not too bad we can load ourselves up and get stuff down quickly. If not we might have to take our time. We can't risk a twisted ankle.'

I untied the trailer and pulled out a couple of tents to carry. The way down to the rock was steeper and more slippery than expected. 'It's a bit awkward,' I shouted back. They must have seen my foot slip as I moved too quickly across the stony decline. I was panting already. It would take ages to get all the stuff down. But, hallelujah, once down on the flat rock I could see the shape of Priest Island, the early sun casting moon crater shadows on its rugged surface. It looked a straight forward run with nothing in the way of our journey.

'I can see the Island straight ahead. And it's a sunny day,' I added, unnecessarily.

Two smiling faces looked down at me.

'It's not easy getting onto the rock, you take the light stuff and I'll do boats and engines.'

Miller managed his gammy leg well on level surfaces, but this terrain would be some trial. The way down was steep and rocky with the slimy, weedy detritus of a tidal loch. You could be on your back in no time.

Five am. We were hungry but breakfast would have to wait, probably until lunch time. The flask of lukewarm coffee still tasted good. We should be over there in a couple of hours or so if the sun, sea and calm weather held. I could be back at Camusnagaul for brunch.

Not a cloud in the sky and we'd predicted, with our scant knowledge, that the tide would be right at about seven am. Only two hours to launch time and the final leg of our escape to Priest Island.

I scanned the opposite shore for signs of life but spotted none. Daylight revealed one or two houses we hadn't noticed yesterday, as if they'd sprouted, mushroom like, during the night. The loch could be a mile wide but without a point of reference it was hard to tell.

Certainly the houses looked the size of those in a Monopoly game. Someone could be standing at a window with a telescope scratching their head, giving the wife a run down before passing the scope. *'What do you make of those three, lassie? Five in the morning and they look like they might be up to no good. Look at the stack in that car and that loaded trailer. They must have been there all night 'cause I remember seeing that yellow car pull in just before dusk. And how do they expect to go anywhere, they dinna have a boat.'*

The weather was exactly what we'd ordered. No doubt Miller and Bellord's metaphysical messages were getting through to the right people.

*What the hell are we doing here?*

Once we'd descended with the first load, we stood and relished the uninterrupted view up the Loch. We checked the map. The beautiful peaks of An Teallach rose behind us on the southern horizon. Opposite, across a mile of water, a single track road appeared and disappeared beneath the northern peaks at Badrallach. From here, there was no road going westward to Scoraig and the mouth of Little Loch Broom, if there had been we would have taken it. The distance then would only have been a 'pond' away. But it's a five mile walk on a simple path that switchbacks toward the tiny crofting community nestling there.

We started shifting the big stuff. I removed the cold stiff tarpaulin from the wooden trailer, folded it, tucked it away and carried the heavy dinghy down the slippery, black, collection of rocks. They saw me struggle and offered to help. I reminded them that if I couldn't manage to get it down on my own, I certainly wouldn't be able to get it back up. Jim and John looked puzzled, as if my journey back had never entered their heads.

It was not surprising that Miller's inconvenient limp and our lack of experience would result in problems getting everything down to the water's edge. Feet gained a cautious hold then, from time to time, one of us would stumble or stand motionless, reaching out for a handhold to steady ourselves. Despite the three of us working full tilt, progress was agonisingly slow.

Fraser Darling had left Dundonnel and Scoraig on different occasions for Priest. But his journey was one of exploration and research, an attempt to gather facts on the flora and fauna that survived on this isolated lump of rock. Aborted attempts to land, due to the ferocity and unpredictability of the weather, had left him frustrated. I began to wonder, that even with his daily vigil and a telescope capable of seeing Priest in detail, whether his knowledge of the north west and its daily seasons made his long awaited trip any more predictable than ours. That sea and weather could change right now.

Despite the difficulty of getting to it, the huge flat rock presented an almost perfect launch pad for our trip. If only it had appeared at the beginning of our search, somewhere a bit closer to the Island.

I unrolled the large dinghy and laid it out. Wrinkled, wet and unwieldy, it stuck fast to the smooth, now dry, rock.

My arms, like pistons, drove the tiny, pathetically inadequate pump. Imperceptibly at first, small flat bubbles of air filled the rubber shape inch by inch, then the floats started to take on their proper form. But by the time the dinghy was fully inflated, a precious hour had passed. I was panting like a dog and cursing myself for not getting a decent pump. The Redstart took about a third of that time.

With large wing nuts and sturdy bolts, I secured the twenty horsepower engine to the laminated wooden stern of the largest dinghy and the two and a half horsepower engine to the smaller craft. We strapped this horizontally to keep it out of the water, to save it getting damaged at sea. There would be no passengers in the smallest dinghy. Jim and John loaded the Redstart with most of the equipment, spread evenly across the width and length. Everything was double wrapped in polythene, placed in storage bags and strapped down tight and low to give as much stability as possible. We checked everything twice, knowing that the Redstart would be towed behind with no chance of making adjustments once we were at sea.

The task had taken two hours. It was now seven am, our predicted perfect launch time. I changed from warm dry clothes into the wetsuit and felt immediately clammy, cold and uncomfortable.

The man watching us from across the loch, if there was such a man, would now be even more concerned. *'Get the phone, lassie, the man's got dressed up in black and they've got stuff hidden in that boat. Must be amateur smugglers, they made a right pig's arse of getting down to the Loch. And one of 'em's a cripple.'*

Gradually the temperature rose between the skin and rubber of my wetsuit. The film of water, warming nicely, made me feel exquisitely comfortable and invincible against the weather and the Minch.

Finally, the Cortina was empty. I checked all the doors and boot, twice, as Jim watched from below. I pinned the car keys into the neat zipped inside pocket of the wetsuit. Losing them would have been the end of it. I wedged the long marine style rubber flippers into the tapering bow of the dinghy. In the event of hitting a rock or being turned over at sea, at least we'd have some hope of survival. I knew I could swim a mile. I'd done it before, in a calm warm sea. Little rocky islands littered the Minch so there'd be at least a chance I could get to land. Right now, looking at the sea and weather, having to ditch anywhere seemed unlikely.

The boat made no sound as it slid gently off the rock into Little Loch Broom. Bellord held the painter, pulling it tight to the rock.

The operation which we initially estimated would only take half an hour or so, had taken three. We'd missed the best tide and lost hours, but consoled ourselves with the fact that, had we left last night as Miller suggested, we'd have approached a black island in a black sea and at night.

One tent and some food stores had been stowed with us in the large dinghy. Should the small craft meet with disaster, at least we'd have some chance. The outlaws and their short term needs, all in the main boat.

We secured the painter of the Redstart to the stern of the Avon S550 and pushed it into the water. I held the craft while Miller and Bellord stepped into the boat. It must have been a first for Miller. He tottered and held onto boat and Bellord. At one point I thought we'd have to fish him out before we'd even left the launch pad.

The man across the way would be rubbing his chin, resting a restraining hand on his wife's shoulder. *'Forget the polis, lassie, get the coast guard and an ambulance, a man's about to drown out there.'*

Miller and Bellord sat evenly amidships to balance the weight. My position astern, as well as giving me an excellent spot to push off from, enabled me to start the engine and steer.

Right up until this very moment, we had not tested the engine. There had been no chance to do so. It must have been the most important thing we should have done regarding preparation for this stage of the journey, but we had not done it. I'd heard that these machines respond well to positive brute force. No point fannying around with a little jerk, this baby needed an almighty pull. That's exactly what I did and was rewarded with a noise something like a new born baby gasping for breath followed by a single smoke ring from the exhaust.

Three determined minds, one or two probably psychic, willed it to start. The second attempt was no better. The cough, if anything, was weaker. Had it been a baby, we'd have feared the worst and moved it to intensive care. The sum of our mental coercion must have frightened the damn thing. On the third sweaty-palmed pull, the engine burst into full life with a healthy pop-pop-pop. A puff of pale smoke disappeared across the loch followed by the comforting sounds of a healthy engine.

We cast off from the rocky shore and moved toward the middle of the loch. It didn't take long to feel the unexpectedly burdensome weight of the smaller dinghy on our little convoy. Manoeuvring was difficult. The drag force of the Redstart delayed response to our rudder control. Even at full throttle, which I thought was worth testing, progress was painfully slow.

I expected to nip along at a fair speed, bow up, skipping along the surface like a speed boat. It was the pace of a lazy Sunday afternoon row. Sometimes it felt like we were going nowhere; partly to do with speed but also to do with the length and width of the loch and the way the wind coming toward us hit the gentle waves, stopping them mid flow like the freeze frame on a camera.

A calm sea and windless weather can turn into a howling gale and crashing waves within the hour but the weather was good right now. It felt like putting along on a boating lake. A light breeze off the mountains ruffled the loch surface, the sun-dappled reflections flashed across our faces making us blink. The air, pure and exhilarating, brought on the early stages of intoxication.

No one spoke. Mint sweets were passed round, perhaps as a distraction. They certainly added an odd dimension; we were tasting and smelling something akin to our surroundings, the sharp 'mint' clean freshness of the sea. The gentle lapping of water against rubber, the rhythmic throb of the engine and a squawking gull overhead were the only sounds. Roads and tracks either side of us were silent. Not a vehicle or person to be seen.

Home and the House slipped into my thoughts. No doubt my delay would be noticed and fretted about. Miller and Bellord seemed lost in the moment, even appreciating the beauty of the place. In a short time they'd be on the island and I would be gone. They had flares if things got tough. I wondered how long they'd last if the weather got bad and they ended up soaked or frozen. They'd have to get help.

Who knows what thoughts were running through Miller and Bellord's minds? They looked relieved, happy, liberated probably. Despite the delays, we'd thought on our feet and adjusted to each situation. Never once had we discussed changing our plan for their stay on Priest Island. Any brief moments of uncertainty were usually replaced with enthusiastic optimism, taking our plan closer to a goal that, in such hopeful mood, seemed inevitable.

The two boats slip slapped their way across the gentle ripples of the loch.

*'They're well up the Loch now, lassie, and moving hellishly slow. Wherever they're goin', they'll be changin' their mind once they hit the Minch. Och aye. Those little play boats won't be goin' far. Better give the coastguard another ring, tell 'em to get ready for a rescue off Cailleach Head.'*

Tanya would be getting the kids ready for school now. Or were they still on summer holiday, about to eat their cereal in the tiny dining room, looking distractedly out at the courtyard garden and planning their day? They're probably not worried at all about their father. Mark wasn't a fan of school, like his dad. Kaz tolerated it but that's as good as it gets for the Green family. I miss them all. Will I be back? Of course, but in the words of Captain Oates, I may be gone some time.

A black shapeless line marked the mouth of Little Loch Broom. As we approached the open sea the gentle lapping beneath us turned to a harsh slapping.

The wind from the north accompanied a heavy swell. The boat rose and fell to a new rhythm, from a waltz to a tango, as gentle loch met the sea proper. Within minutes the rise and fall increased. The little dinghy behind us oscillated wildly, rudderless and cumbersome. It slowed us even more. Once we'd got used to the tango, it wasn't too bad; rougher than expected but nothing really. We were making ground and the weather was holding.

Looking back toward the loch it was impossible to tell where we'd launched the boats. The dinghy at sea level foreshortened perspective. We could easily make out the peninsula dividing Loch Broom from Little Loch Broom, the lighthouse at Cailleach Head and the ominous shape of Gruinard Island. Gruinard, contaminated by anthrax, still has warning notices, 'Do not land. Anthrax. Contamination', prohibiting visitors.

The panorama of yesterday was there. The roads that took hours to travel, the lochs, the sites we searched so hard to find but confounded us, could be seen at a glance.

One and a half hours later and Priest still seemed a very long way off.

*'Can't see them now, lassie. Bobbing along nicely, they were. They won't be once they get well into the Minch; they'll wish they hadn't started it. Whatever 'it' was.'*

Leaving land changed our perception. Without the shore as a reliable point of reference and the vast stretch of sea before us, all sense of travelling toward Priest had gone, we'd stopped moving. At least that's what it felt like.

With the mouth of the Loch between Cailleach Head and Static Point behind us, a string of small islands appeared. To the north, Carn Iar and Carn Deas rocky Siamese twins connected by a tenuous umbilical of raised shingle, then Bottle Island. All were roughly the same size. A smaller island, Eilean Dubh, about one third the size of Priest, was protected from human assault by sheer cliff faces uninterrupted by beach or landing place. This necklace of islands was deceptive, from our sea level perspective they looked closely packed together but it was an illusion.

To the south and some distance away was Priest; alone and isolated, away from the Summer Isles tour trips and the casual adventurer. Almost oblivious to the slowly increasing swell, we'd got used to the rise and fall, we'd failed to notice an increase in the wind. The boats needed more effort to steer and keep on course for Priest. Some waves lifted us to a point where we momentarily lost sight of the small dinghy, which swung wildly with the sudden sea change, tugging alarmingly at the stern of our larger craft. Darling mentions the Island coast here. The Torridonian Sandstone is redder and smoother than on the mainland with strata angled, to form rugged cliffs.

We could make out the south ridge of Priest running the length of it, a dark prehistoric silhouette of Torridonian rock appearing and disappearing as we dipped and dived. No agreeable landing spot appeared. All seemed rising black dangerous obstruction, determined to keep us away. The towering ridge hid what lay beyond, maybe a spot to land or more savage rock to confound us.

Our plan, to cruise the island's coast and find a suitable place to land, was not to be realised. The waves built up underneath us, lifting and tilting the dinghies at precarious angles. Water started to fill the boats. We could bale out our own craft but the small dinghy took on more and more water. The stores were strapped on to the rubber flooring and the food tied on tight to the wooden slatting, a few inches above. The food, triple wrapped and off the deck, must be fairly safe for now, but the tiny half waterlogged craft was proving impossible to control. Like a child tugging its parent in a supermarket, the child was holding up progress.

We headed unwillingly toward the south west tip of the island. The large dinghy so influenced by the smaller, threatened any landing at all. A mild panic overtook us. We considered two choices, keep the two dinghies and chance our luck, or cut one free and have the best possible chance of landing. I looked into the chilling depths of the ink black water and knew for certain I didn't want to be in there at any price. Miller and Bellord were clinging tight to the hand ropes. If we didn't get both boats ashore their survival would be brief. There was only an emergency food supply in our dinghy, enough for a week or so. We had to land both dinghies.

Grey seals swam playfully, adopting the dinghies as their errant young. Were they smiling? It looked like it with their huge glassy eyes above a black-nosed snout and cheerful expression. The sea pounded and lashed our dinghies, driving us toward a rocky cove with its unassailable cliffs, jagged rocks and no signs of a beach. There was nothing Jim and John could do. I had the tiller, the only guiding influence. We held tight, the boat rose high in the water, returning us with a crashing belly dive. I revved the engine hard. At first, the boat was unresponsive then it kicked forward out of the cove, hitting a wave head on and nearly turning us over. The small dinghy was up to its gunwales with water. As it rose and fell, water spilled over the top only to be replenished by the next wave. Surely, even given the meticulous care we'd taken, it could not stand up to such pounding?

The next tiny but unsuitable cove was destined to be our landing place. We were thrown continually against the rocks, trembling with effort and desperation. The small dinghy got the worst of it, corkscrewing over the sea and rocks, bouncing off them and close to getting punctured. We might still have no choice but to cut it loose to ensure our safety. Already a dangerous series of scars had appeared on the rubber floats, some looked about to burst. The sea was now drawing us back toward the Minch. Was it a change in the tide or simply the unpredictable nature of the seas around Priest?

I took the long painter tied to the nose of the large dinghy and dived into the sea. Gasping for breath, I surfaced to a wall of water but kept swimming as flashes of white-faced friends, steep cliffs and foaming seas swung around me. I couldn't hold the boats for much longer. Shoulders and back strained against the weight. If I didn't do something soon, it would be over for us all. Then I felt shingle under my feet. The rope tightened and pulled me toward the sea. There were two rocks jutting from the shingle, their girth too wide for the rope to be tied around them. I wrapped the painter round my waist and started a tug of war with the boats. Miller and Bellord were willing me on. I was almost horizontal, pulling and pulling.

The shingle gave under my feet as I slid back toward the sea before getting another foothold. Inch by inch I pulled myself up the shingle, timing each pull with the mood of the waves, slackening a bit as the wave peaked and pulled when it moved briefly forward. Then I held on tight as the tide attempted to drag me back. I reached the rocks and wedged myself between them. Half a ton of boats, men and supplies seemed determined to win the tug of war. I was holding on but unable to pull the boats in.

Miller and Bellord noticed it first, the rubber nosing ring on the large dinghy was coming away. The painter was attached through the ring and the two men were about to grip the overstretched rope.

'Don't try and hold it,' I shouted, 'you'll get pulled in.'

The blazing sun from the south east backlit the men and dinghies, shrouding them in deep shadow. Beyond them, way out in the Minch, a fishing boat stopped. The skipper would see us struggling, even from that distance. All we needed now was for the crew to decide on a rescue mission and we'd be back in Ullapool in no time, rubbing our sore backs, concocting preposterous stories of our misfortune and waiting for the police to pick us up.

The sturdy fishing trawler rode the swell, pitching up and over briefly, before moving on. Was it going for help? Had they already alerted the coastguard? A helicopter could be here in minutes.

'Jump, John, you have to get in the water, it's not too deep here. I can't hold on much longer.' My spine felt it was about to snap. The boat moved back out, increasing the stress on my back. The rope chafed and burned my flesh under the wetsuit. I swear I could smell scorched rubber along with the stinging salt of a thrashing sea.

John jumped, disappeared for a few seconds, bobbed up again then found his feet.

'I'll hold the boat. Get Jim out,' I said, failing to hide my moment of panic.

'He'll drown,' John spluttered, arms flailing but no signs of fear.

'We don't have a choice,' I shouted. Perhaps he couldn't hear me. More like he had a mouthful of seawater. I shouted louder. 'If you don't get him out now he'll be gone. The nosing's almost off.'

With Bellord's weight out of the boat I managed to pull it closer. He waded toward me, realising Miller would not make it to the shore unless we got him closer. We pulled on the rope together. I wrapped the painter tighter around me, taking up a couple of yards of its length, closing the gap.

John waded out and put his arms out, encouraging Miller to take a leap, but Jim and the boat were already moving away. Then, calm as a diver on a spring board, Miller jumped toward John. The dinghy almost tipped over from the thrust of Jim's mighty leap.

His crippled arm did a weird doggy paddle. His gammy leg gave way as he stood erect before tumbling sideways into the water.

For a man who couldn't swim, and in this sea, it was a brave attempt. John grabbed him by his shirt collar and sleeve as he stumbled and fought to maintain balance on the shifting shingle. I could no longer feel my back or arms; adrenaline had anaesthetised them.

The nosing was leaving the dinghy, the latex glue pulling out the final strands of its attachment. We were all there on the beach. Miller collapsed as Bellord helped me pull the boats closer. The sea must have had a change of heart. A wave reared up, lifting the boats aloft, delivering them with a crash in front of us. We pulled and pulled until the boats slid into the tiny cove and finally onto land. Both the dinghies were full of water, the larger, its contents swimming back and forth in the space vacated by the three of us. We fixed the painter to a more secure part of the dinghy before attaching the free end to the rocks.

# 14

# The Camp

The sun was high. Miller collapsed on the beach but was still breathing. He opened his eyes to see us lying next to him and smiled.

My face burning, scorched from hours of sun and sea, felt tight as a drum, my body steamed from the heat. Our hair plastered against our heads, like threads of coarse twine above red-eyed, unshaven faces. Clothes, now salt-stained and crumpled, felt rough against our sea–washed, sensitive skin. At last we had the haunted look of true fugitives.

My wetsuit dried quickly; I felt like the Incredible Hulk, about to burst out of his day clothes. Either my body was swelling or the wetsuit was shrinking. My groin, balls and armpits were chafed sore from twelve hours of activity in hot sun.

We checked the boats and double-checked the loads. The small dinghy engine was damaged from smashing against the rocks: a bent propeller and gashed petrol tank that might leak fuel but shouldn't be too much of a problem for the two mechanics.

The packages containing tents were soaked. Not a problem,

but the condition of the rice parcels looked doubtful. On closer inspection we could see the water hadn't penetrated the layers of polythene and the emergency flares were safe in their waterproof case. A pull at the dinghies' rubber nosing showed just how close we were to disaster. It came off in my hand.

Grimly, we surveyed our landing spot as the sea pounded our tiny beach. A rocky escarpment, must be thirty feet high, bounded the remaining three sides of our cove. There was no easily visible way up. It would have to be a 'blind' climb.

It was five pm. The sun, now dipping low in the west, skimmed reflections like a flat pebble striking waves, flashing fitfully into our squinting eyes. We'd been at it for twelve hours and thinking of the developing scenario did nothing to encourage optimism.

I would not be going home tonight.

A ragged tide mark ran around the cove. Below it, a nourishing home for marine life clung in abundance. The mark told us that the tide, when it was in, covered the area we were standing in. Not simply covered it, swamped it to a height of several feet. We could leave nothing here.

The first ascent was down to me. Miller and Bellord could not have tackled this on their own. We'd all admitted to a lack of climbing skills but at least I'd climbed ladders and scaffolds—in another life. Ah yes, the other life, the ordinary, cosy life of a man with a small business, a wife he loved, two great kids and a stack of good friends. A man who had thoughts above his station, and big plans. Well, big for me, anyway and with them a hope for respect, kudos, love and a little wealth.

Tanya would be worrying now. One night without a call was forgivable, a barely broken promise. But two? She'd be calling the House and my friends, trying to get contact numbers for my tour up north. Phone Rosko, maybe. That would do it. 'Geoff who?' he'd ask. We'd only met once. I'd be surprised if he remembered that meeting, Miller had taken the floor with his enthusiastic plans for promotional tours.

My kids might be feeling the tension too. Someone might decide to ring the police and hospitals maybe, see if there'd been any accidents or I'd been taken ill somewhere.

I checked the stock of rope, there was plenty for what we had in mind and if things got desperate, more than enough to hang the three of us from the rocks above. Twice.

We scanned the horizon again. Nothing. Emptiness, stillness, sea, a fading blue sky and some relief. We'd made it to the Island.

Every last item would have to be hauled up, including Miller and Bellord. To scale the height wouldn't have been difficult for a seasoned climber. He'd cast an expert eye over the rocky terrain, discern telltale shapes and shadows, note a foot or handhold, spot subtle but dangerous outcrops, put on his climbing gear and harness and make his way up at a measured pace.

I ached from the boat trip, my muscles and back stiff from lying on the beach. I stood and hobbled a few yards, wondering if I'd ever be totally upright again, stretched my arms and legs and breathed deeply, preparing my lungs for the next effort.

John Bellord picked up the sorry-looking briefcase, which had taken in water, and had difficulty opening the salt-dried catches. The wads of notes were wet, clumping together and in danger of becoming papier mâché. He carefully separated them, a note at a time, straightened each one and placed them under pebbles to dry in the still hot sun. It was a ridiculous sight, ten and twenty pound notes pinned in rows along a deserted beach. But this was the only money they were ever likely to have access to and, for once, was irreplaceable.

I swung a coil of rope over my shoulder, walked up to the cliff face and looked up. From this angle it was impossible to spot footholds higher than a couple of yards. The first one, four foot off the beach, stretched my groin and hamstring muscles to unnatural limits. I took a tentative grip on a jagged snub about head height and pulled myself up, remembering not to look down. Miller and Bellord shouted encouraging words, guiding me when they spotted something resembling a handhold.

Much of the time my face was so close to the rock I could taste and smell it: the salty, earthy, ancient smell that had not changed for a million years. Hand grips located the slime of fresh guano or the gritty hardness of yesterday's, dried by the wind and sun, bird shit from the sizeable bird population that inhabited the Island. It's supposed to be good for many things but definitely bad news for climbers. A slip of a foot on the damn stuff and you could be a goner.

A seasoned climber might have looked on amused at my parody. But he couldn't fail to be impressed by my determination. Any thoughts of falling were put aside. My biggest fear was not making it to the top. Two yards, hold breath, foot hold, handhold, pull up again, stop and breathe. I came within reach of my goal and stood on a single foothold, catching my breath before the final push, then reached up to feel dry rock, moss and grass. I peered over the edge at startling green and a gently rolling landscape. Lying prone and exhausted, I rested and took in my surroundings. I was on a narrow grassy ridge that led to undulating terrain. I could see the South Ridge but nothing beyond. No northern or eastern panoramas.

Looking down at the two men now, it seemed a hell of a long way up. I tied my rope to a sturdy rock, checking and double checking, knowing it would be supporting virgin climbers.

'What's it like?' shouted Bellord, 'anywhere to set up tents? Will we manage the climb?' I could hear the animated indistinct discussion of the men below; something about making a winch for Jim. I'd no idea if they'd manage the climb. I'd found it tough enough and I wasn't a cripple. They must be exhausted. They were not young men.

I threw the rope to Bellord. He made a good job of trussing Miller up like a chicken, aware of how fragile and precious his cargo was. He tied the rope and pulled it firmly around Miller's waist and groin before securing a length under his armpits.

'Test it,' I shouted, 'drop your weight against the rope. Pull as hard as you can.'

Without hesitation and with a toddler's courage, Jim dropped his full body weight onto the beach. The rope tightened around the rock, jerking my resting arm. It held. I gave it a tug and watched him twitch with my pull. We could do it.

Cautiously Bellord guided Miller, who was limping badly, toward the first secure grip.

'Look to your left and you'll see an oval dark shadow. It's another hold, enough to get a hand in,' I shouted, 'but don't put your hand in too deep or you'll slice your fingers off.' I'd nearly done it myself, but recalled the relief of seeing that very hold where I'd expected none.

Jim only had the use of one good arm and leg, a more severe handicap than we'd imagined. I kept the rope taut. When he couldn't reach out, or his gammy leg misbehaved, or his weak arm looked about to fail him, I took his weight, half dragging and half swinging him toward the next viable hold. Slowly the exhausted figure made the ridge. Gripping him roughly, part by his clothes, part under the armpits, I gave him one last pull onto the soft grassy strip, on to the tiny island that was to be his home.

Bellord looked relieved. Time was running out, more than that, it had disappeared. We'd not felt it go, but a small part of three people's lives had vanished.

September nights come quickly to the north west and the clouds rolling in from the west hurried it along. We still had to get everything up from the cove. Bellord, working like a man on a chain gang, tied each package to the rope. Miller and I pulled it up, untied it and stacked the stuff in some sort of order before throwing the rope back.

Occasionally a package snagged on rock or swung wildly against the cliff face. Miller and I were aware of the steep ridge behind us as one of the canvas tents rolled away and, before we could get to it, tumbled into a fifteen foot crevasse and stuck there. The climb to retrieve it was even more precipitous than our original climb, but at least it had the advantage of being a tight space between two rocky surfaces, allowing extra grip for my hands and feet.

I doubt Bellord could have managed the final task on his own. I descended to the cove again. With Miller watching over us from above, we folded the Redstart ready to be hauled up. Surprised at how heavy it was, we tipped the remaining water out of the large dinghy and dragged it slowly up the shingle incline to a shallow cave at the head of the cove. We secured it with spare rope to a rock and prayed that the night tide would not take it. I took one more look across the water. A pair of seals surfaced, their cute eyes fixed on John and me looked sad, as if we'd spoiled their fun by taking the dinghies away.

I climbed the cliff again, this time, with confidence and threw the rope to Bellord. I hauled the Redstart up and threw the rope back. He was light, fit for his age and climbed the sheer rock more easily than I'd expected. I'd forgotten he'd been an athlete, a Wimbledon tennis prospect.

Everything and everybody was safe, but darkness was only an hour away and would arrive suddenly as it did yesterday. Carefully we traversed the narrow ridge toward a firm grassy knoll. There, a saucer shaped 'corrie' or hollow looked an ideal place to set up the tents, protected from the wind and out of sight. Even with the tents erected, they would be impossible to spot from the sea. Black clouds were rolling in from the west, merging with a darkening sea, the last narrow band of blue sky shrinking like light beneath a closing shutter.

Would the canary Cortina still be there?

*'They've not come back for their car. They must be in awful trouble to be leaving it there. Have you heard from the coastguard yet? Get the local polis to check the registration. They'll soon find out who it belongs to.'*

The tourist season must be over. A car parked overnight on a lonely road miles from habitation would be shining like a beacon, and what dubious cargo had the gutted trailer held? Once police checked the Cortina's registration it would all be over. They'd know I was in Scotland, close to Miller and Bellord's favourite holiday destination. Local fishermen would be questioned. And one man in particular, the one who stopped his boat momentarily off the coast of Priest, would have a particular tale to tell, of dinghies and men struggling to get ashore.

The two castaways sorted out the stores and equipment; wet from dry, useful from useless. We had three very different tents. One, a tunnel tent, for long term storage, stuff that wouldn't be needed on a daily basis: tinned food, spare gas canisters, stove, bags of rice, polythene sheeting, rope, extra clothing. The second for immediate use: cooking gear, food, etc., and the third for sleeping and shelter. We struck camp in the most advantageous way, tents fanning outward, backs to the south west, entrances facing each other making it easy to get from one to the other in bad weather. Once drenched, it would be almost impossible to get dry, unless lucky spells of sunshine interrupted the winter storms.

We humans are not good at seeing others stripped bare of

dignity and possessions. Miller and Bellord were alone now with little left of their incredible lives. The Island was not up for grabs. It could not be talked round and it didn't need populating to survive. If the truth be known, it wanted us gone.

Bellord unpacked the Calor gas stove. It lit with a resounding pop. We filled a kettle from our flask and set it on the flame. The smell of Oxo brewing was intoxicating. It would be our first drink for over twelve hours and dehydration was a real issue. Since we'd left Little Loch Broom, no one had mentioned needing a loo. There was no piss in us.

What a welcome boost to energy and morale that simple beef infusion gave us.

Miller and Bellord, silently and methodically, started to fill the tents while I collected the collapsible carriers and set off in search of water. There were several fresh water lochs on the island, one of the reasons we chose Priest in the first place. The light, more resolute than expected, gave me a little time, holding halfway between day and night. I left the corrie and passed between a narrow valley formed by two hillocks.

Once I was through, the glory of Priest spun out before me. No signs of human life, no buildings, no tracks, no paths, no fences, no sound. No indication as to whether the ground beneath was boggy or solid. Darling had mentioned this, but he knew what changes in terrain to look for. A few minutes of walking through the soft hilly landscape led to a crystal clear loch. The failing light cast deep black shadows, penetrating the water's depth to form beast-like shapes that slithered with the gentle pulse of the loch. I scooped a handful of water and drank. The liquid ice caught my throat and quenched my thirst.

The Island was bigger than I'd expected. Rugged hills obscured the sea but promised more of the Island beyond. The only feature known to me was the South Ridge, a two hundred and fifty foot high rocky barrier that ran the length of Priest from east to west. For a moment I felt completely still, the rigours of the past days seemed remote, like someone else's experience. The silence was broken by a throaty gurgling as I pushed the plastic containers underwater to fill them.

On the trek back in eerie twilight a coldness came over me and I shivered with the thought that Miller and Bellord may never come back. They may become too weak to make the attempt. The Island had proved a ferocious host, even on a late summer's day. In winter, terrifying winds would roar across the wide expanse of sea, heavy rain and bitterly cold days would keep them huddled in a small tent, unable to keep warm and dry.

They were delighted to see me carrying the full water carriers. At least they would never die of thirst.

No one had mentioned God, bishops, psychology, metaphysics or philosophy since we'd left the House, topics that, up until very recently, had been a constant in our daily discussions. And none of us had the courage to utter the words, organ, money, sponsor or racing. Jim's Magnificent Obsession now seemed a dream away and not magnificent at all, simply an obsession. In all the years I'd spent with Miller and Bellord and despite them revealing that a bishop had been blackmailed following a sex scandal and they'd paid the demand to save him, no one seemed to know whether the bishop had suffered a momentary lapse of judgment or was indulging a lifelong habit. And was there more than one bishop involved? And why was such a sum, a piddling ten thousand pound blackmail demand, made such a lot of? We're talking millions now.

The remains of the day had gone. It was the darkest night I'd ever known. No light lit land, no ship at sea and a sky bereft of stars. The cloud and darkness, total.

My wetsuit kept me humidly warm, preserving me in a tropical jungle climate like a hothouse plant. We crawled into the tent which, fortunately, was big enough for the three of us.

Miller and Bellord, their clothes, stiff and dry from sea water and fierce sun, crackled like crisp packets as they settled down for the night. In no time, I heard the rhythmic breathing of deep sleep.

The muted sound of the waves below and the sound of gulls overhead became soporific. My heavy lids closed and I started to drift off into that wonderful feeling of semi anaesthesia. An explosion, somewhere on the island, woke me. Did the ground move? It felt like it. Darling mentioned this phenomenon in his book: *...a terrible place called the Priest's Hole; a sea cave of indeterminate length on the north of the island. A large chunk of rock had sloughed away to form a skylight. The sea is never calm there and gathers in the mouth of the cave to rush forward—seconds later a dull boom can be heard, smothered by the length of the passage. When the sea is wild, the boom is like a cannon and the rock trembles...*

That felt and sounded like a cannon to me.

The last seconds of a dream disturbed me. It was nothing really, but for me portentous. *A single candle flickered directly in front of me. As I stared at it in meditation, Miller appeared in the tent entrance, shaved and in his smart suit. He blew hard as if the candle was on a birthday cake. The flame went out and Miller stepped back into the night.*

I woke to darkness, relieved to see that Miller hadn't moved. I looked at my luminous watch, surprised at how long I'd slept.

During 'lessons' in our days of the House, we'd touched on the nature of dreams. Man has wracked his brain over the centuries in an attempt to understand the part they play in our lives. Like religion, no one knows, there are only theories. They are, I believe, a continuation of our life in some other form. They bear no relationship to logic or common sense, we cannot control them and most of the time they don't seem to have anything to do with the events of our day. Yet when we are in them we can be active and still be thinking within that dream as if it is really us awake on a bad day. Sometimes they seem so real, so in the now, that we wake up thinking we are still in them. As I did now.

The tent pitched slightly, straining at the guy ropes. A loose flap lashed the side. The two men stirred but didn't wake. I picked my way across their bodies and out of the tent. It was cold and even in the protective hollow of the camp site, the wind was strong. My heart sank as I looked up at the grey voluminous sky, heavy with rolls of charcoal rain clouds. Rain streamed in rivulets off my wet suit as I walked to the highest point of the corrie.

Even before I put my head above the hilly cover, I had to close my eyes against the stinging wind and rain. Once on the brow, I could hardly stand. The battering wind forced me to step back and drop to my knees. I waited a few seconds before moving to the top again, ready for it this time. White-capped waves, sea the colour of lead and pounding surf, crashed around the rocky coast. My worst nightmare had survived sleep and become reality. Whatever the conditions, I had to leave. Now.

# 15

# Rougher Sea

Miller and Bellord's haggard, unsmiling faces did nothing to cheer me. They'd heard the wind and rain too. If our physical transition toward the persona of fugitives was in any doubt yesterday, it had been completed by the passing night. Three days of scruffy beard, a darkening around glassy eyes, a confused forlornness that comes from poor sleep and deprivation and clothes no charity would risk taking. We smelt bad.

'It's not good out there,' I didn't need to say. 'But I have to go.'

'Look at it,' said Miller, waving his arm at the weather but not venturing outside the tent.

'You can't leave now, you'd never make it,' he reasoned, eyes full of concern. 'Give it an hour or two and see what it's like then. You never know, the weather might improve.'

Yes, I was certain he really cared. 'Suppose it gets worse?' I said. 'Then we'll all be in trouble. This could last for days, or weeks. There's no choice, I have to go.'

Miller looked to Bellord for support. Bellord lowered his eyes but said nothing. He knew I had to leave.

'Don't forget I'll have the big dinghy to myself. It'll go like a rocket, I'll be back in no time,' I said, unconvincingly.

Miller gave me a puzzled look. 'I thought you'd take the small one, we should have the large one here in case...' he said, catching his breath, stopping mid-sentence, perhaps realising his selfishness.

'There's no way I can take the small one. I don't even know if the engine works now, it got quite a bashing against the rocks.'

'That means we'll be stuck here without a boat.'

This was the first sign of any significant disagreement. I didn't quite believe they'd let me find my way back in a tiny rubber boat that would hardly get me out of the cove in this weather, never mind back to Little Loch Broom. 'If I don't get back we'll be sunk, maybe literally for me. You have flares if you get into trouble, but you're safe for a while. I think it's only a bent propeller on the little motor. You know about mechanics, you have tools, you could fix it. You'll have plenty of time. I don't have any. Everyone will be wondering where I am. I have to get back,' I spluttered, in short breathless sentences.

Nothing on earth would keep me there. I had no illusions about the dramatic weather and sea changes in this part of the world. I'd had enough experience to know that what you observe at any given time cannot be trusted to last.

Our sombre mood continued as we sheltered in the lea of the largest tent, brewed tea and ate a few biscuits. A silence had fallen since we'd discussed the dinghy.

I don't usually do guy hugs, unless they are sons, or friends in crisis. I guess this situation qualifies, but it didn't happen. Goodbyes are never easy, but to be leaving these two in such isolation in so remote a place was tough. In all the years we'd been friends, they had always supported and helped others. It looked different now, but I knew they'd be back. I'd need patience and bravery to keep that belief going. They'll have some peace at last, all the time in the world for a crystal clear analysis of what they'd done then work out a plan for vindicating all those left to face the music.

My emotional parting was overshadowed by a gnawing trepidation. I was about to launch a tiny boat in a fearsome sea and dash for my life.

Miller reached into his pocket, opened his wallet and gave me twenty pounds, apparently unaware of his meanness. He didn't look embarrassed but I was choked. I had no money, a Cortina running on almost empty and over eight hundred miles to drive. It might just about cover the petrol but there would be nothing for food or emergencies. I thought about the empty Cortina tank, then about the tank of petrol that got us here. Was that close to empty too? I'd not thought about cash for myself. I had none. He saw my face and gave me another twenty. The man who had been so generous, now miserly.

I checked I still had the car key, retied it to a belt loop and dropped it inside my wetsuit.

Taking the flippers and life jacket I started toward the ridge, praying the boat hadn't been washed away with the night tide.

Despite the risk of getting wet and unable to dry out, Miller and Bellord walked toward the ridge in waterproofs. Red eyed, damp eyed but without tears, we said goodbye.

The cove looked bigger than I'd remembered it. The heavy grey sky and pounding seas reflected its mood and I wondered what would have happened if I'd been talked into taking the Redstart. How could he have suggested it? I was still seething. The only plan we ever had for it was fishing on a calm day. The flares were the best bet for any future escape.

They watched as I slowly descended the cliff, Bellord ensuring the rope was secure. The dinghy was there, albeit thrown several yards up the shingle toward the shallow cave, its tie strained and twisted.

Untying the dinghy was a devil. The sea had caused the rope to swell and knots to tighten. Eventually it was free and I dragged the two hundred and fifty pound boat down the shingle. Okay, it was downhill but it seemed to make little difference. With the engine strapped on and the boat half full of water it must have added another hundred pounds at least.

I stopped to secure the can of petrol which was floating back and forth in the waterlogged hull. I bailed out as much water as I could before checking the tank, connected to the motor by a thin rubber tube. It was less than half full. Was there enough to get back in such seas? The journey across had taken its toll. With only one person in the boat, less the weight of stores and drag effect of the little dinghy, I wouldn't need so much petrol anyway, I'd virtually fly back. But just in case, there was a single oar for emergencies.

An incoming wave caused the bow of the beached dinghy to lift high off the shingle. Two small figures in the landscape gave encouraging semaphore-like signs from the ridge. Gulls flew back and forth across the cove, no doubt hoping my activity would encourage fish. I gave the boat an almighty push and jumped in, using the oar to push against the threatening rocks. The waves bucked, forcing me first up and then back in a half somersault. I reached for the starting rope on the engine, leaving the oar wedged under the bow. Another great wave tossed me upward and threatened to wash me back into the cove. I pulled the starter rope. The engine fired first time and with unexpected power, the boat lurched suddenly forward, out of the cove.

Miller and Bellord were still on the ridge, semaphoring away. I had no idea of the message except it must have included, goodbye. Take care, even. As I turned south eastward out of the little bay I lost sight of them and wondered if I would ever see them again.

The gravity of leaving in such haste became apparent. The

dinghy hit the first waves of the 'real' sea. The light aerodynamic shape of the dinghy, deprived of its cargo, began to lift as the wind got under it. The dinghy skittered along like a trained dolphin, bow in the air, stern deep in the water almost upright as we rode each wave. To save the thing turning over and dumping me in the sea, I flung my body face down, head toward the bow, increasing the dinghy's stability. But it didn't stay tight on the water for long. The boat couldn't cope with the big seas. It lifted and crashed wave after wave, the engine spluttering, misfiring and threatening to die on me. When it hit the sea after riding high it would surge forward suddenly at what seemed a shocking speed.

The rain was torrential now and, aided by the waves, filled the boat. The petrol tank, loose from its tenuous mooring, floated freely stern to bow, side to side, zigzagging back and forth. Still belly down, I tried to steer and keep an eye on where I was going while steadying the petrol tank. It proved impossible. Any suggestion of land evaporated, hidden by the perpetual valleys of water. The vicious wind sliced the tops off the waves creating a stinging salt spray, momentarily blinding me. We'd forgotten that most essential piece of equipment, a compass. It would have been invaluable now.

Wind was my only guide. The tall seas, black skies and sheets of rain kept the land from sight.

The abysmal conditions persisted for the next hour, like riding a watery switchback. Suddenly the rain ceased, the wind dropped and the temperature rose. A sea mist descended and shrouded everything.

The silence, as they say, was deafening: the sea mist and quietude, as distressing as the foul weather. Vision, zero. Throbbing engine, muted. No waves to tack and no wind to guide me. Gradually, sun burnt the mist away and I could see further north and, almost directly ahead of me, the landscape gave way to the mouth of Little Loch Broom. It was still some distance away and difficult to judge how long it would take to get there. There were no fishing boats around the mouth of Loch Broom. It must have been a hell of a morning here too.

The skipper witnessing our landing on Priest must have been part of the Ullapool fishing fleet. He'd have told his mates about our stupidity. They'd be having a laugh. Or maybe he told the police and coastguard. On the other hand, silly sods trying to land on Priest might be a common occurrence, enjoyed as a local sport and regular topic of conversation in the pub.

The stern of the boat dipped, the tiller snatched from my hand. I slid forward, forced by the sudden backward jerk. The engine misfired, made an odd kind of strangling noise, blew a puff of blue smoke and stopped. A buoy behind the engine bobbed and dipped as it moved closer to the dinghy. A fisherman's net. I didn't want to damage it and I didn't want to be seen messing about with fisherman's property. They might take me for a competitor and harpoon me, or whatever they do to saboteurs in this part of the world. The main rope framing the net had bound itself to the propeller. The net itself, tightened around the shaft, coiling layer on layer like a snake choking its prey, until the engine gave up. It was now a solid mass.

It took the best part of twenty minutes to untangle it. On inspection, the engine looked no worse for the experience and, as far as I could tell, no one had spotted me. Apart from a few boats going about their business off to catch fish, and a wisp of smoke from a distant chimney, the landscape looked empty of human activity.

The engine started on my first fresh pull. The little craft glided forward, along with the sigh of a grateful man. The sun shone as brightly as yesterday. Yesterday? It seemed a week away. I hoped Miller and Bellord were bathing in the same sunshine, relaxing beside the tents with a brew, cooking a hot meal. They'd be planning a move to a different part of the island. The spot we landed was too near the coast and the prying eyes of passing boats.

I could visualise Bellord off to fetch water, discovering the terrain for the first time, perhaps scouting around for a place to call home. The stone bothy at the island's centre would be the perfect place, if anything of it was left standing. Darling had already discovered it was roofless, but if some of the walls still stood, the two would be sheltered from the worst of the winds. And if tents could be put up inside, they would be positively comfortable. Miller would be impatient to inhabit it.

The engine coughed again, twice, then remained silent. Nothing had fouled the propeller, no horrible mechanical noises emanated. It had simply, and not too surprisingly, run out of petrol. I reached for the oar, tapped the empty petrol can, which rang hollow, and rowed.

The landmark features of the rocky slopes were unrecognisable travelling in the opposite direction. It was an oddity, remembered from my trekking days. Always look back. If you don't, you will not recognise the spot you are returning to. We had failed to do that.

I couldn't see the canary yellow Cortina, it must have been towed way, the police hiding behind hillocks preparing to nab me as I stepped off the boat.

*'Gimmee the scope, lassie. One o' them's come back. He's on his own and there's only one dinghy. They must have been dropped off somewhere. Priest most likely, it's the only place with water and a landing spot. But they couldn't have landed yesterday, even the fishing boats didn't chance it out there. Maybe they died trying. Any news from the polis or coast guard?*

I couldn't see the little road circling the loch from here. As I edged closer, a single car traced its contour, appearing and disappearing as it rode the rise and dips of the road. I strained to follow its course until the car disappeared seconds after passing a startling flash of yellow. The Cortina.

The last few yards seemed endless and silent, apart from the gentle splish, splash of the single oar. I grabbed the painter and jumped onto the flat rock we'd launched the dinghies from yesterday. It took some time and strength to get the heavy boat out of the water. My muscles trembled with the effort, my legs weak from hours at sea and the cliff climbing of the past twenty four hours. The loch was calm with no sign of traffic along the coast road. Smoke continued to rise from the chimney I'd seen earlier.

*'He'll never get that boat up there. I'll take bets on it. He's had it. The polis will be here any minute.'*

I put the wooden seats, spacers and engine to one side. An engine twice as heavy as I remembered it. Getting air out of the damn boat was harder than putting it in. I stamped, pressed, squashed and rolled until it was flat enough to roll up.

Up hill, with such a weight, was a real problem. I could only move a yard or two before being forced to rest. The boat took an hour to haul up with a further twenty minutes for the engine. By the time it was all packed in the trailer I could have lain right there and slept. Then came an exquisite moment: removing the car key from the string that held it safe. The sun was strong now, the wind light. Inside the Cortina was hot. I moved the seat back, sunk luxuriously into its warmth and, with some difficulty, peeled off the wetsuit I'd worn for thirty six hours.

With the heat of the car wrapped around me, I couldn't remember the last time I felt so good. My white prune of a body sang with a new energy. I was going home.

The car seemed as I'd left it. No police warning pinned to it, no one had tried to break in. And in all the time I was dragging stuff up from the loch, not a single vehicle or person passed me. This was indeed a remote landscape.

A second exquisite moment came when I put on warm dry clothes. I felt where every soft fold and shape of shirt, pants and jeans touched my skin. In fact, all my senses were sharp and clear: hearing acute, eyes like a hawk and the presence of my own body, uncannily alive.

I set the driving seat back to upright, ready to move off. The hairs on the back of my neck prickled, sending a shiver down my spine. I felt a human presence behind. After knocking the rear view mirror getting into the car, I could only see a section of roof lining through it. I turned, expecting to see Jim and John sitting in the back seat, but no one was there. The experience of the past few days had 'retuned' me in some inexplicable way. Had Jim and John somehow transmitted this 'energy' to help me, some esoteric, mind-body stuff? It felt like nothing I'd experienced. But if I'd learned one thing during the time I spent with Miller, it was this. Don't ever believe you can work any of it out with logic. No one can.

I'd been warned that Cortinas were prone to starter problems but I'd never found it so, the car started on the button and I moved smoothly away from the shore toward Dundonnel.

I hadn't contacted anyone for three days. I'd not eaten, washed or shaved, yet felt oddly fresh and grateful that I'd survived. My trouser belt was slack, a few pounds had come off. Gradually a gnawing, physically painful hunger developed. My front bone was touching my backbone as the saying goes. Half an hour later, I pulled in to a small parking area where a caravan set up selling tea and cakes. This was illusory, remarkable, as there was no one here to buy anything. No cars and no walkers or visitors of any kind.

The wispy haired old lady with sharp eyes, a floral apron and rolled up sleeves, smiled at me kindly. Grandma made a fresh pot of tea and put a small tin tray of homemade cakes before me. I hadn't spoken a word. She made no comment on how I looked, but those eyes wouldn't have missed a thing. I needed to go, but standing in the peace and grandeur of that beautiful place, the mountain peaks sharp, the sun on my back and an appetite needing attention, I stayed a few more minutes to scoff cake and chat. We discussed weather, tourists, and her little business. And we never saw a soul.

I was driving too fast, desperate to get to a phone. A cafe in a small village provided my first meal and it was substantial. The plate piled high with the 'special' followed by a dish of apple crumble and more tea. My stomach groaned with the weight and solidity of its unexpected treat.

I found a public phone screwed to a wall across from the service counter. My call would not be private. Tanya picked up after a couple of rings.

'What's happened?' she said, her voice clear but emotionally distant. Cold. What did I expect?

I could hardly hear her. I covered my ear in an attempt to shut out chatter drifting from the busy cafe. 'I picked up some sort of bug and had to take to my bed for a couple of days.' A long silence. Empathy or suspicion? 'But I'm on the mend.'

'Where are you, when will you be back?' she asked, softly.

I only picked up on, *where are you?* 'I've just filled up with petrol and stopped at a café to ring you. Sorry, it's really noisy here.'

'I said when will you be back?'

'Tomorrow, before lunch hopefully, depends on traffic. How are the kids? Can I speak to them?'

'They're round at Mum's.'

'Any phone calls?'

'Who from?' she said, sharply. It was a reasonable question.

'Anyone. Marion, the House, stuff to do with work?'

'No calls, some post, nothing important. A postcard from Miller and Bellord.'

'What's it say?' I heard her rustle through the post which was always piled up next to the living room phone waiting attention.

She sighed heavily, pointedly, like she was in a hurry to end the call. Pissed off, probably. 'Looks like Miller's writing. Says they're having a nice break. Decent hotel, weather good. Don't work too hard. See you soon.'

'That's nice.'

'We're at Mum's for lunch. Try and make it. Love you,' she said, cutting me off before I had a chance to reply.

'Me too,' I said, to the dead phone.

On the face of it, our adventures of the past few days had slipped unnoticed by the world at large. The card was interesting. I knew the House would get one, that was part of the deception, but why me? I suppose it made sense, compounded their alibi and it might look good if I handed it to the police when questioned.

It hurt to walk to the car. My shrunken, cramping, stomach now so full it wanted to burst with the sudden burden of food.

At the first motorway stop I bought a disposable razor. The guy in the washroom mirror was definitely not me. His face was burnt by the sun, yet thin and jowly. He had a thick black growth of beard and red, sore, bloodshot eyes. Once he'd taken his shirt off, his body smelled like mouldy rubber, and there were peculiar marks, fresh scars across his back and shoulders; burn marks from the ropes used to pull the boats in on Priest. They were already scabbing up, not unlike the attack of shingles I'd had two years ago caused, so Miller had assured me, by protracted emotional stress.

After washing my hair and body down to the waist I spent an inordinate amount of time trying to wet shave my bearded face. Resilient patches confounded me. After a few nicks and spots of blood the skin was, more or less, hairless. I splashed with cold water to stem the bleeding and the change was remarkable. I now looked like a lean sunburned traveller. My clothes looked pretty good too, I'd made sure of folding them carefully in the boot when I'd put the wet suit on.

Memories of the past few days came in subliminal flashes. In my semi hypnotic state, the effects of dehydration, days with less than a pint of fluid, I drove onto the busy motorway. In no time at all, I was hungry again. Starving, with an elephant's appetite and a camel's thirst. My second gigantic meal at the motorway lodge wasn't a patch on my village feast. That didn't stop me stuffing myself and drinking three cups of tea.

Before I hit Sussex there were a few practical considerations. I needed to hide or flog some gear. Hide for now, but where? We'd not considered this part of the deception. Our plan had, oddly, not given a great deal of time to what I'd do when I got back; apart from delivering letters to the company directors. But that wasn't to happen until the end of their holiday, in less than ten days' time.

I'd be broke by the time I got back, but the trailer, dinghy, engine, life jacket, flippers and wetsuit, might fetch a few bob. Maybe there was enough to pay me until the holiday period was over. After that, I'd be out on my ear or in prison, if the cops were hard on the case.

Selling stuff would be risky but I'd be a fool to dump it all. I would have to hide it first, come back when the dust settled, sort out buyers and negotiate a best price.

Along the A24 toward Worthing, an idea, albeit a risky one, started to form. I took the coast road toward Brighton and pulled into Kingston Beach parking lot. A little unmanned lighthouse overlooked the harbour casting its life saving beam toward the English Channel; lighting up Miller and Bellord's return route to the UK.

Shoreham Lifeboat was stored close by, in its well-worn boathouse. To the right was Shoreham Rowing Club, an ugly block of a building, the scene of many raucous goings on, not all of them related to rowing. More your drinking, groping, Saturday night shenanigans, known as Rowing Club Socials. The club had a decent car park occupied mainly by boats and trailers.

I reversed the trailer into an empty spot, released the catch, took off the number plate, ensured the load was strapped in tight, and drove out. This I did with the air of a man who frequents the place. It would have taken a very observant soul to spot the brief moments of uncertainty, the shaking hands and the beads of sweat running down my forehead. If the whole lot disappeared in the night, too bad. It would solve one problem but deprive me of cash. It was reasonable to assume the theft of a dinghy from this area was unlikely. Fishermen and rowers left gear here all the time, because they trusted each other.

# 16

# Dark Stranger

No matter how slowly I drove, there was no escaping lunch with mother-in-law. I owed it to the family. The kids would be there and I'd get all the questions over in one go. Ha ha. I would rather repeat the past few days than face up to this lunch.

Frank answered the bell. He was, of course, smiling and friendly. 'Hello, mate, blimey, you look well. Where yer been? Costa Brava?'

We shook hands warmly. Five faces greeted me; Tanya, smiling weakly, the kids, beaming, mother-in-law Madge, making sure I knew how she felt, her eyes boring into mine and through the back of my head before she smiled, thinly. Madge of the dyed black hair, the razor tongue and her ability to spot a lie from twenty paces, would give no ground. Despite an unshakable belief in her powers of deduction, she often got it wrong. She could tell when someone was lying, I'll give her that, but the devil was in the detail. The actual lie itself often remained undiscovered. Now she was prepared to condemn me based on instinct alone. Her unblinking stare had already warned me. Anything I said throughout the meal would be viewed as a lie. I couldn't blame her. I'd worked out roughly what I'd planned to say but it wasn't that convincing and she'd know it.

Tan gave me a peck on the cheek, the kids kissed and hugged me, Frank smiled and nodded, as if to say, *all the family together, how great is that*. And Madge went to check on the meal.

My relationship with Madge, up until fairly recently, had been good. She was physically stiff with everyone. Even when she hugged the kids, there was a certain lack of commitment to the embrace. I'd heard she'd been abused as a child. Hasn't everyone? Madge does not forgive. This may be the key to her inability to let things be and a total ineptness when it came to showing physical love.

She came into the dining room smiling. What had changed? Cooking food for people was the only way she could really show love. She piled plates high, poured large glasses of wine, baked enormous apple pies and gave seconds you dare not refuse. We all knew that she loved us but simply couldn't say so.

'How did you get the tan?' asked Frank, innocently.

'I caught some sort of bug and had to rest up for a couple of days. I just sat out on the hotel balcony. Amazing weather.'

'It's rained nearly every day here,' said Madge, pointedly, implying that if it rained down here in the south it must have rained twice as hard up north.

'You've lost weight,' said Tanya.

'As I said, I've been ill.'

'What with? Did you get a doctor out?' said Madge, sniffing while cutting me another huge slice of pie.

'No I didn't see a doctor. I had a day on the loo, then started to feel better.'

'You could still have rung and saved Tanya worrying,' she said, giving me a fresh napkin whilst pouring nearly a cupful of cream over the pie.

By the end of the meal, despite the fact I'd sidestepped

some dodgy issues, my future relationship with mother-in-law looked decidedly shaky. The plate of food and extra pie were not to be misinterpreted. It felt more like the last indulgence for a man on death row.

My first uneasy day back from Scotland and the first day for years without Miller and Bellord at hand, was coming to an end. I couldn't wait to get to bed, but Tanya wanted to know about the Rosko tour. I put the 'innocents' to bed, lit the fire and spent the evening lying. It sounded unconvincing to me, but Tanya seemed to swallow it. Or was she aware something was seriously wrong and decided now was not the time to start a row?

I picked up the mail, checked the postcard from Miller dated the day we left for Scotland, and put it safely in the sideboard drawer.

Sleep was a long time coming and when it did, produced sea monsters from deep black waters. I woke cocooned in bed sheets, soaked with sweat, in a state of fear and panic. I'd been shouting, Tanya said.

'What about?' I asked, terrified of what I might have revealed.

'A load of rubbish,' she said, laying a hand on my forehead and asking if she could get me something. 'What's wrong, I've never seen you like this before? You look awful.'

'I have been quite ill, you know.'

The bathroom mirror did me no favours. My dark-rimmed, baggy-eyed image stared back at me. I showered, went back to bed and slept till five.

The morning clouds scudded across the distant seascape. Our view from Highways looked down the hill across to Portslade, Shoreham and the Channel beyond. Miller and Bellord would be waking to their second morning alone, free from all that was about to happen in Sussex. I would be experiencing the day to day collapse of a small business empire and a whole lot more.

Everyone at the House would be eager to question me. They would have received postcards and talked about how safe and rested the two men must be. Right now they would be content in the knowledge that Miller and Bellord were resting in France and that once they returned, the two magicians would pull rabbits out of hats to the relief and applause of everyone.

Miller and Bellord wouldn't leave me to face the music alone for long. Of that I was certain.

*

The office was busier than usual. Phones never stopped, morning mail piled high, meetings arranged for days and weeks ahead and already, at eight in the morning, a group of immaculately dressed men were waiting in the grand hall. No one there I recognised, and they weren't happy.

Margaret and John, secretary, director and power behind the orphaned business, listened to the brief hurried account of my trip up north. None of us had time to spare. Even then I wanted to spill the beans, tell them what we'd done, save them from at least some of the anguish. I wanted to reassure them that the pair were safe and only doing this to protect us all. And that, even now, they were preparing a plan to come back, like cavalry over the hill, to put everything right. The trouble was, even while I was thinking it, a nagging doubt nibbled the edges of my optimism, a doubt that would visit me often.

As I looked out across the back lawn of the House toward the wood and the ice house, two figures flitted across the gravel and into the trees. Not the fabled monks, but flesh and blood human beings, one limping, smoking a pipe, the other dapper, with an urgent gait. A trick of the mind, something my subconscious hoped to see, then in a second, they were gone.

During coffee break I checked my mail, returned urgent calls and set about preparing for a busy racing weekend; issuing press passes, organising trackside advertising and wondering how on earth I was going to keep it all running. Miller and Bellord's two week holiday period was half way through. It had taken five days plus to get them to Priest and get back again. A week tomorrow things would start to get serious at the House while Miller and Bellord sipped tea outside their tent, looking across the Minch on a kind September morning. Maybe even from the outlaw's bothy. Or, perhaps the season ends early in the Summer Isles and they would be battening down the hatches in preparation for the first winter gales.

My first days back were not so bad. There was loads going on: twitchy banks, skulking finance companies, unease amongst the Southern Organs shops and staff and more visits to the loo than usual for company directors. Whatever was brewing in the heartless world of finance, restraint, at least until the two got back from 'holiday', was being shown.

By the end of their fortnight's break and their subsequent failure to turn up, the extent of their crime would gradually unfold. But we had yet to learn the extent of it.

Before they'd left, we'd discussed the number of unpleasant tasks I would have to perform. The financial detail was left out. I would be playing the innocent.

Prize money for drivers was due for championships and much more. I had no idea what had been paid or to whom. At least this dearth of knowledge would confirm the fact that I was a harmless and financially powerless puppet ready to act as a punchbag for all the anger due from certain quarters, namely drivers and the motor and air racing fraternity. As the racing promotions manager, I'd been much like a waiter in a posh restaurant, of no consequence to most, but bearing a gourmet meal. And all eyes had been on the feast. Miller's cash.

Finals of the Formula One Air Racing Championships were due to take place at Sywell, Northamptonshire, the following weekend. It was the biggest event in the Popular Flying Association's calendar. This local aerodrome on the edge of Sywell village, served Northampton, Wellingborough and Kettering and had an auspicious history. It was utilized as a training ground for Tiger Moths during World War ll and a base for manufacturing Wellington bombers. Many aerial shots for the film Battle of Britain were taken from here. It boasts an interesting Aviation Museum dedicated to wartime history and a 1930's Art Deco hotel with bar and restaurant.

The day after Miller and Bellord were officially due back from France, I had to attend the final race of the Southern Organs Formula One Air Race Championships. Already speculation about Miller and Bellord's true whereabouts was emerging. They had never been late for anything in their lives. They'd played truant on the odd occasion, like the time they bunked off to watch the Le Mans film, but never late. They would have phoned. For Miller and Bellord to be late could only mean one thing. Something terrible had happened or they'd legged it. Most of the staff came down on 'the something terrible has happened' side.

It was the end of a hard year's work for the pilot owners of the racing planes. Formula One Air Racing was a far cry from the Formula One Motor Racing scene with its teams of mechanics, rich sponsors and high-performance cars. These planes were built, tested and maintained by the pilots who flew them. They relied on pooling resources, sharing the modest income from the Popular Flying Association (PFA) and practical help from fellow racers and enthusiasts.

The weather was fine. A light wind lifted the air sock and planes were parked smartly on the broad grass runway. Tom

Storey, current championship leader, was there in his Airmark Cassut as was the Red Baron, in old pilot flying leathers, his fiery red hair and beard, fluorescent in the sunlight. The race, as always, thrilled the crowd. Something about pilots getting into single seat aircraft on a grass strip reminded me of Spitfire sorties during the war. Decades ago these PFA guys would have been those very pilots, passionate enough about flying to fight their battles from above.

Their engines turned and the almighty power thrust took them forward. As the planes roared down the sward and up into the pale blue sky, hearts leapt and the crowd cheered. I wanted to run, but it was my solemn duty to present the winner's trophy. Solemn, because the five thousand pound prize money had disappeared.

My anguish and the lies I'd rehearsed so many times clouded my presentation. The moment, however, will stay with me for life. I remember Tom Storey, six foot plus (I'd always wondered how he ever got into that tiny plane) and ramrod straight, stepping up to the podium with his clean cut good looks and beaming face, savouring his big day. The upturned expectant faces of the exhausted but excited pilots froze, as I delivered a completely fabricated tale of why their prize money was missing. It tore at my heart. I wanted to throw up. The colour drained from their faces, mutterings and anger emanated from the floor. It must have seemed incomprehensible, their promotions manager, spokesman and front man for the racing programme, turning up penniless. It was an awful moment. A friendless chill pervaded.

After the presentation, comprising a small silver plated cup but no prize, no one approached me. It had been a depressing day. I attempted to keep eye contact as the men parted to let me through their gauntlet of disappointed looks and angry faces. I failed. I picked up my briefcase, walked, weak-legged to the back of the room, collected my coat and left. It was the longest walk of my life.

This pattern of disappointment and betrayal became familiar. Once plans have been formulated to deceive and defraud there is no turning back. Further criminal acts are crucial to ensure earlier deeds remain undiscovered.

Now the time had come to deliver Miller's letters to the company bosses. The directors had been on the phone, worried to death about their future and speculating like everyone else about what might have happened.

The letters were handwritten in Miller's confident large looped style and sealed with extra tape. Suicide notes, that's all I knew, an attempt to buy more time in the hope that their apparent death would mean the end of the case. This part of the plan worried me greatly. To leave someone a suicide note was a terrible thing. The implications, that there were two dead men, God knows where, knowing family and friends were out of their minds with worry was bad enough. Then to turn up months later, healthy as could be, was enough to give anyone a heart attack. No one would ever trust or believe in them again.

Miller had persuaded me the ploy would buy them time and finance companies would then call it a day, because their guarantors and fellow fraudsters, Miller and Bellord, had died or disappeared. Surely the money men would have to concede defeat and write off the debt.

The only men likely to respect their suicide notes were the heads of the Japanese export companies. In Japan, when men at the top cause a company to fail, suicide is considered honorable, desirable even. I wondered how the Japanese would feel when Miller and Bellord turned up again three months later. Suggest *hari kiri* I should think, death by falling on their sword.

The drive along the Sussex coast from west to east should have been a pleasure, but delivering suicide notes reduced it to a grey endless journey. I remember walking through a stylish entrance, being greeted by a receptionist who smiled but had no need to ask for my name. Other than that, I only vaguely remember the surroundings in which I found myself. Plush leather chairs, Venetian blinds and expensive carpet. For the millionth time this morning I patted the slim envelope tucked inside my jacket pocket.

Then I stood in front of the grim, pale faces of men in hand-tailored suits and silk ties, who seemed to have forgotten their manners. They decided not to shake my hand and assumed I wouldn't be there long enough to want a seat. I handed the letter over. They took it across the room to catch the light, opened the blinds a little wider, adjusted spectacles and slit the envelope with a paper knife. The letter, neatly folded in three, was opened quickly. One man leaned over the other and they read. Then read it again before folding it and placing it back in the envelope.

They appeared to be having some trouble deciding whether to turn and face me and stood staring out of the part-opened blinds for what seemed like an age. Neither spoke. Their faces looked even paler and grimmer when they finally turned toward me.

'Is there anything else?' one asked.

'Nothing else, I'm afraid. Do you have a reply?' I didn't want them to know that I had an inkling of what the letter was about. And they weren't about to tell me.

'Who gave you the letter?'

'Jim and John. They left several for me. I'd been travelling up north. They were on my desk at the House, in a large envelope, when I got back.'

'I suppose that large envelope didn't happen to have a stamp on it?'

'No. It was a plain, brown and addressed to me.'

'Why you?'

'I'm their friend.'

They gave me an affronted look. 'So are we!'

Another overwhelming desire to tell my secret sank, unspoken, as they showed me the door. 'No need for an answer,' said one.

'We'll get our secretary to deal with it,' said the other.

Suicide notes without bodies were not going to work, that was obvious. The police would still search for corpses or walking, talking, criminals. But it might buy the outlaws a little more time. I doubted if the banks and credit companies would drop their case. And yet, with the guarantors and perpetrators of the scam gone, there seemed little point chasing nominees who would never be able to pay back the huge outstanding debts. Wasn't it obvious that these men of money knew the score, knew they were bending rules and collaborating willingly in making a fast buck? Surely they'd have to back down and swallow their losses?

The weight of evidence against the financiers seemed overwhelming: the reams of contracts guaranteed by only two men, the incestuous parties and entertaining at race tracks, the fact that nominees, refused credit for small items, suddenly became creditworthy for thousands of pounds purely on Jim Miller's sanction.

By nature, police and media cannot afford to waste time. They need to be off the blocks at the first sniff of lawlessness or scandal. And they were.

Police officers and reporters descended on the House like a plague. Staff were interviewed by the police. The media picked off individuals one by one, first at the House, then at any address they'd managed to extricate from whistleblowers. The writs poured in from the credit companies putting the blame squarely on the shoulders of the nominees.

Tanya was devastated. I think she believed the suicide. Madge was incensed. They'd taken her money. I kept the lies going. It got so easy it frightened me, because once this was all over, once Miller and Bellord came back, regardless of the outcome, many of my friends and colleagues would never trust me again. Mother-in-law would castrate me, Frank would forgive me, Tanya would want a divorce, and as for the close friends who'd lost money…

Norman Luck, crime reporter for the Daily Express, rang and asked me for an interview. He called at my home in Sussex and plied his trade. I felt the interview went well. In my favour in fact: Norman was sympathetic, empathetic even. I was an ordinary guy, an employee who'd been duped. But that's the way these guys work. They are quite brilliant psychologists who befriend, check out stories with others, then print something juicy for the masses.

Naivety is not helpful when dealing with the media. In no time at all you find yourself sweaty-palmed and in deep doo-doos. Norman Luck wanted a further interview. I expected him to turn up alone. He introduced me to his 'colleague'. A dark mysterious stranger, whose hair swept tightly back, accentuating deep piercing eyes, serious eyebrows and a pale face. His black beard ran thinly, in a neat line from ear to jaw, thickening at the chin to spring upward either side of a full mouth to form a moustache. He sat silently, with a fixed stare.

If this was a reporter, I'm an honest man. He looked more like a magician or hypnotist. His dark clothes completed the picture. Norman Luck did some polite interviewing before introducing the man as his colleague but did not name him. The mysterious man proceeded to question me. His interrogation, so direct and rapid-fire, confused me. I managed to keep my head by adopting tactics I'd used in the police interview: let the interviewer do the work and only answer the question, as succinctly as possible. He gave me a tougher time than the police ever had and left me exhausted after accusing me of lying. How would he know, he's not a bloody mind reader. He's not Miller. I hadn't cracked or said anything stupid. Not even reddened at his directness. In fact he accused me of being a pretty cool customer. I took it as a compliment.

The press photographers asked me not to smile and chose unguarded moments to take shots for the next day's paper. It always puzzled me why, with all their expensive cameras and equipment, newspaper photographs of criminals never look any good, as if they'd been taken with a disposable camera. The picture is deliberately blurred to give it a rushed look, as if the subject is trying to escape the lens, conferring immediate guilt. The style, apparently, sells papers.

On the sixteenth of October 1975, a month after the two disappeared, the Daily Express printed a front page scoop. *Three Million Pound Help the Church Organ Fraud,* followed by an article printed on the seventeenth of October updating the figure to five million. The article went on to mention that more than four hundred people and twenty finance companies were involved. Also that two attaché cases, filled with cash, had disappeared with Miller and Bellord. Television, radio and the rest of the media took the story international.

For the first time, perhaps for Miller and Bellord too, the enormity of the fraud was revealed. It had never crossed my mind that so many people were involved and all had been drawn to easy money.

It began to appear as if Miller's wealth had been an illusion, borrowing large sums of money then paying it back to create a healthy credit rating. It looked pretty certain that the banks, finance companies and sponsors had discovered the goose that laid the golden egg and were reluctant to give the money machine up. That is, until economy, politics and the law caught up with them. Then, oh, how squeaky clean we all wanted to be.

Friends and staff gave up their Calais postcards for scrutiny and Miller's handwriting was authenticated. Interpol and the fraud squad were on the case. Miller and Bellord had been 'spotted' across Britain, Europe and as far away as Australia and Africa. Some of the more speculative sections of the media suggested a criminal link with Lucan and even the Great Train Robbers.

The Lucan 'link' did have certain parallels. All three, suddenly and completely disappeared with no real clues to their whereabouts. And there followed, in both cases, a heavy police presence at Dover: reported sightings of the three men in more or less the same countries and Lucan's car was abandoned at Newhaven, a few miles up the road from Miller's Eastbourne Finance Company. Psychic detectives were rubbing their hands with glee. Add to that Detective Superintendent Roy Ranson's comment when asked whether he'd give up looking for Lucan, now it was likely he was dead or had committed suicide: 'We're still looking for Lucan all over the world and until these sightings run out we'll continue to follow every single one up.'

The detective constable on Miller and Bellord's case said virtually the same thing.

# 17

# Betrayal

Scotland kept coming into the picture. Virtually everyone, including the police and media, knew it was their favourite holiday destination, so it seemed the obvious place to search. But why would they choose somewhere so obvious? Favourite haunts are usually the first place to look, so they did. Hundreds of police were deployed, questioning and searching around Ullapool, only twelve miles away from Priest Island. If an officer stood on the braes above Ullapool with a telescope and Miller and Bellord stood atop the South Ridge, they could have semaphored each other.

Not a single clue turned up. The word would have spread across Wester Ross, yet neither the guy across the Loch, (*they'll no be comin' back now, lassie*): the tea lady, (*I was her only customer*): the caravanners, (*did they ever spot us anyway?*): the petrol station, (*nothing unusual about a car and trailer buying petrol at the end of a season*), or café, (*unlikely to remember one man buying sandwiches*), reported sightings.

Six weeks went by and the police and media had got nowhere. Nevertheless, two people had got a tenacious grip on the mystery; Marion and Norman Luck's strange colleague. I'd discovered that the dark stranger was psychic detective, Bob Cracknell. Norman Luck had already warned him he'd gone too far in the interview and I could have filed a complaint. I hadn't and wouldn't. Now the police were interested in Cracknell's claim that he'd had psychic clues and that they might be interested in what he had to say. They weren't interested in psychics but they were interested in clues, from wherever. The police and media had run out of ideas. The police deal in facts and that's it. So when Cracknell started talking psychic speak about seeing water and somewhere isolated with a religious connection, and came up with Scotland; really? They began to lose interest.

Despite Cracknell's tenacity and the relentless hunt for Miller and Bellord, the two men remained undiscovered. We'd chosen our hideaway well. It surprised me that, having taken the trouble to employ a psychic detective, notably in the light of his powerful impression that I was lying, no one questioned me further about Miller and Bellord's whereabouts. Even my fictitious trip up north seemed to have escaped scrutiny. It was never mentioned again, at least, not to me. This was not what I expected. In all the newspapers and books I've read, and all the films I've seen, once such juicy clues were declared, the police and press ground the suspect down with a barrage of questions, accusations, phone tapping and threats.

Marion's insistence that I was being particularly secretive came to me via the grapevine. Face to face she had been sarcastic, oblique, sometimes direct, but observed a polite and necessary caution like a mouse skittering around a sleeping cat.

Writs were arriving by the cartload, alarming documents, accusing and sentencing at a stroke, to intimidate and strike quickly, hoping to induce panic and the knee jerk reaction of an early settlement.

Targetting my friends seemed the pits. Many had signed as

nominees, earning a few bob on the side whilst creating cash for banks, kudos for Miller and organs for churches.

The nominees formed a 'fighting group'. They employed a team of solicitors in the hope that a large number of defendants acting together would be better placed to fight cases and expose the banks and finance companies for malpractice.

I had a real dilemma. I could join the group and say nothing, extend my traitorship, or come clean about Priest and give Miller and Bellord up. It would give them a chance to clear our names and take the blame. Somehow, I couldn't do that. It would kill them and in the meantime may complicate things further. We still believed that as guarantors Miller and Bellord would remain culpable and if so, were best left undiscovered on the Island.

Bob Cracknell had got his psychic foot in the door at the House, and was allowed access to Miller and Bellord's flat. He opened wardrobes, touched clothes and belongings hoping for vibrations, psychometric clues, and anything else that might be floating around his invisible world. The police used more practical methods in their search. They ripped wood panelling from the walls, turned out cupboards, took furniture and fittings apart, and rolled up carpets. They must have guessed the missing cash would not be found here. But they had a routine to follow. Equally there were no other clues. All Miller and Bellord's clothes and belongings remained as if they really had gone on holiday and were expected back.

A disturbing copy of a letter from one of the shop managers, to the solicitors and group of individuals who'd joined forces to fight litigation, dropped through our letterbox.

*Dear Mr. Green*

## Re: SOUTHERN ORGANS

*Towards the end of last year a meeting was to be held of all those concerned in this matter, but unfortunately this had to be cancelled at the last moment.*

*As the whole business is now reaching a crucial stage, it is obviously highly desirable that another meeting should take place, along the lines of the original gathering at the House. I have discussed this with my own solicitor (Mr. Alexander of Rawlinson and Butler) who is of the opinion that such a meeting would be beneficial to us all.*

*As there are a number of solicitors representing different people in this matter, I have undertaken to arrange the meeting independently.*

*As most of you will know, Mr. Alan Chase (Miller's friend and Company Director) and myself are to go for trial in the High Court in the near future, to defend the action brought against us by Progressive Supply Limited, an actual date has yet to be fixed.*

*It appears that our worst fears are to be realised, for I understand from Mr. Alexander that the solicitors representing the consortium of Finance Companies have a huge pile of writs waiting to be served on, presumably, each and every one of us. They are apparently waiting only for the result of the forthcoming High Court case before instigating proceedings.*

*Since writs were served on Mr. Chase and myself by Progressive Supply, the situation has developed as follows:*

*Progressive claimed the amounts 'supposedly' owing plus, in each case, damages of one thousand pounds. We both lost our first hearings and were recommended to appeal against the judgment. Despite the fact that this appeal was pending, Progressive succeeded in sending in the Sheriff's Officer to my home with the intent of obtaining the full amount 'owing' or failing that, seizing goods of equivalent value. Fortunately we were able to stay this action until after the appeal.*

*Our appeal was heard and once again we were unsuccessful. The only course left open to us under the law was to appeal for the right to trial in the High Court. This we were recommended to do and the appeal was successful. We are now waiting for the date of the trial to be set.*

*It would appear at present that everything rests on the results of these High Court trials. If we lose the case, it seems certain that the majority, if not all, the Finance Companies will commence proceedings against us all. For myself certainly, and I suspect for many others, the result of such action will mean bankruptcy. Mr. Chase and myself have defended Progressive's actions through the normal channels i.e. in the law courts. Right up to our High Court appeal no real consideration has been given by the courts to the moral aspects of the matter or to the fact that so many other people's futures depended on these judgments.*

*Pessimistic though it sounds, my opinion (born of personal experience) is that if we try to defend these actions individually in the courts, we will fail. However, the 'strength in numbers' principle has been proven time and again and I believe that if we joined together now with the spirit of determination that was apparent at the original House meeting and brought our case back into the public eye demanding to be heard and given real justice, then we would have a good chance of success.*

*I am hoping that at this meeting we can elect an action committee; arrange for representatives to put our case to the press; arrange a petition; formulate some system for keeping in touch so that ideas and suggestions can be discussed and put into action as soon as possible.*

*Obviously I could not contact you all individually, so a time and place has been arranged which hopefully will suit everybody. I feel sure that all those involved will want to attend. If you really cannot be present, perhaps you would be kind enough to let me know. Details of meeting on rear of this page.*

*I for one don't relish the thought of having the rest of my life literally ruined by bankruptcy. Let's take action now before all those writs start dropping through our letterboxes.*

*Ashley Rose (Southern Organs Shop Manager)*

If I'd had my fingernails pulled out one at a time, followed by toenails and teeth, I could not have felt more pain. Every event, every confrontation, every meeting, every chat with friends, every lie, knowing what 1 knew and what was happening because of my duplicity, was eating me from the inside out. Miller warned it wouldn't be easy but begged me to have faith in their plan. It was getting harder by the minute. But no one had been charged and each day drew closer to Miller and Bellord's planned return. Then the onus would be on them and they would drag their banking friends, kicking and screaming, through the courts.

The process of law, protracted and enigmatic, became irritating and corrosive, wearing us down and devastating our lives.

Any relationship I had with the motor racing world was history. Incredibly, to me at least, the effect of the whole affair wiped out my brief career at a stroke. Once the search for Miller and Bellord had started in earnest and the nominees and racing drivers were targeted as potential criminals, the phone in my office stopped ringing and I was unemployed.

Margaret and John were fighting for the House as well as their jobs and integrity. John Howell had been kept in the dark too. He'd been denied access to transactions within the companies and had no knowledge of the dodgy credit arrangements. Even worse, the accounts and ownership details of the House remained a messy mystery. Margaret and John's hands were tied by the lack of transparency, accurate records and missing documentation. Perhaps it was Miller's plan, that if there were no records, no one apart from them could be blamed.

Margaret had more to lose than anyone. Her home was built in the grounds of the House, her job was there and Miller had tinkered with her mortgage arrangements, as he'd done with others. She was stuck.

Despite the turmoil, Margaret and John helped save my skin. They employed me to do building and maintenance around the House. Kindly, they said it would be an economic option for them too. My return to the building trade was sobering and my guilt, working for Margaret and John knowing I'd helped Miller and Bellord escape the law, gave me even more sleepless nights.

The outside of the House needed painting. A twenty-six bedroom mansion is no mean task for one man. It didn't daunt me. I bought an old banger for a couple of hundred quid, stuck a roof rack on it, picked up a couple of ladders from my old garage and started work. Over the years I'd decorated the House several times, inside and out. I knew its restless plumbing, its passageways and rooms and its impressive hall and staircase like the back of my hand.

The only part of the House that ever disturbed me was the boiler room and to this day I don't know why. It was accessed from outside by a narrow staircase into the bowels of a basement labyrinth. The entry was through a peeling dark wood door. Steel bars covered the small aperture where glass had once been, giving it the appearance of a prison cell. Lit by stark clear-glassed bulbs, emitting a poor light, the two boilers were fed from a stack of coke, metres high, stored in a corner of the dingy, underground utility. It was roasting inside the boiler room but any sweat from the experience felt icy cold. I had nightmares about that place and its stack of fuel. Ghosts or bodies loomed in those dreams but not in reality. When the store of coke ran low, all that remained were blackened rendered walls. Could I have been experiencing some psychometric effect from the Tredegar days?

Through long nights I painted the kitchens. Chef provided a midnight feast before he went off duty and the night staff would take their coffee break with me. Never once did I see ghosts on the lawn. Of course I imagined them, especially in the middle of the night when trees rustled, owls hooted and deer wandered softly out of the woods to linger in the ice house mist.

Every part of the estate, every room I worked in, resonated with Miller and Bellord's past presence. They'd be asleep now, tucked up in a tent somewhere on the Island, in a gale perhaps, buffeted by wind and rain, but warm in their thermal sleeping bags. It wasn't hard for a wandering mind to think of other possibilities. Perhaps they were already back on land, hiding out with newfound friends, or old ones, from previous visits to Ullapool. They'd been to Scotland enough times. Maybe they were abroad in another land, sipping cocktails on a beach with a stack of money. My imagination couldn't quite stretch that far.

Miller poured scorn on any man who took his own life. He believed that we had to live with and solve life's problems no matter how dreadful they seemed. But people change. Perhaps the suicide notes were genuine. Maybe right at this very moment, while I was painting the kitchen, two bodies were hanging from rocks by the very ropes we used to climb the cliff, or floating face down in the still waters of a loch. Or they'd taken the little dinghy out to sea and perished in the deep icy waters of the Minch. Less dramatically they could simply have died from exposure, their tents swept away in a storm, rain-soaked bodies backed against a sheltering rock, unable to dry out. Or a virulent bug attack on their weakened immune system finished them off.

*Evening Argus—October 1975*

*Sussex Bosses Hunted in Multimillion Pound Organs Riddle.*

*Interpol have still not located missing directors Sidney Miller and John Bellord who vanished on September 10th 1975 before the money tangle was discovered.*

*Today Southern Organs shops were closed as police and receivers went through the books. Security guards and dogs were called in to watch over the stock.*

*Mrs. Olive Leong, wife of the chef at the Nursing Home said:*

*'Miller and Bellord have been good to everyone. This has been a shock because they were such nice men.' She added, 'Now they have disappeared everyone is running them down. I think it is wrong. All the time they were giving, people were happy.'*

*Her husband has been chef at the House for fifteen years. Mrs. Leong said that when her daughter Tina married two years ago, Mr. Miller let her use his Rolls Royce for the wedding and gave her a present. He also gave her son Kevin a present when he married last year and helped him find a house.*

*Brands Hatch has struck the name Southern Organs off two championships being staged at the circuit on Sunday.*

*Meanwhile the Air Racing Association, which was promised thousands in prize money, has not been paid.*

# 18

# The Gone Men

I have no problem feeling love and warmth for another human being, it comes easy. As my marriage looked even more likely to crumble, my affairs with other women became inevitable, vital even. Tanya had shut down emotionally, steering the relationship toward a brother and sister act that denied sexual intimacy. Who could blame my wife for her affair? I had betrayed her and everyone else for Jim Miller. It wasn't looking good in the morality department. The children realised things had changed. The family lived within a fragile structure kept together by nothing more than the innate human desire to hold onto memories. We all still touched, smiled, joked and respected each other. It was a reasonable formula for continuing sanity.

Then a breath of something good, Margaret Cutler and John Howell had managed to save the House from being sucked into the black hole of Miller and Bellord's debts. This not inconsiderable achievement secured Margaret's home for the foreseeable future and her continued employment at the House.

We'd all got used to writs and the detritus of legal documents, solicitors letters, and the perpetual speculation about the final outcome. It became increasingly unlikely that the legal system would be satisfied with anything less than the full story and that would be impossible. Without Miller and Bellord to tell their side and reveal collusion by the money men, things were likely to remain unresolved. The resulting farce would be like trying the outlaw's family because the outlaw had disappeared. Even if some of the cases were won, the legal bills, unemployment, mortgage arrears and endemic depression would cost us dear, maybe even our lives. I wanted Eddie to turn up on his Norton, tell me to hop on the back, get real, and make like a rocket for the open road.

A current affair with a close friend, who'd also signed up as a nominee, made me ripe for confession. At first my story came in drips, titbits of enticing but not very revealing information. Then a trickle. Then it gushed out, unstoppable, how close I'd been to Miller and Bellord, how they'd helped everyone and tried to do some good in the world. When I heard they'd needed help, I'd offered it.

She nodded sympathetically, in all the right places, understanding my dilemma, because in the heat of sexual intimacy we all become loose-tongued and empathetic.

'They're not coming back, are they? They've been gone nine months and we're all going to end up in court. We'll lose everything,' she said, blinking back a tear. 'I'll stand by you, whatever, but I think you know what you have to do. You're the only one who knows where they are, Geoff, the only one who can move things on.'

'It might not help our case,' I said, less certain than ever of any plan Miller and Bellord had to save us.

'They guaranteed it all. Surely if they come back and point the finger at the crooked banks and credit companies, name names, there'll be an almighty public outcry. The press will have a field day and we'll have a better chance of winning, because the banks and fat cats will be exposed as the true villains of the piece.'

She looked sad, so small and vulnerable. I had got her and her family into this. Okay, she could have said no to the easy pocket money. But my friends signed because they trusted me and genuinely felt they were helping churches.

'Think about giving them up, for all our sakes. They've betrayed us all.'

When I'd dropped Miller and Bellord on Priest Island, we'd anticipated the food supply would last about two months, three at the most. A longer stay would only have been possible if they'd managed some fishing on calm days and harvested edible plants from the island's rich flora. Even so, surely they would not be able to survive for too much longer. Something must have happened and I was less certain of their whereabouts now. How could they have possibly survived a sub zero winter on Priest?

Our semi at Highways was a new, open plan, three-bedroom house. The ground floor comprised lounge, dining room and kitchen on a single span. The floor to ceiling panoramic windows looked across bungalow roofs that clipped the edge of the South Downs and the view toward the sea: the Channel.

I was trying, unsuccessfully, to read the paper. The children were asleep upstairs and Tanya was preparing tea in the kitchen. The phone rang. I raced to it, a habit I'd got into.

'Geoff?'

I'd know Jim Miller's voice anywhere, despite the poor line and words resonating, like his head was stuck in an oil drum.

'Yes,' I answered quietly; shaking and angry. For the very first time I could willingly have wrung his bloody neck. Tanya clattered about in the kitchen, only yards away.

Anyone could have picked up that phone. I tried to ignore the dizziness and sudden weakness in my legs. I wanted to crumple into that chair, the one I could put a hand on but not quite get my body into.

'Are you alone, can I talk?' he whispered, his voice so soft now, I had trouble hearing it.

Surely he must have heard the commotion from the kitchen.

Where were his psychic abilities now, his skill at reading situations, picking up nuances in voice and conversation? Would it have been beyond him to realise that after saving their lives from the pounding seas around Priest, I may not have survived the journey back.

Someone must have told them of my return. Maybe he was in touch with an old and still loyal friend, communicating easily between Ullapool and Sussex. Johnny and Marion maybe?

Miller and Bellord must now have grasped the magnitude of their crime and that I would be facing the aftermath alone. I wouldn't have dreamt of putting that burden on anyone. I couldn't speak, not just then, I wanted to ask so many questions. *Are you coming back? It's tough here, can't you come and sort it out like you promised?*

The call truly shocked and confused me. In the end I decided not to ask him a thing, a decision I knew I would regret.

'We're on the mainland, in Ullapool. We're desperate for money, can you send some? I'll give you the address...'

He mentioned Moss Road in Ullapool. They were in a caravan in the grounds of someone's bungalow for a few days while they picked up provisions. They were returning to Priest Island. How did they get back? Not by that damaged dinghy, I know. Who picked them up? Whose caravan and house were they hiding in? Their secret was surely over, or someone they trusted had decided to shelter and protect them. They were never coming back. I knew that now.

'I haven't got any money. I'm broke. Things are bad here...' Tanya came out of the kitchen. I said a hasty goodbye and put the phone down.

Bob Cracknell was still ferreting around and having a bad time of it. The police had labelled him a crank which is, apparently, the worst thing you can call a psychic. His marriage was under strain, he was severely depressed and close to a nervous breakdown. Much peeved about the police slur on his name, he made an official complaint and received a public and written apology. It did not alter the fact, the police still held the same opinion. It was a hollow apology delivered under pressure. That wouldn't have suited me at all. I think if I'd been Bob, I'd have kept quiet.

If I'd had my brain in gear I would have asked Tanya to let me alone for a moment. I could have asked Miller more questions, pressed him as to why they hadn't come back, why they'd betrayed us all. And had they any idea what we were all going through? But now I knew where they were, what was I to do? I felt ill with the burden and the dilemma I faced. It was impossible for me to understand why a man who lived and taught the things Miller had spread amongst us, would eventually leave us to stew. If they'd come back I'd have defended them to the bitter end.

My lies and deceit were always inexcusable. But the plan was so simple and promised a solution for everyone. Pop Miller and Bellord across to the Island, bit of peace and meditation, come back with a magic solution, expose the money men for their greed, they'd drop all charges against everyone and all would have been well. He'd said it would!

What of the bigger picture, cause and effect, karma, the Magnificent Obsession? Even now I held back from giving them up. Miller's voice had evoked powerful memories and emotions. The phone call, like a hypnotist's cue established long ago, triggered a known response in a credulous patient.

Morning sun streamed into our small kitchen-cum-breakfast bar. Tanya sat opposite as we silently picked at our breakfast. A nightmare few days and nights had left me with something close to the worst hangover in history. But I hadn't drunk a drop. During the past week I could easily have been convinced that I'd had spectral visits from Miller and Bellord during the night; they'd put up arguments, begging me for my continued silence. They'd show me their camp on the Island, tents set comfortably amongst the bothy ruins, the Elsan toilet in a quiet nook of its own. They needed more time. But their astral visits would not reveal the quiet road in Ullapool where they waited, hoping for more cash to arrive.

I held Tanya's hand as she held mine. We looked at each other, eyes tired of it all, the failing relationship, the writs, the default on the mortgage, the escalating bills, and the worried friends. We both felt ill. Only the joyous innocence of our kids lightened each testing day.

Tanya guessed something was up. She must have seen me shaken from Miller's call even though she could not have known who'd rung. That's the thing with being together for years. You know when something is wrong and when your partner is being deceitful or secretive but you can never be sure what the deceit is covering or what the secret is.

The media pressure died down but melancholia weakened me and left me ripe for further confession. This must be the moment interrogators wait for, the prisoner on the edge of divulgence, when the questioning and mental torture over long periods of time suddenly bear fruit and the prisoner tells all. In fact the confession pours out unstoppable, like a washer-less tap.

Tanya sat passively, listening without comment, encouraging me with her silence. For a minute she looked as if this was no surprise. She neither smiled nervously, which she sometimes did, nor did she cry, which was likely. Weirdly, there was a look of relief, her face softened and her shoulders relaxed as if some painful spasm had left her. No doubt her understanding and calmness had been made bearable by the new love in her life. There would be much comfort in his sympathetic arms, enough to sustain her throughout the ordeal. In a way I was pleased, my burden of betrayal marginally eased.

She didn't push me to give them up, which was quite something, given that friends and mother-in-law were impatiently awaiting justice.

Although police action, court appearances, bankruptcy, decimated relationships and unemployment became routinely predictable, what had previously been uncertainty and speculation, regarding the extent of the fraud, suddenly became reality. Most of the nominees knew what they owed. The writs and demands were drafted, delivered in hard copy and read many times. It looked as if the wheels of litigation, for most, would grind exceedingly slow. Not least because of the energetic disputes those individuals and their solicitors, fuelled by various fighting funds, would throw before our faceless enemy.

The unscrupulous are used to winning. The big boys employed the best lawyers and pooled enough money to enjoy the luxury of patience. It was a most effective combination for winning against the man in the street, who winced at every solicitor's bill and wanted it all to end quickly. Some did end it quickly. Unable to stand the pressure and decimation of their lives, some nominees took the best deal going. This usually meant agreeing to a reduced settlement figure paid over years with interest. Or a lump sum paid up front to drop the case. Occasionally a nominee would receive encouraging news from a solicitor only to be disappointed by a further missive declaring things hadn't quite gone to plan.

Not once did these money men acknowledge they'd made a fortune out of Miller over the years, millions from their dodgy transactions. Banks don't change. They do some very dodgy stuff and collude with gusto if they see an opportunity but protect themselves with small print and bullying letters if things go wrong.

*...we are withdrawing your overdraft facility...due to the current economic climate we are reviewing our business account arrangements with you...we have no alternative but to...if you do not settle within thirty days we will have no other choice but to place the matter in the hands of our legal team...*

Banks, apparently, can blacklist anyone they like, refuse credit and call in debt at a stroke, without pity. They can ruin lives and credit ratings for years. But, whatever the crime, no one can blacklist a bank!

Every day on Priest Island the two must have thought of what they'd left behind. Thinking and problem solving is what they did, and with time on their side they must have thought very long and hard indeed before deciding that coming back was, after all, not an option. Maybe they'd heard about Bob Cracknell rooting around the mountains, lochs and islands. They would have sniffed at his credentials. Psychic detective, solver of mysteries.

Perhaps it was inevitable that I would give them up. The task they'd set me was too great. It had gone beyond anyone's reasonable expectation. It is not possible to lie and deceive on such a scale without losing reputation and respect, hard earned over years of loyal friendship. Who would believe me now?

Before I gave them up, I had onerous tasks to perform. My arrest could be imminent.

Firstly I needed to seek advice from a neutral solicitor, someone who'd not represented anyone else involved with the nominees or banks.

My friend knew of a reputable solicitor.

Buildings that house the legal profession have hefty entrance doors, a labyrinth of corridors and staircases, embellished with dark oak panels, and stern, knowledgeable receptionists whose fixed smiles instill something resembling paralysis. We waited anxiously in the empty reception room preparing our pitch. There was no easy way to tell it.

Reassuringly, certificates of expertise decorate the walls. Amongst them professional propaganda and adverts of services: how to make a will. Have you been involved in an accident? Going through a divorce? There's plenty of money to be made from others' misfortune.

Mr. Rogers, our chosen one, was a young dynamic partner in a respectable firm of Worthing solicitors. He offered us seats, made himself comfortable, relaxed into his green leather chair and cleared his throat. We were ready.

He couldn't have helped being taken aback by my story which, at first, sounded like a synopsis for a half-baked bank heist. I expected him to stop me midstream to say that to deal with such a complex dilemma was beyond his expertise. But he didn't. His face grew more serious as I explained my connection with Miller and Bellord's disappearance. He knew about the fraud, the international search for the men and also knew they were still at large.

'This won't be easy. You are an accessory, at least. You might even have to stand trial alongside them.' He fiddled with a pen and sucked the end of it absently, giving me a moment to take in the facts. I'd already thought of prison, many times, and seriously considered it might not be such a bad place to be.

'What goes on in here is absolutely confidential.' He removed the cap from his pen and made brief notes. He numbered each hastily written paragraph as he went and underlined the finished page with a flourish before removing his glasses.

'You need to think very carefully about what I am about to suggest. It may not save you from prison but it will give you the best possible chance of doing so.'

My friend slid her hand into mine and squeezed it gently.

'I happen to have some knowledge of the officers running the fraud squad. I want to chat to the case team off the record and let them know you are prepared to give Miller and Bellord up. I hope to convince them that you are totally aware of what you have done and what you might be charged with. Everything you say in the interview must be totally open and honest. If they find out you are lying, they'll throw the book at you.'

'What are you expecting them to do?

'In return for your confession I want them to consider leniency. I want them to do their best to keep you out of prison. We do have a chance, because I know and they know that without you these men might never be brought to justice. The police have got nowhere with this case and I don't intend to reveal your name unless they are willing to strike a deal.' His voice rose with undisguised excitement.

'Before we arrange an interview with the police, there are certain things I must do,' I said, dreading the confrontations ahead.

'We can hang on for a few more days, that won't be a problem, but don't leave it too long. Miller and Bellord may have plans to move on. While you're doing what you have to do, I'll sort out the official paperwork and prepare the way. Don't worry, you won't be mentioned by name, not yet,' he assured me. He stood up ready to draw our meeting to a close. 'Can you tell me what it is you have to do?'

'Many of my friends signed these bogus agreements. They made those choices of their own free will but I introduced them to Miller. Now they will know I've betrayed them by choosing to take Miller and Bellord to Priest Island. I don't expect them to understand why. I'm not sure I would, under the circumstances. I need to confess to all of them before I give those two men up.'

'That'll be tough. We don't know what Miller and Bellord

will say when they are arrested. They'll get to know who shopped them eventually and as for friends, they'll find out about your part soon enough anyway. Once the two have been caught the police will be knocking on doors and contacting the media, so be prepared for a tough time.'

Slapdash attempts at meditation and giving myself a damn good talking to helped prepare me for the next few days. It had to be the most difficult thing I had ever done. Or hopefully will ever have to do.

A few friends thought I was much stupider than I looked but stood by me. Many were hurt, appalled, disgusted and could not forgive me.

When I knocked on doors, stood in lounges, hallways or kitchens, depending on friends' reactions and sense of hospitality, my confession became a script. Words repeated at each visit with ever more sorrow and contrition.

'There's something I have to tell you. It won't be easy and I don't expect you to understand. But you're my friends and I wanted to meet you face to face so that at least you will credit me with that much courage.' Most looked completely bemused at this point as if I'd lost it and finally flipped.

'I helped Miller and Bellord escape.'

More often than not, faces turned ashen. Some turned an angry shade of red. One or two guided me swiftly toward the door. In each case, I stood my ground and finished my script.

'When Miller and Bellord thought of all the options, we agreed it would be best if they were out of the way. They assured me that with them gone, the finance companies and banks would be powerless to sue anybody. They knew Miller and Bellord had signed each and every agreement as guarantor and that was the key. None of the sponsors had enough money to buy such expensive items, we all knew that. All the money men had to do was check credit records but they didn't bother, didn't think they needed to. They took Miller's word and guarantee because they trusted him and they were greedy. Miller was wrong to assume his signature would save us and now we are all facing prosecution. They promised to come back and sort it out but they haven't and that's why I am giving them up now. We all trusted them. Even you,' I said, hoping for a hint of understanding.

'Why didn't you give them up sooner and save us all this grief?'

'Because I thought it would eventually come right.' I really did. 'If it's any help, I would have done the same for you or any one of my friends in trouble. I know it looks as if my loyalty was to one person, that I chose Miller above you, that wasn't what I intended. I honestly thought I'd be saving everyone.'

Each visit to a friend felt like more nails and teeth being extracted. Many of them did not challenge me directly at the time, they were probably in shock. But the gradual withdrawal of friendship did come. With some it took months before the final break, others just stopped inviting us to social occasions. Phone calls dropped to a trickle, people crossed the street to keep out of my way and ignored me in restaurants. A sea of whispers washed around me wherever I went.

Mother-in-law would never forgive me, that didn't take a great deal of working out. Miller had stolen her money, I had lied to her and betrayed everyone and my marriage to her daughter was on the rocks. Enough reasons for any sane mother-in-law to cut you adrift. She did have a bash at cross-examining me about the affair, questions, questions, questions. It all seemed a little pointless now. After all, the whole thing was built on a pack of lies so how would she know if I was telling the truth? I attempted again to reassure her that, however it looked, I never intended to hurt anyone.

Mr. Rogers and I met with the Fraud Squad. He interrupted

the proceedings when the interview veered off course. The police finally agreed to leniency in exchange for information, though leniency seemed less important now

I wanted it over with.

# 19

# The Arrest

On Friday thirtieth of July 1976, a small police convoy wound its way through the Highlands, down through the Braes of Loch Broom and along Moss Road to pull up a hundred yards from. Roselea, Mrs. Mackay's guest house. Her modest bungalow, nesting in a small piece of ground, was their target. On the front lawn, alongside the path, stood a smart caravan, the place where Miller and Bellord had phoned from.

Obviously I was not there to witness the scene, but I conjured the moment up in crystal clear definition as I lay in bed, depressed and spent. Uniformed police officers surrounded the building, hiding behind hedges, trees and in neighbours' gardens. A couple of plain-clothes officers approached the front door and two more made for the caravan. Miller and Bellord didn't resist arrest but they were shocked and found it impossible to believe anyone had given them up. The two assumed it was the tenacious search by police and the media, or a word from a suspicious neighbour that instigated their arrest. With gaunt pale faces, the two betrayed men stepped out into the cool highland air, handcuffed and duly warned: anything you say may be used in evidence against you in court. Mrs. Mackay stood aside, crying and wiping hands distractedly as if she'd recently finished baking. Their ignorant saviour would never get over it.

My sense of treachery would be slow to leave, if it ever did. Police protection, at least in the short term, worked well and my name was not mentioned. Miller and Bellord were kept in a cell at Horsham police station and then moved to Lewes, ready to appear in court the next morning.

Lewes Prison lies in a pretty Sussex town overlooking the River Ouse. The guidebooks brag about fortifications, the castle, the Viking raids and their vicious deeds, but the town did not brag about its prison. The building is excluded from most tour books, as if that would make it invisible.

The paperwork following Miller and Bellord's arrest must have been horrendously complicated and as things hotted up, the paper trail became ever more fictitious; false documents, deceitful letters and lying statements. Criminal bankruptcy charges were filed against them. Each disclosed debts of one and a half million pounds with assets of only two and a half thousand pounds. The fraud squad unearthed nearly three thousand fictitious hire purchase agreements requiring over fifty thousand pounds a month to service them. The total, including transactions settled over the years and now forgotten or spirited away, would have been staggering. Already seven million pounds was being estimated. With such a huge cover-up, we will probably never know the exact figure.

There was little evidence to support their claim that they'd made sizeable donations, given gifts and made loans. The official receiver disclosed that people replying to his letters had denied receiving any money at all. They would, wouldn't they? I found this sad. I knew for a fact, they'd been generous to many people. And I wouldn't mind betting they'd never asked for receipts. They'd given freely, they'd taken freely.

Miller and Bellord denied the lavish parties and jet-set life style. I could see why they were quick to play it down. They lived humbly in their little flat, ate simply, and drank very little alcohol. Their clothes were M&S. Entertaining was lavish at times and I could never be quite sure what most of that was for. Of course they would have to put on a show for the money men, the celebrities and potential investors and they loved to see others enjoying themselves. I also think Miller craved a following. He had a Magnificent Obsession and everyone was going to hear about it. Most of us had, and benefited from it.

Eventually the case went to trial. Miller and Bellord were given six years each for a number of charges including: stealing from the House trust, obtaining a pecuniary advantage by way of overdraft facilities, defrauding finance companies and forgery.

Forgery? It was the first hint, at least the first open accusation, that some of the documents may not have been signed by the nominees. This was a real turn up and if it could be proven by expert witnesses, the prosecutors might be compelled to drop the case.

I could see Miller, prior to his flight to France, puffing at his pipe, John Bellord, head buried in paperwork, trying to plug all the leaks in their scheme should it ever come to this. Well it had come to this and maybe they knew the forgery issue was bound to come up. They might even have set out to produce a whole bunch of forgeries to muddy the legal waters. It would be complicated and difficult to separate the true signatures from the forged. The system would go into overload and implode under the sheer weight of it all.

*DAILY EXPRESS Wednesday January 5th 1977*
*The Express reveals the amazing story of fake suicide Crusoes*
*who hid for 262 days on remote island*

## £3m CON MEN CASTAWAYS - by Norman Luck

*Two men who fled their crooked millionaire lifestyle by faking suicide and becoming castaways on a remote island ended up in prison yesterday.*

*Behind them middle-aged bachelors Sidney (Jim) Miller and John Bellord left the ruins of a £3 million fraud and faint footprints in the sand of Priest Island.*

*Now they start a six year jail term not far from the Sussex mansion where they lived.*

*At Lewes Crown Court it was said that Miller and Bellord were only trying to meet their 'insatiable urge to help people but they ran into a mysterious blackmail case which led to long term fraud over the sale of organs to churches'.*

*The story of their company, Southern Organs, mixed in with the use of the Horsham Mansion as a nursing home, was first revealed in the Daily Express in October 1975. The details of the final plot—get away to France, faked suicide, castaways off the Scottish coast—are even more bizarre. For as survivors Miller and Bellord were cast in a Robinson Crusoe mould that made a commando want to use them as instructors.*

*In March 1976 Royal Marine Sergeant Bade Curtis, with another sergeant commando, landed on Priest Island reconnoitering for a survival exercise for their men. He found Miller and Bellord to be experts on survival. 'They made tea out of roots, knew all the plants (winkle stew was a specialty) and advised us on the best water to use. They had rebuilt parts of a stone hut and made it into a kind of a cave by lashing polythene and driftwood across for a roof, topped with dry ferns for insulation. Their tents were pitched in the ruins and they had a proper chemical toilet. I told them I wished they were available to instruct my men.' By the time Sergeant Curtis returned with his men, they'd gone.*

Norman Luck's story gave a fine snapshot of the scam and escape to Priest Island. There were some inaccuracies, as there often are when several people give an account of the same story. I certainly did not pilot the getaway helicopter, nor did I destroy vital documents relating to financial agreements. Although Norman Luck had been the one to employ Bob Cracknell, the psychic's name was never mentioned in the article.

Miller spoke to Norman Luck while on remand in Lewes.

'It was a hard life,' admitted Miller. 'We wanted to get away to be quiet and think. When we arrived at the end of summer, the Island was calm and peaceful. We had plenty of provisions to last us for a while, but eventually they ran out. We did manage to get to the mainland twice to get extra provisions, but when the winter set in we had to start living on the natural resources.

We did very well for shellfish but even though we had fishing rods, we didn't catch many fish. After a while we got to know all the plants. Some made excellent tea and others made a kind of vegetable broth. We didn't attempt to hunt the bird life. There were hundreds of gulls but even in desperation we could not have killed them.

Both of us lost a lot of weight. Most of our time was spent writing our story and resting, otherwise we cooked and explored.

The winter was bleak. Violent storms forced us to stay inside the ruined crofter's bothy huddled around a fire. Neither of us could have faced another winter out there.'

The second part of Norman Luck's scoop was headed.

*The Isle of Raw Survival*

*Two fraudsters took to jail yesterday, the secret of a womanising church leader, it is said, they'd saved from a scandal.*
*This helping hand for a wayward cleric was the beginning*

*of the long, long trail of trickery followed by Sydney Miller and John Bellord. It lasted twenty years and snowballed into a mammoth hire purchase swindle involving 20 finance houses and innocent victims who thought they were helping to buy organs for churches.*

*For Miller, 56, and Bellord, 48, directors of the firm Southern Organs International, the price was six years each. For the churchman—high up in the uppermost echelon of the Church of England—it meant his good name had been preserved by their silence.*

*They gave specific instructions to their defense counsel, Mr. John Elliot, not to make any specific reference to the bishop after they'd pleaded guilty at Lewes Crown Court to plotting the fraud, theft, forgery and obtaining money by deception. All Mr. Elliot would say was: 'Late in 1959 they were confronted by blackmail demands. It had nothing to do with them. They raised the money to pay the blackmailer off.'*

*Now the full story may never be revealed. The church leader himself died with his secret some years ago.*

*In a bid to protect his memory a number of bishops visited Miller and Bellord whilst they were in Lewes gaol awaiting trial. And none of them will talk about the matter.*

*The only known fact is that one of a number of women the cleric had affairs with made a £10,000 blackmail demand.*

*Miller told me [Norman Luck] when I visited him in jail: 'If I revealed any details of the scandal all our work would have been wasted. We have struggled over these 20 years because we helped a friend.'*

*In court Mr. Elliot told the judge: 'These crimes were not for personal gain. They gave moral and spiritual help to people. No one was turned away'.*

*The former Bishop of Woolwich, Dr John Robinson, now Dean of Trinity Chapel Cambridge, also spoke up for Miller and*

*Bellord. They were, he said, 'hardworking and dedicated to the House trust'.*

*But Judge Edward Sutcliffe QC told them: 'You had built up this image of yourselves as big charitable figures—images you were not prepared to drop. The only thing I can think of is that you got some self-satisfaction out of this'.*

What I have never been able to fathom out, is how a ten thousand pound blackmail demand can have been such a protracted burden. Simple maths make the whole thing seem ludicrous. They bought the House for something like seven and a half thousand pounds in the 'fifties, which was a stack of money in those days. Then they built up a multi-million pound business and pulled off a huge fraud which must have easily swallowed a mere ten grand blackmail payout. Some of the fake organ agreements alone were worth close to that and yet the secret of the wayward bishop was still used as an excuse for Miller and Bellord's plunge into decades of debt.

*Dear Mr. Green,*

*With reference to our meeting last week, I confirm that that you have left two letters and a short document with me.*

*I have read through the papers and in particular the letters. Clearly, Messrs Miller & Bellord would like to see you.*

*In one of the letters they suggest that they will be sentenced to long periods of imprisonment. Once they have been sentenced, there will be little or no opportunity for you to see them until they are released from prison. If therefore, you would like to visit them, you should do so before they are sentenced.*

*The decision as to whether or not you see them is entirely yours. After they have been sentenced, if they go to prison, then you may come to the conclusion that you would have liked to have seen them before they went into prison. They know where you are and they know how to contact you. In the circumstances, I do not think there is really any harm in your going to see them. However, I would suggest that you see them at the last possible opportunity, that is, during the week prior to the trial.*

*Of course, in all the circumstances, you may decide that you do not want to see them at all.*

*I await hearing from you as necessary in due course.*

*Yours sincerely,*

*Robert Rogers*

In the main, Robert Rogers handled the whole thing well. I couldn't fault his judgment or ability to handle the case, apart from one thing. It seemed odd, to say the least, that my solicitor should even contemplate a meeting with Miller and Bellord. We had betrayed each other and they were in jail because of me. In addition, court cases against me were pending and it would be an uncomfortable and ill-advised farce for the three of us.

Mrs. Miller, Jim's mother, must have gone through hell. Her cosy home, standing in a converted mews across the covered courtyard, was only a few yards from Miller's flat. She didn't deserve the suffering weighted on her over the past year and I should not have prolonged it. This tiny, bright, stooped lady of uncertain age with blue rinsed hair and matching poodle was an eccentric, son-loving mother, but completely innocent of any wrongdoing here.

She was kept in the dark regarding the depth and scope of Miller's beliefs and work. She would not have liked it: the secrecy and the discomfort of those who dare argue with his philosophy. Equally she would have no idea at all about the skullduggery of the business side of things. She simply enjoyed the company and lifestyle that such gregariousness and generosity produced.

It must have been a cruel blow indeed to see the respectable and only son, the philanthropist that any mother would have been proud of, carted off to prison following the terrible news he'd committed suicide. The tough part for her now would be living amongst the sympathy and gossip that inevitably followed Miller and Bellord's arrest and imprisonment. Staff at the House rallied to support her, despite the fact they would be facing serious charges themselves for signing agreements.

At least the elderly mother could now visit her son and support him, having agonised over the past year that she may never see him again. What on earth would they talk about?

Margaret took Mrs. Miller to Lewes Prison every week. I tried to imagine this frail lady walking through prison gates for the first time: the noise, the bars, the smell of crowded cells, the uniformed officers and the stark, glossy-walled interior.

The letters referred to in Robert Roger's correspondence were written in John Bellord's neat, regular hand on standard prison notepaper. The two men would have been sitting on their steel-framed, grey, blanketed beds, neatly made and turned back. Maybe a few personal belongings helped to give the place an identity. There would, I imagine, be a lot of letter writing. But letters don't influence like the stare of persuasive steel blue eyes. I reread the letters, the carefully chosen words, kind words without admonishment, but I did not want to see Miller and Bellord, or answer their letters.

The rot had not stopped as we'd expected it to. Their confessions and collaboration did nothing to affect the small army of bankers, solicitors and finance companies with their writs, prosecutions and self-righteousness. Such was the lack of response to their capture, it was as if Miller and Bellord had been arrested for a completely different crime, not the one that plagued us now. Their containment and statements made not a jot of difference.

They were safe now, dry and fed, cocooned from what the

rest of us were going through, protected from their angry victims by steel bars and the law. There were, however, certain things and people they would not be protected from.

One day a very unexpected visitor turned up to see them in Lewes. I doubt either of them would have predicted it, not in a million years. So when mother-in-law Madge walked into the visitors' room and sat squarely in front of them, Miller and Bellord must have come close to melt down. I'm unaware of prison etiquette, but they would have agreed to see her, wouldn't they?

Even now, I could never be sure why she decided to visit them, they had no money. Perhaps she wanted to grill them about son-in-law's activities and what part he'd really played in the whole thing. I'll never know. What I did know was that she asked them what had happened to her investment, her thousand quid. Their answer stunned me and, hopefully, her.

'We gave the thousand pounds to Geoff, didn't he give it to you?' said Miller, so it was reported.

Madge relayed her prison conversation to Tanya, who then told me. In addition, Miller and Bellord, in their defence, may well have pointed out that they'd paid her monthly interest in cash, ten pounds a month, one hundred and twenty pounds a year, twelve percent: a very generous arrangement indeed. The ten pound note was always put in a brown envelope, paid on the dot each month, and given to me to pass on. They paid, right up until the day they disappeared.

Whether Madge quoted Miller's response to her question verbatim is academic. Nothing would save our relationship now. In the end she didn't know who to believe. Everyone was lying. I did not have the thousand pounds and was never given it. So Madge had the courage to face Miller when I could not, but she didn't know them, they were strangers who'd taken her money. This detachment, this emotional distance between them made it easier to give chase to the thieves who'd grabbed her savings and left her short. Equally they had to face her, even though they probably had little choice in the matter. They may have panicked and blurted out my name, taking the heat off them but crucifying me.

My impending divorce from Tanya only added coal to an already raging fire. Madge had even less reason to keep friendly. Now she'd have another bone to chew. She knew Tanya's latest love and didn't think much of him, so Tanya would be getting it in the neck too. Her new husband would face a generous dose of disapproval. As far as mother-in-law was concerned, he did not exist and would never be accepted into the family.

Allegations from my enemies came sneaking out of the woodwork. These enemies had no face. Self-appointed messengers decided I should know that certain people thought I was part of the scam from the very beginning, that I stole one of Miller's cars and had a load of money stashed away ready to be picked up once the dust settled. And that I alone had pushed Southern Organs Racing beyond Miller and Bellord's financial means, purely for my own interests. They didn't know me. The only person I have ever pushed to do anything is myself.

Like all anonymous accusers, their stories could be as fantastical and defamatory as they chose. The bigger the lie, the easier it rolled off the tongue, certain to find credibility with the scandal-hungry media and minds fertile for planting seeds of gossip.

Bob Cracknell, hoping to get credit for his role in the story, was disappointed. That he guessed roughly where they were, nearly had a breakdown and predicted when they would be caught was not enough. And who did he tell that to? He had spoken to Marion and Johnny and followed his psychometric impressions after going through Miller's flat. His idea that they were living some kind of monastic life in a cave had something going for it but there were some inaccuracies in his account. He said Miller used a stick. Perhaps he had, over the boggy and sometimes treacherous island landscape. Could Bob Cracknell have sensed this? We certainly didn't take a stick with us, and Miller had never used one in all the years I'd known him, apart from the time he fractured his hip, falling over a briefcase John Bellord left in a doorway. John Bellord was fastidious about everything and for him to have placed that case so carelessly was an indication, to Miller, that things weren't right in the psychic awareness department. But that use of a stick was only for a short period of rehabilitation, years ago. Yes he'd come up with the fact that Miller had been disabled, but that was common knowledge.

Bob Cracknell repeated his claims in an article for Prediction, a monthly publication devoted to the occult and astrology. He gave an even fuller account of his role as a psychic detective in his book, Clues to the Unknown. He claimed to have played a significant part in getting the men arrested, predicting the time and place of their capture. That couldn't be true, it was never mentioned by the media, newspapers or anyone else and only revealed in Cracknell's book a year later. However he couched it, no one knew where Miller and Bellord were until I confessed all to the police. He also told of the two men evading Interpol for eighteen months. It was in fact nearer half that time, ten.

He omitted to mention in his book that I had given their whereabouts to the police the day before they were arrested. According to Cracknell, John Bellord had strong suicidal tendencies. Exactly the opposite was the case. I'd known John Bellord for fifteen years, he was one of the bravest and most upright characters I'd ever met. He faced things head on and when Miller chose to escape, it was John Bellord who wanted to stay and face the music. Okay, Miller overruled that and some may say it was weak of John Bellord to give in, but only those who knew Miller would understand how powerful and how trusted he was and, most of the time, how right he was. If he could fool bishops and bankers, he could fool anyone.

# 20

# The Psychic Detective

Bob Cracknell talked about the two men hiding in some sort of cave on the side of a hill and revealed that I'd rowed them across to the island from Ullapool, a distance of twelve miles. In reality our journey had been in a dinghy powered by a petrol-driven engine and launched from Camusnagaul on Little Loch Broom, many miles from Ullapool.

Marion, she of the now low profile, had every right to say to the world, 'I told you so.' She'd been distracted by all the effort put into searching for the castaways, the hubbub, the media, the police and the wronged parties in general. She'd befriended Bob Cracknell and grew ever more fascinated by his confidence and air of mystery. Airs of mystery were welcome at the House. It's what we'd all grown up with.

To be fair Bob Cracknell had, in great earnest and dedication to his art, spent a considerable time travelling up to Scotland, questioning the locals, sensing things and following his nose. He came across a ferryman who'd admitted to spotting Miller and Bellord when he'd been employed sailing to and from Ullapool. Normally this ferryman worked the Iona to Oban run and confessed to being a special constable.

It seemed more than odd that this PC, who must have been around when Miller and Bellord escaped, would not have been suspicious at the time. Miller and Bellord's descriptions had been circulated, there was a huge police presence in and around the north west for months. Add to that, the newspapers and TV promoting the fact that Miller and Bellord loved Ullapool and the north west. Yet, it seems, it was only Cracknell's questioning, months later that jogged the ferryman's memory.

It didn't add up. There were no other major crime investigations in the area at that time, nothing that would have diverted attention from the big manhunt. The local police, including the specials and the close knit community, should have spotted even the mildest out of place ripple amongst its community: strangers on the scene, a canary yellow estate car they'd never seen before, parked in a remote place for thirty six hours. The ferry would have been a particular focus. It was often the only means by which locals crossed from island to mainland. Most passengers would have been regular native travellers, greeting each other and showing signs of whispering interest should a new face appear.

As far as I can make out, there would have been no reason at all why Miller and Bellord would have taken that particular ferry, unless they'd had a complete change of plan to escape the rigours of life on Priest. Or were they out to confound me, the only person who knew their plan? Or was I? If they'd returned to Ullapool twice for stores, they must have made jolly good friends and in the process stirred up local interest. I can understand them trying the trip once out of desperation and risking capture, but twice? Did they use flares? Did a fishing boat pick them up? I bet they didn't risk the tiny dinghy. Even on a brilliant day, there would have been no guarantee they could have got back. And if they had risked it and couldn't face the return trip, who would they have stayed with? Someone must have helped in a big way. What stories had they told? What reason did they give for being on Priest Island?

Cracknell also revealed, quite openly in his book, that the case had left him moody, depressed and put a strain on his home life. Unbelievers of such an inexact science were bound to give him a hard time. Now and again everyone gets powerful feelings, instincts, and premonitions. Miller had an extraordinary ability to 'see inside' people's lives and help them in remarkable ways. But things can go wrong. Feelings and vibrations can let you down on a bad day at the psychic office. Because there is too much stuff out there, and the more stressed you are the less likely you are to pick up subtle clues. This may have been what happened to Cracknell. So much negative stuff was coming from those around him, sceptics, police, media and me, that he'd experienced a psychic overload and blown a fuse somewhere, rendering his skills weak when he needed them most.

In hindsight, he would have been better off tracking Miller and Bellord down on his own. It would have saved him the ignominy of rejection by the police and others. Didn't his psychic skills alert him to the negative police vibrations? Surely a signal to pull back!

*

Once their kids have grown up, most adults are anxious about them leaving home. Some are glad. I bucked the trend and left my kids before they left me. It wasn't a choice I wanted to make but it turned out to be the right one for all concerned. My life was a bit of a wreck and the children were too young to get into the whys and wherefores of why loved and trusted adults fuck their lives up in full view of their loving offspring.

My wife and her new man were about to get married. I left the family home so he could move in and give the kids the best shot at a stable environment. I use the term loosely as he wasn't their dad, he was a stranger sleeping in their father's bed. As far as I could reason it was still the best solution, a solution that needed some working on.

Away from the case, good things were happening in my life. I bumped into Carol, a girl I'd met through one of my building clients a year or two back. We'd hit it off and now we were both going through a divorce.

If we'd had a chance meeting once, probably nothing would have come of it. But it happened repeatedly and in the most unexpected places. I'd visit a shopping precinct I'd never been to before, Carol would be there. Tanya and I were invited to a dinner dance, not my favourite leisure pursuit, at a Brighton hotel, which happened to be on the same night as Carol's father's company bash. Carol and I floated coyly past each other in our best dinner dance gear, avoiding conversation, uncertain of our ground, aware that Tanya was there too.

Weeks later, I bumped into Carol again. That was three times in a row. If ever there was a sign, this was it. I invited her to dinner, she accepted and we were on the road to the longest courtship the world has ever witnessed. Keen to start a new life together, we both declared our interest in health care and were eager to begin new careers. We worked out costs, commitment and the effect on family lives, before deciding; osteopathy for me, acupuncture for Carol. She had two very young boys to consider. Academically, she had a head start, a string of 'O' and 'A' levels, so she was ready to go. I returned to school to get mine. It was tough but much more exciting than when I was a sickly kid struggling through my school years.

The court cases, investigations and interrogations had run out of steam. No vast sums of money found, no secret offshore bank accounts and no other devious means of securing a fortune had been discovered. The accelerating interest rates, the huge financial commitments and Miller and Bellord's naive generosity had used it up. Not to mention, the Winds of Global Change, a phrase coined in the 1970's to encapsulate the predicted economic and political disruption worldwide.

The nominees, however, still had their battles to fight, still had to salvage what they could to avoid bankruptcy and their homes being taken away. It was every man and woman for themselves, Miller and Bellord were not going to save them now. The fighting band of solicitors and lawyers had to find an agreeable way out. Some nominees left the comfort of organised fighting groups to pursue their own path, employing fresh legal blood in the hope that a new eye over the problem would make a difference.

No such luck. Many nominees decided to compromise and meet the finance companies in a deal that would reduce their debt but tie them to high interest repayments for years. Others made one-off payments that left them broke and, in my opinion, let the money men completely off the hook. After all, these financiers were complicit and had been caught with their trousers down. But as bankers do, they managed to pull their pants up quickly enough to look respectable before they got anywhere near a court.

My day in court was yet to come. There were murmurings. If Geoff Green could be nailed it would be a huge coup for the prosecution and may even be the beginning of the end for the nominees' fight for any sort of justice. What the final bill for all of us would be was impossible to gauge. Most had signed multiple agreements with different companies. As soon as someone was successfully taken to court and agreed a settlement, another company would crawl out of the woodwork and go after their share. For nominees, the process was ruinous.

This bullying injustice was wrong and I would never give

in to the financiers' hypocritical demands. My building society wanted their house back. Luckily my wife's new husband-to-be agreed to take on the mortgage. I'd have no home but my wife and kids would. No one could squeeze me for cash, I didn't have any. Assets? None apart from an old banger, a two hundred pound Vauxhall Viva. I'd cashed in my life insurance policies, stopped paying into pension schemes, and had no employer to subtract money from my wages. Great. They'd get nothing.

With divorce, bankruptcy and impending litigation came a surprising liberation. Despite being without my wife and kids, and some of my friends turning against me, it was the most liberated I'd felt in years. Images of my wife's new husband sleeping in my bed and winning the affection of my children with treats and the inexhaustible attention of someone desperate to be accepted, should have been painful. But by the time it actually happened, my sleepless nights and knotted gut all but disappeared. The arrangement was a poor alternative to traditional family life, nevertheless it had a better chance of success than the pretence of the past few years.

I knew Miller and Bellord would make the best of their incarceration. They'd been moved from Lewes, first to Wormwood Scrubs, then to Ford Open prison in Sussex, half an hour's drive from where I lived. They would befriend the prison staff and the prisoners. Inmates would get due attention and find Miller and Bellord damn good company. I couldn't help but wonder how they'd portray themselves to the other prisoners. How much they would tell and how much blame they'd be taking. Don't prisoners always protest their innocence? Would Miller turn out to be a Don Corleone or a Robin Hood? They would get time off for good behaviour. They would be the most perfect prisoners that had ever been. Once they'd left Lewes, their letters to me stopped. I hadn't replied and as yet, had no intention of visiting them.

Years slipped by. Miller and Bellord were likely to be out before all the nominees' cases had been brought to court. Where would they live? Would they 'set to' and have a crack at sorting things out for us: the cavalry coming over the hill? Unlikely now. With all the bad vibes from the nominees and the disillusioned, they might be tempted to disappear again. The BBC were waiting for them when they got out and made a programme, Miller may have directed it. He certainly had a hand in the editing. Quite obviously it was from his viewpoint. Past patients, the Bishop of Woolwich and a grateful actor, sang his praises on camera. The episode included an interview with crime reporter Norman Luck, who described Miller and Bellord as the most unlikely criminals he'd ever met.

The programme was put out on a Sunday night between the Ten O'clock News and, ironically, Claire Rayner's Casebook in which the advice columnist meets people who have faced up to personal crises in their lives.

Sunday 30th November 1980<br>BBC EVERYMAN<br>Miller and Bellord

*An act of Christian charity, a miracle cure, an unorthodox but successful healing practice, the support of distinguished churchmen...*

*Startling facts combined in the lives of Jim Miller and John Bellord, yet such simple separation of right and wrong seems to fail in understanding their nightmare story which led five years ago to front page headlines and public disgrace.*

*Now in this Everyman film people who have known them piece together the clues of this extraordinary partnership and as Miller and Bellord themselves sit down to confront their past for the first time, they uncover a confusing pattern of motives, spiritual claims and moral judgments.*

It was an unsettling, surreal experience indeed, to see them again: talking, smiling, relaxed almost. Miller looked wan but spoke animatedly and affectionately of their stay on Priest Island. The BBC had flown them out to Ullapool and the film crew had staged a remarkable scene of the two men, ferried by a local fisherman, stepping out of a rowing boat onto the slippery, rock strewn cove of Priest. The sea looked calm as a millpond and the shot made it look like they were tourists paddling on a boating lake; exactly what we had expected when we planned our trip in 1975.

Bellord, a little of the pale prisoner deprived of fresh air about him, spoke up in the most endearing terms about Miller. They both admitted to the crime, Miller blaming people's greed for some of it and Bellord simply admitting to it. Bellord added that it wasn't like an ordinary crime, not like robbing a bank, because no one was really losing. Either he didn't get a chance to talk about collusion or they'd edited it out. It seems the only thing that ultimately brought it to an end was the panic caused by the banks' kneejerk reaction to the developing UK economics and the horrendous interest rates.

The programme was heavily biased; we'll tell you our story, you film it. Or so it seemed.

The opening scene of BBC Everyman, Miller and Bellord, covered the early years of their lives, in what seemed like seconds. They were both seated, relaxed in someone's lounge, Bellord operating a slide projector showing scenes of the House, their healing practice and the motor racing all accompanied by Miller and Bellord's voice-over. The programme moved on to interviews with grateful patients talking about their miraculous recovery and a shot of Johnny driving his taxi, telling of Miller curing his limp. The rather grave looking Bishop of Woolwich, unable to understand what came over his two friends, emphasised they were good, hardworking men, which they were. Norman Luck repeated what he'd said in one of his articles, *what unlikely criminals they were*. Then, Everyman is not particularly noted for its radical reportage. Bob Cracknell was left out of the production.

Miller did not come across well on television. He looked effeminate, stern, touchy even, and less charismatic. Any contrition shown, and it wasn't much, appeared defensive.

John Bellord seemed his old self, confident, charming, reasonable and suitably contrite. He said he'd felt unbelievable sorrow for the problems they'd caused.

Seeing Miller had unsettled me. That's how he affected people: that's what made us all wake up and take notice. We were either intrigued, motivated, or plain scared. Seeing John Bellord simply made me feel sad. There was no bitterness in him, no sense that he'd had a rough deal, only a tough time coming to terms with it all.

I was looking forward to the whole mess being over, when a small finance company, fighting for its life, persisted in making a claim against me. Probably because it had nothing to lose, its back was truly against the wall. So was mine. They were determined to take the matter to court and extract due compensation for the alleged fraud I'd committed against them.

The company, Langtonian Finance, had been convinced of the benefits of motor racing sponsorship by Jim Miller. The boss was told of the particular advantages of having a car with his company's name on it flying around a race track, a track that would have thousands of potential customers standing or sitting around it. He could entertain in the hospitality suites, chat to other wealthy money men and their rich friends. Our rich friends. In hindsight the deal was no better than sponsoring a bullet with your name on it, and it would go straight to the heart.

My sympathy for the boss of this small company was genuine, but I could not accede to his request.

# 21

# The Forgery

Then something completely unexpected happened. Langtonian's solicitor sent mine a copy of a dodgy HP agreement with my name on it. But the signature on the contract did not appear to be mine. The name was right, G C Green, but the writing was not. It did not compare to some of the other documents I'd signed. These letters, unlike my scruffy hand, were too carefully formed: they had a measured sharpness and were indented, as if the signee had pressed too hard on the paper.

This was a real turn-up. I was expecting to conduct my defence on the grounds of the finance companies collaboration, but now a more exacting defence had turned up. My signature looked like a forgery and if it was it could be proven. The news filled me with new hope, not only for myself. Others could study their signatures to see if they were fraudulent too. Maybe the courts would throw out all pending cases in the light of such ambiguity.

Could this have been Miller's plan from the start? If it was, my conscience might have some serious battles ahead.

Their story of collusion with the banks didn't hold up. The power of their guarantees fared even worse but perhaps this forgery was exactly what was needed to shake the money men. Perhaps all the nominees would get their money back! In my dreams.

Langtonian Finance wanted half the amount I allegedly owed as settlement. Some sponsors were keen to say yes to this kind of deal. They could pay instalments at a reasonable rate of interest over many years and then they'd be worn down by protracted litigation from other claimants. I'd made up my mind, I was not going to play ball.

In return for the substantial sum I allegedly owed, payment for goods I hadn't even seen let alone owned, they promised not to inform other finance companies of our deal. This hardly seemed like the money men sticking together as expected. So far, the finance companies had collected their evidence and pooled resources to allow their lawyers optimum chance of success. For those who weren't getting results fast enough this new strategy must have held some appeal. Over a cup of coffee or a stiff drink in comfortable surroundings, smiling credit company bosses would hand out cigars and offer each individual a special deal. They'd tell the nominees how the company was bending over backwards to solve the problem. Meanwhile, behind the scenes, the next company would be preparing their own special deal.

There followed some heavy correspondence, interminable phone calls and meetings with solicitors. The Langtonian 'targets' had the most reason to worry. Langtonian had already taken a similar case to court which they won on the balance of probabilities. This meant insufficient evidence, so the fault was placed squarely on the shoulders of the nominee who'd signed the hire purchase agreement.

However, this balance of probabilities did not include the added weight of an allegedly forged signature. Forged or not, I would still have refused to pay. My argument was and always would be that, the nominees, the finance companies, the banks and Miller and Bellord had all done wrong. We had all gained some illicit financial reward. We should all say so and stop putting the blame on any single organisation or individual. The fiasco should slip quietly into oblivion and allow us to lick our wounds and get on with our lives. That would have been just.

Mr. Rogers received a phone call from Langtonian's solicitors informing him that they had a private detective agency carrying out discreet enquiries as to Geoff Green's financial standing.

Any case heard in a court of law would have to consider collusion and the prosecution would, surely, have to prove that goods were actually purchased and delivered to ensure transactions had been completed. As it turned out there was no such evidence. No delivery notes and no deliveries. None of the company vehicles could produce a log that gave their whereabouts with times, dates and delivery address.

My solicitor, Mr. Rogers, was as excited as me about the counterfeit signature. An independent forensic handwriting expert was called in. He applied to my bank for a copy of my signature and requisitioned past HP agreements and letters written around the time of the alleged forgery. The documents and samples were used to compare my real signature to the forged one. In addition I had to write numerous samples in front of the forensic examiner, copying words and sentences from a prepared script. Once completed the samples were removed, in case I copied them, before a fresh lot were set out before me. After that we moved to a new stage of analysis. The handwriting expert uttered commands that had to be written quickly, as a signature would be, under his steady gaze, ready for comparison to other documents.

I hadn't imagined it like this. I expected high-tech analysis, clever sharp-eyed certainty by the forensic expert. It was a painstaking job. Was my writing flowing? Was I trying too hard? Did I hesitate slightly at each attempt? Did he know I was having grave doubts about the signature and thinking that, after all, it may be mine? Then the waiting game. He tucked all the documents neatly inside his black briefcase, spun the combination lock and reassured me he would complete his report as soon as possible.

The instructions to the expert were: to examine and compare the above documents in order to offer an opinion as to the possibility of common authorship of known and questioned signatures.

No timescale was given as to how long it would take the handwriting expert to arrive at a conclusion. It was reassuring to know that any further legal action could not be taken until the results of the forensic analysis were known.

Carol and I, in the heady energy of our new relationship, set about the task of choosing our college courses. In between building work I ploughed through 'O' and 'A' levels. It was not so onerous really, I enjoyed working with youngsters and they must have found me amusing. Why would a forty year old want to sit exams designed for teenagers?

Carol, with two children to look after, could not afford the choices that were open to me. The hours had to fit in with children's school and family life. She chose a four year course in Chinese medicine and acupuncture. My choice was the British College of Osteopathic Medicine in London. As we waited to start the courses, we hoped the Langtonian affair would be tied up before the start of term next year. Surely the forgery revelation would finish it.

*31st January 1983*

*Dear Mr. Green*

*The handwriting expert's report is to hand and I enclose a copy. The solicitors acting for Langtonian have also been sent a copy and no doubt they will obtain their client's instructions in the near future.*

*On perusal of counsel's advice it seems to me that we should have a complete defense to the Claim and if they do not agree to withdraw, we must press on with all speed. I will wish to instruct counsel to advise whether in the light of the report we ought to seek a hearing of the Court to determine as a preliminary question whether in the absence of any evidence that you signed the Hire Purchase Agreement, this matter should be allowed to proceed. I will keep you informed of developments*

*Yours sincerely*
*Bob (Robert) Rogers*

I couldn't stop my hand trembling as I picked up the report. It had taken so long.

*R.W. Radley*
*Forensic Handwriting and Document Examiner*

### REPORT
*Geoffrey Colin Green and Langtonian Finance*
*Instruction*

*To examine and compare the above documents in order to offer an opinion as to the possibility of common authorship of known and questioned signatures.*

Then followed a blow by blow account of the meticulous document analysis. It must have taken days of scrutiny.

*Summary of opinion*

*I can find no significant evidence to indicate that the signatures in question are authentic writings of Geoffrey Colin Green.*
   *R.W. Radley.*

Surely it was in the bag. Irrefutable evidence had been produced and not a court in the land could find me guilty of the crime Langtonian were accusing me of. Robert Rogers was away when Langtonian's response dropped on to his desk. It had to be humble pie for Langtonian's lawyers, what could they possibly do now? Mr. Cudlipp, Mr. Rogers's colleague, let me in on the news.

*23rd February 1983*
*Dear Mr. Green*

*I write in the absence of Mr. Rogers from the office.*
   *Langtonian has taken the unusual step of instructing their solicitors to obtain their own handwriting expert's report. We have loaned them the documents used by Mr. Radley and have asked that they obtain their report as quickly as possible.*
   *Personally I do not see the necessity for obtaining a second opinion, however, they are perfectly within their rights to do so and all that we can do is to ensure that there is no unnecessary delay.*
   *Yours sincerely*
   *R. Cudlipp*

Damn.
   I could see the sense of a second opinion, from their point of view, they had nothing to lose. If I won my case, Langtonian

would be in serious trouble and the company might even fold as a consequence. I could not be certain to what degree, but the amount of business put their way by Jim Miller was substantial and a good slice of their turnover. If the new forensic expert found against me, the writs from Langtonian, sitting in the business pending tray waiting for my case to be proven, would be on their way to other nominees.

Things were getting silly. I'd had enough of the three year argument with Langtonian. Now I'd take a leaf from Miller's book. When you need something sorted, always go to the man at the top. Surely to do this you needed authority and clout. Miller had it in spades but I would be viewed as a minion and not worthy of a managing director's exclusive time. But wouldn't the weight of my case be disturbing him? Even if his forensic expert decided my signature was genuine it would be a one all score for the expert witnesses, another impasse. How would they resolve that? A third expert witness maybe. It could take years. Expert witnesses are not in a hurry, because their reputation is at stake and their findings must be open to the most thorough and public scrutiny.

Surprisingly, my appointment with Mr. Isaacs, head of Langtonian Finance, was set without too much trouble. The arrangement was to meet him alone at his offices in Sussex.

The drive, which could have been agonizing, was nothing of the sort. I was calm, collected, focussed and not thinking too specifically about how I was going to play things. I had to keep the script flexible as there were a few possible scenarios. Would he really meet me on his own or would he suddenly decide it was too risky? He didn't know me well enough to anticipate the mood I might turn up in. I might get angry, attack him even. He might have decided to employ security men, respectable bouncers, ready to give me the old heave-ho if I got physical. Perhaps he'd employ a whole team of lawyers to sit in a row behind a protective boardroom desk waiting to intimidate and persuade me to back off.

No one checked for weapons or recording equipment as I walked confidently through the entrance doors of Langtonian Finance. I was greeted respectfully by the receptionist and shown to Mr. Isaacs' office. The whole workforce must have known why I was there. Were they holding their breath, or chuckling confidently behind closed doors?

Mr. Isaacs and I had met before, at the racing circuits. I remember his undisguised excitement when his sponsored car was revealed for the first time, the Langtonian Finance legend emblazoned along the pristine white bodywork of the Formula Atlantic racer. I remember too, his delight at being wined and dined in the hospitality suite with a trackside view of his car rocketing around the circuit, his company name flashing subliminally and memorably, in the eyes of the crowd.

Politeness and restraint was in the air. We almost bowed, Japanese style, as I approached. He was a neat wiry chap with wispy grey hair and a friendly smile. With his rimless spectacles and intelligent, studious face, he looked more like a university lecturer than a financier. He appeared too kindly to have been the author of the brusque instructions delivered by his lawyers. *Beware the wolf in sheep's clothing*, Miller would have said. I also assumed, because of the gravity of the situation, that our conversation might be recorded. I hoped it would be, because nothing I had to say was untrue and I would not hold back on my accusations. In fact I would be happy for every single word to be on record. Perhaps Mr. Isaacs suspected that I might be recording the meeting too.

How many of the racing drivers were involved in nominating organs through Langtonian contracts, I wondered? And if they were, would they be coughing up? Did Miller target any of the Formula One Air Racers as nominees? I've said it before, if he'd deceived bishops and bankers, what chance did they have? Miller's patients would be rooting for him, wouldn't they? And the more casual acquaintances, those who'd managed to avoid becoming nominees and keep their distance—Portsmouth Football Club, Alvin Stardust, Emperor Rosko, John Surtees, the police, Lady Cawley, a raft of celebrities, and countless others, would be breathing a sigh of relief at their lucky escape.

The meeting with Mr. Isaacs was amicable. He suggested several ways forward for bringing our impasse to some agreeable resolution and put it to me that we were all culpable and that it would be only fair for me to pay at least part of the sum owing. I disagreed and dug my heels in.

There was no way I would pay him a penny. I reminded him that he was one of many who'd had full knowledge of what was going on with the nominees and that he was part of a conspiracy to make a stack of money from 'pyramid' selling products that didn't exist. Because if he'd looked at his company's transactions individually, carried out a few spot checks, knocked on a few nominees' doors, he'd have found out mighty quick that all was not well. But the financiers didn't because, like everyone else, they trusted Miller. Not that they thought him honest necessarily, but trusted him to be in control of what was happening. No one at the time doubted Miller's ability to make them a stack of money. And if there were suspicions they were quickly put to one side. Banks and money men do this all the time. They play with money that doesn't belong to them and when it goes wrong wheedle their way out of it. Everyone knows that.

Thirty five years later in the years 2008—2011, the general public trusted these huge profit makers with billions and when it all went wrong the government used our money to bail them out. Even then, they still thought it was their God-given right to dish out huge bonuses, fabulous pensions and pay offs. And nothing will ever stop the trend because in some perverse way we still have to trust them to make the world go round. The system is flawed, dirty and corrupt.

Hang on a second, the bankers would counter, you all signed documents you shouldn't have, took money that didn't belong to you and convinced yourselves that your tiny indiscretions were excusable.

Yes it's true, we all did what we did for money and that's the nub of it. We can cry about the injustice of it but hey, look at us, look at how indignant we are about those other cheats. No one should put their name to a document without seeing the goods or making sure they exist. In my own defence, I had delivered some of these nominated organs, dropped them off, seen them signed for and used my experience to reassure friends and others of their existence. Easy to realise, in hindsight, that these paltry few deliveries were simply sprats to catch mackerel. And now we know for sure that in some cases, as many as ten agreements for the same organ existed.

The meeting with Mr. Isaacs ended with a handshake and something resembling a smile from both of us. His because he'd been beaten fair and square, and mine because I'd won. Not too many days later, Langtonian's solicitors rang Mr. Rogers to tell him the results of their discreet enquiry about my financial status. That Geoff Green was broke, divorced and living in a single room on the edge of Hove. Ironically, Langtonian ended up paying my costs which must have been the last straw for Mr. Isaacs.

These times were not as hard as they appeared. I could start again with a, more or less, clean slate. Rather than feeling confined by a single room, after the luxury of a three bed-roomed house, I felt liberated. Miller and Bellord must have felt liberated too. Tanya remained friendly enough and that allowed me frequent contact with my children.

# 22

# Return to Priest Island

Years rolled by. Apart from two letters and their debut on the BBC TV programme, I had not seen or heard from Miller or Bellord since the awful night they'd phoned from Ullapool, asking for money,

In 1987 Carol and I qualified in our respective courses. I built up a practice of several thousand patients, received my first class honours degree in osteopathic medicine and had my research published. Carol and I finally married in 2005 after thirty enjoyable years of courtship. In all that time, the spectre of Miller and Bellord never left me. Their philosophy and teachings gave me the self-confidence and drive to pursue any path I chose. So the Welshman from a council estate, who never imagined being so fortunate as to have such opportunities and adventures, was grateful.

I will never know what made Miller and Bellord's life's work and teaching take such a turn and drive them along such a materialistic path. Surely it could not all have been blamed on the struggle to pay off the bishop's blackmailer.

Miller and Bellord's life, once they'd left Priest Island to settle on the mainland, remained a puzzle. Their repatriation mystified me. Who they got to help them and how they managed to evade the law and Bob Cracknell for such a considerable time, bugged me. There was only one way to find out and that was to go back to Ullapool and do some detective work.

Carol was enthusiastic, as she was about everything. All the way through she'd supported and encouraged my desire to write the story, tolerating my obsession with Miller and Bellord and our odd past. While we were in Ullapool, I wanted to return to Priest and explore it; experience what they must have felt during the first liberated days on their stunning hideaway.

This time I would be doing it the easy way. We flew up to Inverness from Gatwick and hired a car for the duration of our trip. On the plane, I reread part of *'Island Years'* by Frank Fraser Darling, the book that gave me inspiration for the perfect hideaway in 1975.

*'The steep hills make Little Loch Broom a dangerous place for a boat when the winds blow, but from this perch behind the Brae House the sea looks calm enough until you put a telescope on it. If the day is clear you can see the Outer Hebrides and pick out the shapes of the hills in the Forest of Harris. And from farther up the hill, where the view is unhindered, the crofts near Stornoway, over forty miles distant, are visible through the glass. There is an island between there and Little Loch Broom, and its long shape cuts off part of the Hebridean view. It is about eighteen miles from this rock behind our house, and now, after our years of island life, I do not care to look at it through my glass, for if I see the surf beating up in white puffs, distorted by mirage, I am reminded of anxious days of wishing to get there and knowing the swell would not allow; and if the sea is flat calm and the sun shining, I wish I was going anyway.*

*The island is Eilean a' Chleirich.' Priest Island.*

I hadn't really paid enough attention to that passage before.

If I had, things might have turned out differently.

The journey from the tiny airport and out onto the quiet road is unlike any other airport exit route. It was completely hassle free, like our own private landing strip. And already we could see bright swathes of yellow rape seed, decorating the sharp lichen green landscape. The evening was drawing in rapidly, the lights of Inverness, a warm glow on a hillside, welcomed us. The hotel on Ness Bank overlooked the river. We collapsed into our bed and woke early for the drive to Ullapool.

The trip along the A385 passing the Corry Bridge over the Braes of Ullapool seemed even more beautiful than I'd remembered it. The pretty whitewashed village as welcoming in the sunshine as it had been two decades ago. Time for a cuppa. A small cafe welcomed us in and Carol sat in a smoky corner, stretched her legs and opened our neat little Ullapool guide book.

*In 1755 Captain John Forbes reporting to Commissioners handling the Scottish estates following the clans uprising in support of Bonnie Prince Charlie, described Ullapool and the surrounding district. 'Nothing but necessity makes strangers resort here...The roads are mountainous, rocky and full of stones, and no bridges upon the rivers, and for a great part of the year, the area is almost inaccessible...' Yet later goes on to say. 'I am humbly of the opinion that a village should be erected at a place called Ullapool.'*

We sipped our tea. How incredible it must have seemed then. Even now you could get lost in these hills, and much of the surrounding landscape makes travelling tough.

*'...later, Ullapool farm was divided up and twelve soldiers returning from the Seven Years war are given crofts there, small enclosed fields where a home and a living could be built.*

*The best fishing in the Western Highlands tempted colonisation of Ullapool. This started mainly in 1788 when a ship, the Gilmorton, left Isle Martin with masons, joiners, other tradesmen and their families to build a community in Ullapool.'*

They'd have a fit now. Klondykers anchor in Loch Broom, mainly from Eastern Europe, but also from as far away as Taiwan and Egypt. Russians, Nigerians and other nationalities wait for 'sea taxis' to take them back to their huge ships, floating factories that buy herring and mackerel from British fishermen in the Minch. Each of these craft sucks up hundreds of tons of fish from UK ships before freezing and processing their catch.

This floating, multicultural, multi-racial gathering of men briefly swell the population of Ullapool then leave with their holds full of Scotland's fish. A bit of smuggling went on and maybe sailors and merchants fell in love with the local lasses whose language would have baffled them, as it baffled me.

Miller and Bellord may have seen the remnants of this passing trade and had they parted with a few quid could have been whisked off by an amenable captain to Russia or Taiwan.

Shore Street was our destination, firstly to charter a boat to take us to Priest then to trace the current owner of the island and get permission to land and stay, a courtesy that never entered my head when I took Miller and Bellord.

Shore Street runs almost parallel to the Loch and I remember only too well the Captain's Cabin on the corner of Shore and Quay Street. From the outside it looked the same today, but inside, things were different. In 1975 we'd stocked up here for our trip to Priest and I remembered all the things we'd missed; a good local map, decipherable tide charts, a compass. Now it was more of a general camping and hardware store, DIY rather than chandlers. Whatever it stocked on its shelves, the Captain's Cabin was and probably still is a meeting place, known locally as the 'Corner of the Store' since 1798. It was the place to look for casual labour, something we needed to do now. We had to find someone willing to take us to Priest. The staff in the Captain's Cabin didn't know of anyone willing to undertake the trip. We asked who owned Priest Island. No one in the store had a clue. We scoured the town. Even the local tourist office didn't know.

Striding onto the broad 18th Century pier we spotted the bulky hull of the Stornaway Ferry, the crew were loading fuming cars and trucks up the rattling iron ramp to take the three and a half hour trip across the Minch to the Isle of Lewis. Harbour offices and kiosks flanked the Shore Street side of the pier. It was May, too early in the season for tourists, so an air of solitude hung around the quayside. We noted from kiosk adverts that none of the Summer Isle tours ever ventured out as far as Priest.

Low clouds, wind and a brief glimpse of sunshine gave the impression of uncertain weather. This was typical for the time of year in Wester Ross. Fishing boats were getting ready for tomorrow's catch. A leather-skinned local, a sailor, left the rail he was leaning on and walked across to us. He puffed on his pipe and moaned about foreigners fishing around Ullapool and the North West. But this was not news.

*'Four hundred years ago the fishing fleet was Dutch. The Scottish Parliament in Edinburgh tried to stop the foreigners and in the 16th Century, passed an act penalising the Dutch for fishing there. In the18th Century the government called for a report on the commercial exploitation of herring and formed the British Fishery Society.'*

*Source: 'Ullapool' by, A. Barnes, Pub Eagle Eye Press 1991.*

The sailor drew fiercely on his pipe and muttered through the exhaling smoke. 'We thought we were secure forever, but oh no, now we're fighting off the bloody Spanish.'

Strolling past the decks of trawlers we stepped over a tangle of wires, nets and unrecognisable paraphernalia. Gulls screeched overhead, diving and skimming boats and buildings. We headed toward a couple of fishermen repairing a net. They were concentrating, counting the net squares before lining them up to repair the ragged tears. They didn't acknowledge us.

I coughed. 'Know anyone who'd take us out to Priest Island?' I asked. One of the men looked up, squinting as the sun came through the net and struck his face. He looked friendly, a hint of the Mediterranean in his tanned handsome features. His accent was not broad and I guessed he wasn't a native.

'I will take you,' he answered, looking back to the nets, checking his repair. We could not believe our luck; we'd barely arrived and we'd secured our charter to Priest Island. 'I am Marius and this is Virtuous,' he said, waving casually toward a nearby boat with the painted legend, Virtuous.

We explained to Marius, our skipper, that we wanted him to drop us off on the island and return the next day to take us back. We said we were doing research for a book. He nodded but didn't press for details. We needed to talk about money which is always difficult for me and, apparently, for Scottish gentlemen too. I asked how much the charter would cost.

He stroked his chin, stared past me across the Loch, and said, 'I might shock you.'

'Try me,' I urged, expecting the worst.

'One hundred pounds,' he said. Was that each, one way or what?

'One hundred for the whole trip,' he said, rather nervously, as if expecting us to haggle.

I shook his hand. 'That will suit us fine,' I said, not troubling to hide my smile of relief and pleasure. We thought it would be more than double that. Carol was smiling too.

'When can you take us, we're here for the week?' I said, hoping it would be soon.

He looked at his watch. 'We'll leave at six, today,' he said, coiling up the remnants of his repair.

Tonight? Around the same time Miller wanted to leave in 1975.

'If the weather gets bad, we might have to change our plan. Meet me here and we'll decide then. We won't get close enough in this boat. I'll need to pick up a fibreglass dinghy off the beach before we leave. We'll have to anchor off the Island and row the last bit.'

If Carol was nervous about the loose arrangements, it didn't show. Considering the dramatic weather changes that occurred when I took Miller and Bellord, which I'd told her about, she must have felt some apprehension. Things could change in a minute here, or the weather might blow up while we were on the island and we could be stuck for days.

Eve and Duncan Stockall owned Ardvreck House, the place we were to call home for a few days. They would remain our friends for long after we'd left and have remained so ever since. Their imposing guest house sat on the edge of Loch Broom, literally. Walk down the slope from Ardvreck House, past the grazing sheep, and you will step onto the narrow shingle beach and, if you so desired, dip your toes in the icy waters. Look east and you could see up the Loch toward Ullapool and the Braemore Hills, look west and the mouth of the Loch was visible, spilling out toward the Summer Isles. Facing us were the spectacular rugged mountains dividing Loch Broom from Little Loch Broom with its view toward Priest Island.

The panorama and thoughts of the journey we were about to take, sent shivers down my spine.

Duncan was a fisherman netting langoustine for shipment to the luxury restaurants of Spain. We assumed it must have been quite tough, uneconomical even, until Duncan explained that Scottish langoustine are probably the best in the world. Top Barcelona restaurants were willing to pay premium prices.

We told them about our charter to Priest Island. Duncan knew Marius, they'd fished together and he praised Marius's seamanship. We told them about the book I hoped to write and promised to tell them more of my adventure later. I think Eve and Duncan were surprised to learn that we would not be staying that evening.

Duncan reminded us to take flares to the island, in case of an emergency.

We dropped the cases in our bedroom at Ardvreck and left the rucksacks out ready to pack with our basic two man igloo tent and sleeping bag. Trying to get everything into these two bags was ambitious, and shopping for the trip would need prudence. I knew how difficult it could be transferring stores from dinghy to the Island in a heavy swell. The more compact the rucksacks, the easier they could be tossed ashore if we got into difficulties.

Back at Shore Street, though we didn't feel hungry, we had a quick bite. At the grocers we bought some ready to eat pies, coffee, Oxo, chocolate, bacon, eggs and beans. Outside The Captain's Cabin a busker in a battered felt hat and ill-fitting clothes played his accordion. How desirable his simple life seemed. He grinned and nodded as we chucked some change into his tin.

The Cabin supplied us with a simple gas burner, flask, matches and a torch.

The anticipation, the wait for six o'clock, seemed an age. I felt as if I had flu and a temperature, but it was psychosomatic following a moment of self-reproach and panic. I wanted to turn back and stop this silly trip, right now. What on earth did I think I was doing and what could this possibly achieve? So what if Miller and Bellord had help getting to and from Priest and things were not quite what they seemed? It wouldn't help to know now, would it? But in the end, despite the reasoning, I had to find out how they did it.

We spotted Marius walking toward the Loch, with children. He shouted across to us. 'Be back here in an hour.'

Marius turned up at the quay side spot on six o'clock with his two children, who wanted to come for the adventure. We waited in the sunshine, looking down on the crescent of shingle where a blue fibreglass boat was tied to a block. Marius and a friend turned it right ways up and winched the ten foot dinghy onto the deck of Virtuous.

The plan was to drop us on the Island and pick us up the next day at five o'clock. He suggested we stand on the cliff top above the boulder beach where he would be taking us and wave him in. On a clear evening we should be able to see Marius and Virtuous passing the mouth of Little Loch Broom on their way from Ullapool.

Winching and placing the dinghy on board seemed surprisingly awkward as it swung and banged the side of the trawler. The two men guiding it had to make sudden manoeuvres to avoid being trapped by the wildly-swinging craft, and went to great lengths to tie the dinghy securely. Space on deck was at a premium and it looked like this was the first time such a craft had been taken on board. We carried our rucksacks down the worn iron staircase that zig-zagged from the pier to the boat below. It smelled like a fishing boat and one could easily trip over the winches, creels, nets and ropes that covered most of the deck.

Marius checked everything at least twice before starting the engine. Clouds of blue-black smoke rose skyward in the still air. We cast off and in no time, we'd pulled away from the quay and were sailing past Ardvreck House and up toward the mouth of Loch Broom. I am no seaman but felt curiously at ease on the Virtuous. I have the greatest admiration for fishermen. It is a hard life and they only get paid for each catch, not for the number of hours they put in, or their bravery.

It felt a longish trip even though we were motor-driven and the boat seemed to be nipping along. Things at sea are deceptive: a racing engine and waves running at you give the impression of speed. But it is impossible to tell how fast you are travelling. It is only when you pass something solid, a rock, a buoy or another boat that you know what kind of progress the boat is making.

The children, especially the girl, were shy and hid for a great deal of the trip in the fishy hull of the boat. She looked every bit the tomboy and ventured out occasionally to climb masts with a baseball cap, peak down over her eyes, totally at ease on the undulating boat. Ross, the boy, almost a young man, shook hands vigorously before disappearing below. Their presence made the trip seem more ordinary, like a family outing.

As soon as we rounded Ullapool point we felt the unexpected chill of a light wind channeling down the Loch and were ushered into the warmth of the cosy wheelhouse. There was barely enough room for the three of us. We were intrigued by its contents; charts, sonar navigation, flares, extra clothes, life jackets, manuals and a reassuring crackling radio that emitted comforting information from shore and fleet. Occasionally a message was exchanged and a note written in the log, AWO, all's well on board.

Marius was good company with tales to tell: A badly-aimed torpedo ended up travelling straight down the Loch only to be discovered by fishermen. Once, a depth charge was found floating in the Loch. A couple of locals, unaware of what it was, took a hammer, spanners and a chisel to it, to find out what the drum contained. Thankfully, the crew of a passing boat recognised the depth charge and stopped the men blowing themselves up.

We cleared the mouth of the Loch at Rue Lighthouse and headed south west toward Priest. Now we were in choppy waters, like the seas at the beginning of my trip with Miller and Bellord in 1975. Marius made coffee. Spray hit the wheelhouse, momentarily blurring the seascape. We spotted Isle Martin to the north and then the Summer Isles. They look romantic from a distance but apart from the largest Tanera More with its small population, they are isolated, uninhabitable and unapproachable.

Eilean Dubh appeared and could have been mistaken for Priest at this angle. Then tiny Bottle Island, really a large rock, appeared, two mile distant from our destination. Then, in all its splendour, Priest Island. The Island captivates, thrills and terrifies in one complex emotion. No one could deny its awesome beauty, the place for adventure. For some time the Island appeared to be getting no closer, as if we weren't moving at all, yet the engine was still chugging, Marius was still steering and there were no complaints from below that we'd stopped.

Two hours after leaving Ullapool, Virtuous dropped anchor safely, a couple of hundred yards off the coast of Priest. The sun came out and turned the water a startling blue. We could have been in the Mediterranean about to land on a Lilliputian Corsica or Sardinia. Marius said the swell made it too risky for the three of us to make the journey in one go. There were rocks and eddies to contend with. We decided that I should go first, partly for the occasion and partly to ensure I'd be there to help Carol when she came ashore. Once I stepped into the dinghy and Marius started rowing, it felt like 1975, approaching Priest for the first time.

This was where we should have chosen to land in 1975: a boulder beach, rough and rocky but leading up in a gently rising slope to the Island proper. No cliffs to climb and the swathe of coarse grass on a small plateau would have been the ideal place to set up the tents. I would have been driving home the same day.

The rowlocks of the dinghy were loose, Marius had a

problem keeping the single oar located and we nearly lost it. One oar and no spare...

The boulder beach looked easy to negotiate but I had thick rubber soles and the massive pebbles were slimy with seaweed. I slipped and fell with a crash, twisting my ankle. My boots and jeans were soaked. I had no change of clothes. Boots full of water and no way of drying them was not good and the thought of being airlifted off with a fractured ankle now, would have been just too much.

It seemed an age before Marius got back to Carol. As she stepped cautiously into the bobbing dinghy, I imagined how she must be feeling, ready to land on Priest for the very first time after hearing me rattle on about it for years. It was easy, as an observer from the land, to realise how tricky it really was trying to guide a small craft into the cove. Each gentle swell nudged the dinghy toward a spiteful rock, the oar jumped out of the rowlock at each manoeuvre, forcing Marius to push off from the approaching rock. Eventually I caught the painter and pulled the dinghy in. Carol arrived, flushed with excitement, and helped me straighten up. After testing the ankle injury with a cautious hobble, I was fine.

It felt odd, to say the least, standing on the boulder beach alone. Not scary, but certainly unsettling. We threw our bags containing the tent, food and equipment onto the beach and waved Marius off. Back on the Virtuous, Marius and the two children waved back. 'See you tomorrow,' he shouted 'If the wind and weather changes I might need to pick you up from another part of the Island. Stay alert.' We'd know which part of the Island to be by noting the direction of wind and waves. I gave him the thumbs up. We'd agreed that if the weather turned impossible, we might even have to stay an extra day, or longer. Marius had offered us flares, in case of emergency. We forgot to take them. But we did have matches and a torch so could easily make up some sort of beacon or rough signalling flag if all else failed.

The moment was not easy to put into words. It was exciting and gut-wrenchingly sad all at once. Carol and I were going to spend a night and day on this uninhabited island, the same that Miller and Bellord stayed on for nearly a year. We were about to explore where they had explored, literally, following in their footsteps.

We watched Marius and the children sail out of sight as we lugged our stuff up the gentle slope to our chosen site. With Carol experiencing it with me, it felt wonderful. Seals played in the cove, birds soared and the choppy sea, swirling the green seaweed, foamed along the boulder beach.

# 23

# A Night on Priest

The preparation for this trip to Priest had, in some ways, been more thorough than the one in 1975. I'd had more time to write and contact the various bodies in Scotland regarding the Island's history, and it was with great pleasure and renewed interest that I re-read Fraser Darling's Island Years.

A few of the caves, particularly those on the south east of the Island, easily missed, showed signs of human occupation. Smuggling and whisky stores were lucrative pursuits after the First World War and during Prohibition in America.

Soft green mosses, lichen-covered rocks and moorland stretched over hills. Rocky bluffs and crags spilled down toward lochs. This wilderness has been interrupted by visits from man throughout the Island's history. In 597AD a clergyman, a student of Saint Columba, once inhabited the Island. He'd been banished for his 'distasteful' mode of living and forced to stay on Priest until he changed his ways.

An outlaw banished there by the locals for sheep stealing under the old clan law built the stone bothy. Its ruins were chosen by Miller and Bellord to shelter through a harsh sub-zero winter.

There is evidence of the Mackenzies having lived on the Island during the 18th and 19th Centuries after being driven from the mainland. They moved from cove to cove, as weather dictated. Records show that cove was taken to mean cave in this context—though coves, as we understand them, often ended in shallow caves. It seems the whole recorded history of Priest speaks of escape, incarceration, exile, reflection and hardship, either self-imposed or dictated by law or religious order.

With our rucksacks checked and secure we walked the slippery boulder beach to a soft grassy mound dotted with alpine plants and dry heather, then up and over the hills. We puffed and panted our way over the testing ground. To the left rose the towering South Ridge, its spine running the length of the Island, obstructing our view of land. Light was fading and we needed a camp site. The soft terrain, like thick pile carpet, sprung our step. Lochan Fada, the long loch and the largest area of water, appeared as we traversed the first hillock, its beauty sudden and dramatic. Carol didn't utter a word, but I could tell she'd been moved. A light wind ruffled her hair as she drank in the atmosphere and the silence.

The Island was ripe for cliché: spellbinding, awesome, welcoming, enigmatic and threatening all at once. Any new experience has its own magic, but this!

We came across another four lochs, all smaller than Lochan Fada. Most sites we considered for our camp were either too boggy, too rocky or on too much of a slope. We turned back to the little boulder beach and pitched on the dry grassy slope, the place we should have opted for in the first place. We dropped the igloo tent next to hundreds of bluebells, our own garden, the vivid blue stretching almost to the beach.

As I pitched the tent, Carol unzipped the bags and started to rustle up some food. There was no gas. The shopkeeper had left it out when he packed our goods in the Captain's Cabin. It was annoying but not disastrous. We had plenty to keep us going, including a flask of hot water. So we drank Oxo and ate chicken pasties.

Sitting on the grassy slope looking past the narrow channel of sea lapping the cove, we watched a baby seal play, dipping and diving in a display of graceful seamanship.

The setting sun threw deep shadows on the hills west of Lochan Fada, casting black spectral shapes across the eastern slopes. Beyond that, the South Ridge was lit with an orange brilliance, a combination of the Torridonian stone and the remnants of a setting sun. Light faded quickly and the sky darkened with night and cloud.

Slipping inside the womb of the igloo tent, we curled up together, fully dressed apart from our boots and coats. My jeans, still wet and cold from my tumble on the beach, clung like a soggy bandage to my legs. Sleep did not come quickly. We chatted about our adventure so far and prayed for good weather tomorrow. Eventually, Carol fell asleep. I listened to her rhythmic breathing, a comforting sound when the mind starts playing its devilish tricks. Gulls screeched overhead followed by a total eerie silence before the wind picked up, vibrating the tent, loosening the outer skin and allowing it to flap endlessly as rain followed wind into the night.

These were identical conditions to those experienced in September 1975. I felt the same anxiety, not knowing whether conditions would allow us to leave Priest the next day. Carol slept on. I tossed and turned through the night, listening to the rain and the wind, thinking it was abating before a thorough squall shook us again. I wondered if the little tent would hold for the night. I began to question my risky escapade again. Why risk Carol's life? Why not leave the past alone? What was the point? The point was simple. I needed closure. I needed to feel what they'd felt exploring the Island for the first time and find out what happened to them between leaving Priest and their arrest.

Lying in a minuscule tent on half square mile of rock in the midst of a ferocious sea is an intimidating and unforgettable experience. I imagined looking down, bird-like, from above and seeing the igloo tent braced against the wild weather: the storm-lashed lochs and hills and the foaming sea pounding the rocky coast, booming cannon-like as it gushed through the Priest's Hole.

The tent proved substantial and weatherproof. It didn't let us down and not a drop of water passed through the fabric. Our 'home' turned slowly from black to a pale blue as the early dawn lightened it. We brushed our teeth, ate a breakfast of bread, cheese and dates and drank Oxo stirred into the tepid remains of our flask.

Within yards of leaving the campsite the weather and our mood improved. Leaving the north west of *Lochan Fada,* deep blue lochs met grey bald rock and steep cliffs plummeting to rocky coves and swirling, pounding seas.

Dry heather sprung our step as we walked toward *Lochan na Glean*, Loch of the Glen and then *Lochan Iar*, the Western Loch, before turning north into the heart of the Island. We climbed to the top of a small hill. There, before us, at the edge of *Lochan na h'Airdhe*, the Loch of the Shieling, nestled the outlaw's bothy. Its remains looked as eternal as a Stone Age fort.

The bothy was about thirty feet by ten. Dry wall rocks formed the sides of the building to a height of six feet. There was no roof, only the remains of a hastily made wooden frame draped with torn plastic sheeting, the only sign of Miller and Bellord's stay twenty years previously. I could feel they'd been here. It was like they were here now, sitting outside the periphery of vision, sensed but not seen. Then I touched the walls they'd touched, trod the impacted ground they'd trod, moved from end to end as they must have done a thousand times.

Three distinct areas were evident, one, presumably where they pitched the tents (only room for two by the looks of it), the other for cooking and a small recess formed on three sides by loose stone walling was, presumably, the toilet area which must have contained Jim's beloved Elsan toilet. They would have been protected from much of the wind but I doubt the polythene would have lasted long in the inadequate frame displayed before us. Perhaps it had been more substantial then.

I visualised them trying to keep warm, cooking simple meals, writing diaries. But on sunny days next to the pretty loch, this would have been a seductive place and most likely the time when they felt most at peace. It would also have been the time they would have talked about what they'd done, meditated with the sun on their faces, thought about coming back, maybe. Or were they making other plans, secret plans.

It started to rain heavily, giving us some idea of how difficult it must have been for Miller and Bellord to keep dry. The impacted ground in the bothy would have turned to mud without a proper roof and stepping from the tents in a winter storm would have been thoroughly depressing.

Once again, making our way across heather and boggy ground, we set about finding the place where I'd landed with the two men in 1975. It started to rain again then stopped suddenly to reveal a clear sky. Twenty years is a long time and I had only seen our landing cove under stressful conditions. Not a reliable state at all. Now every dip and cove along the coast seemed like 'the place'. The west coast in a brisk south westerly was a different land, the seas more fierce, the rocks blacker, the flora sparse and scrubby. There was no gentleness here.

Two shags perched on a high black rock, oblivious to the wind. The Island is a paradise for birds, with over thirty species, including two and a half thousand storm petrels and the occasional buzzard and peregrine. They give the Island its life and its sound along with the pounding sea lapping in the East Bay, crashing in the Cauldron and rushing, gurgling and exploding in the Priest's Hole.

Then I saw it, the gentle grassy slope across a craggy cliff where we first set camp in 1975. We ran toward the spot and peered into the cove below with its familiar tide mark of marine life, the rocks I'd wedged myself between to hold the dinghy back from certain disaster and the shallow cave where we tied the boat up for the night. The scene played out before me: the dinghy swamped with water, the painter tearing away from the bow, the panic to get the two men and stores ashore, the climb up the cliff, the failing light and the realisation I would not be able to return that day. We could so easily have died.

Maybe it was lack of food, tiredness or the sudden emotion, but I felt dizzy and leaned into Carol for support. She held me until I'd recovered, which took only moments.

We continued our trek around the island, through bog and rock interspersed with heather and coarse grass. Unbelievably we'd been trekking for over six hours and got lost more than once.

Anticipating a hot meal of bacon and eggs, we gathered driftwood. The long trek and the emotional experience had tired us. We were beyond tired, we were exhausted. Carol trailed behind as I covered the last couple of hills before descending to the cove and boulder beach. With scraps of toilet paper, dry heather and driftwood we got our little fire started. The smell of bacon is enough to get the tastebuds going at any time. But I have to say, after our day on the Island in exhilarating air, rain and sunshine, with all the excitement and our hunger up, our bacon and egg, speckled with heather and wood ash, was truly divine.

We'd planned to climb the South Ridge, where Miller and Bellord strode out for the BBC Everyman film crew in 1979. But we were spent. A gloomy damp afternoon forced us into the tent where we fell soundly asleep. Even before I opened my eyes I could tell the weather had changed. The bright interior of the tent gave off a steamy humidity brought on by the warming sun.

We left the tent to stroll along Lochan Fada. Carol spread herself onto a boulder at the water's edge and closed her eyes, letting the warmth and the moment seep in. I sat a hundred feet away looking down the loch. The low sunlight reflected off the rippling water, making me squint. It really is the most magical place and for a rare moment I felt perfect peace.

A spell had surely been cast on this place. I looked across at Carol and knew that she had felt it too. Fraser Darling, in his book, talks about the magic and healing qualities of the Island, particularly this Loch and we were lucky enough to be experiencing it. Miller and Bellord, during the making of the BBC Everyman programme, confessed to never having been ill in all the time they'd spent here despite the sub zero winter, the often damp conditions and implacable storms. They hadn't even caught a cold.

On lighter days they may have reminisced about their parties at the House, the splendid food, the prestigious guests. Roy Plomley, one of the guests and creator of Desert Island Discs would find it ironic, that Miller and Bellord had actually stayed on a deserted island.

What a programme it would have made, what tales they would have to tell. And at the end of the show, Roy Plomley would have asked Jim Miller the usual questions;

Roy Plomley: *What piece of music would you take to the Island?*

Jim Miller: *Bach's Toccata and Fugue in D.*

Roy Plomley: *What book? You already have the Bible and*

*Shakespeare.*

Jim Miller: *White Fang by Jack London.*
Roy Plomley: *What luxury item would you choose?*
Jim Miller: *An Elsan chemical toilet.*

We'd probably have lived to regret our attempt to scale the Ridge. Marius would be here in a couple of hours and the wind had changed direction so we had to be prepared to scramble to a different part of the Island. We ran out of time and as the wind held we climbed the fifty foot bluff that overlooked the east bay. Marius should be here within the hour. We trained our binoculars across the Minch toward Loch Broom but there was no sign of Virtuous. We sat in the sunshine, waiting. Then we spotted her, chuffing steadily toward us, reassuring puffs of exhaust smoke trailing back toward the Loch. Almost to the minute we'd planned, Marius anchored Virtuous off the bay.

The sea was choppier than it first seemed and Marius was having some difficulty negotiating the rocks to the boulder beach. I grabbed the painter and towed him in. Our relief at seeing Marius safe and smiling as he ferried us back to Virtuous was total. Unexpectedly, we both admitted to feeling sad at leaving Priest Island. It had cast a spell on us and no doubt, had cast one on Miller and Bellord too.

Marius had woken in the night to the bad weather and thought he might have had to leave us on the Island a bit longer. He'd even considered coming back to the seas around the Island to signal he'd be back when the weather changed. We certainly appreciated his concern. That round trip would have taken at least four hours and a considerable amount of fuel.

We were cold, tired, hungry, thirsty and feeling melancholy. The trip back to Ullapool seemed endless. Even snug in the wheelhouse, we could not get warm. This must have been how Miller and Bellord felt on many of those days on Priest, hunkering down and waiting for daylight so they could get up and move around the Island to get their circulation going.

Marius, relieved we were safe, told more stories of life at sea. But nothing lifted our mood. All we wanted now was food, drink and sleep. It was quite emotional saying goodbye to Ross and Marius as we left Virtuous. They had been our staunch, reliable companions on a difficult journey. We gave Marius an extra thirty pounds and ten to split between the children. They were as delighted as we were about the whole deal.

We headed straight for the fish and chip shop on the corner of Shore Street and, too tired to talk, drank a couple of glasses of lemonade, two mugs of tea and polished off a huge plate of fish and chips. We glowed with the effects of highland sea and air, a full stomach and the satisfaction of achieving our trip to Priest. Then came exhaustion. The short drive to Ardvreck House was silent.

We tried not to disturb Eve and Duncan, but they'd heard us come in and invited us for a nightcap. Explaining the real reason for our visit to Priest and the adventure of twenty years ago to strangers, did not come easy. But a scotch or two, Eve and Duncan's genuine kindness and interest and the fug of surreality that comes with fatigue, loosened my tongue. Duncan was twenty at the time. He remembered the massive police hunt and the media coverage.

I made some enquiries and found out there were at least three people in Ullapool who might have helped Miller and Bellord. Both Marius and Duncan had mentioned Billy Macrae, skipper of the Kittiwake, who had taken two men off the Island twice during their incarceration. Billy, it was said, could be found on the pier most days.

Ian McLeod, a resident of Achiltibuie who ran local boat trips, spoke of stormy days fishing off Priest. One particular day he was passing the south west side of the Island and saw a small barefoot figure running down the grassy slope toward the sea, signalling frantically for Ian to take him aboard. This must have been Bellord, Miller couldn't possibly have run. The sea was too rough for the boat to get any closer, so Ian McLeod informed the rescue services as soon as he returned to Ullapool. The next day two men were taken off the Island and back to the mainland. Ian McLeod vaguely remembered the two outlaws. Not surprisingly, the true facts had, with time and the telling, become distorted. He'd heard that two murderers were living on Priest Island...

Billy Macrae did not do business on Sundays so we had a day to look elsewhere for clues to Miller and Bellord's life on the mainland.

Ullapool Museum occupies the old parish church. The building looked uninviting and we were in half a mind to walk on but the rain came down and changed our mind. We expected nothing more than a brief local history with a few fishing nets and the paraphernalia and artifacts of a fishing community. We were wrong. It was a fine museum with moving exhibits, computer accessible information, models, audiovisual presentations and a newspaper archive in the library section.

There was not a single line of newsprint, not one photograph or reference to the castaways Miller and Bellord. As far as the museum was concerned, nothing happened here in 1975. There was nothing about the biggest manhunt in Wester Ross, no mention of the men's ten month stay on Priest Island, or their sheltering in Moss Road just a mile from the museum. Nothing.

Early, on a cold, lead grey Monday morning, we walked across Shore Street in search of Billy Macrae. A sullen fisherman leaning against the pier rail was eyeing us but turned his back as we approached.

'Good morning, we're looking for Billy Macrae, is he around today?' I asked.

He pointed to a young lad about to load something into the

back of a small truck.

'He works with Billy,' said the man, returning to his meditations across the water. He was probably the first unfriendly character we'd come across in Ullapool.

'He's due soon. Regular as clockwork he is, be here in about twenty minutes or I'm a fisherman,' he said, laughing at his own joke.

We took a brisk walk around the pier to warm up and on our return came face to face with a red tractor driving down the middle of the pier toward us.

A heavily built man in his sixties, weathered with the complexion of a man who'd spent a life in the open air, eased himself out of the cab. He looked unapproachable.

I said we were old friends of Miller and Bellord and asked him if he knew them, adding that someone told us he'd met them.

'If you're friends with these men, why don't you question them?'

'We lost touch years ago. I wondered what happened to them.'

'Well, they certainly aren't in this part of the world now,' he said, with absolute certainty.

On closer questioning Billy seemed vague about dates and events and I began to wonder if he was being deliberately evasive. Maybe there was a genuine blank spot in his memory, but that was hard to believe. Older people are more likely to have problems with recent memory rather than events of decades past. Age seems to bestow a particular sharpness for certain things. Old aunts and uncles can recite poems from childhood. They can remember who was at whose wedding or christening and spats with old adversaries verbatim. Ask them what they did yesterday and they look blank. Billy either could not or would not tell us about the two outlaws who landed in Ullapool two decades ago and mixed with its tight knit community.

Billy, like a thousand others, may have fallen under Miller's spell. He described them as gentlemen who had paid well for his services, without going into detail as to the extent of those services. Whatever was or wasn't said or remembered there must have been an element of wanting to help us, because he gave us the name of Danny McKenzie, a local taxi driver. Apparently Danny had been Miller and Bellord's chauffeur whilst they were in Ullapool.

Billy couldn't remember where Danny lived but within five minutes of searching the local Post Office directory, we came up with his address and a telephone number. The call was going to be difficult as my first sentence needed to hook him quickly enough to stop him slamming the phone down. No doubt he would rather forget what happened twenty years ago, especially, as it turned out the two were arrested and sentenced to six years in prison. Danny may even have been questioned as a suspect, someone who'd aided and abetted in a minor way, delayed their arrest and wasted police time.

The phone rang and kept on ringing. He must be out. Then someone picked up and a throaty voice, from a lifetime of smoking at a guess, answered.

'Yes...Who's that?'

'Good morning, Mr. McKenzie. My name's Geoff Green, Billy Macrae gave me your name.'

'Did he now? What for?'

'I'm writing a book about events that happened in Ullapool twenty years ago. He said you were a local taxi driver and knew most of what went on in the town.'

'So does Billy. He knows more than most of us.'

We didn't mention Billy was having trouble in the memory department.

'Well he must have thought you'd be more helpful because

he gave me your name.'

Danny moved the phone away but I could still hear him coughing, which he did without pause, for a minute or more.

'Come round tomorrow. Elevenish. I can't promise anything,' he said, breaking into another bout of phlegmy coughing.

Danny lived in the tiniest guest house I'd ever seen. It overlooked Loch Broom on a long straight road at the western reaches of the village. We'd parked two hundred yards away. I left Carol to stroll around and explore a part of Ullapool she'd not seen.

On the dot of eleven I rung the bell, twice. I heard shuffling and mail being cleared from the door mat. A frail looking man with round shoulders and tired eyes blinked when he saw me and seemed to be having second thoughts about letting me in. He didn't smile and for a moment he didn't speak. Perhaps this wasn't Danny. He looked as if he'd no knowledge of my call and his first words confirmed my theory.

'I'm sorry but I can't stop now,' he said.

*Then why invite me in the first place?* I thought.

He just stood there, unable to think of his next line it seemed. Eventually, he waved me through.

The parlour of the guest house could have been the museum of a collector. Not a collector of antiques or specialised objects but of cheap mementos and ornaments; fairground figurines and bits of china, holiday souvenirs perhaps, and old aunt's keepsakes from long ago.

He didn't offer me a seat.

'What do you want from me?' he said, his mouth dry of saliva, and eyes pink with weariness.

I may only have minutes with this guy and they needed to count. 'I was a friend of Jim Miller's. He was here in 1975 before he was arrested. Big story. Billie said you'd ferried them around a bit when they came off Priest Island.'

'That was a long time ago. You're not a reporter digging up dirt, are you?'

'I'm writing a book,' I said. 'There are a few gaps about the time Miller and Bellord were here in Ullapool. I was hoping you'd be able to clear a few things up. I only want to write the truth.'

'If they're your friends and you're so keen for the truth, why don't you ask them?

The population of Ullapool must have prerecorded that question.

'Because I haven't seen them since 1975. They started a new life when they left prison. That's what we'd all do, wouldn't we?' I put this to him but didn't wait for his answer. I needed to keep him going.

'Besides, no one knows where they are now,' I said, which did have a ring of truth to it.

'They were good generous men,' he started.

*Really?*

'I first picked them up in Achiltibuie,' said Danny, 'I'd dropped a fare off and they waved me down just as I was on my way back. They looked a bit rough but sounded like a couple of toffs.'

'How did they say they got there? Achiltibuie is a long way from Priest Island or Ullapool.'

'They said they'd rowed across from the Island in a rubber dinghy.' He coughed.

'Weren't you surprised, or a bit suspicious? I would have been.'

'Not really. I didn't see the dinghy, it could have been a big one for all I knew.'

'Coming all the way from Priest, I mean, two elderly guys, southerners, suddenly appearing out of the blue.'

Something was wrong here. If he hadn't seen the dinghy, where was it? Would they have got in the taxi and left it? No, I don't believe they arrived in the dinghy otherwise they'd have guarded it with their lives. They needed to get back. The most likely scenario was they'd hitched a lift on a fishing boat and found out the skipper was going the wrong way, to Achiltibuie not Ullapool. They would then have had no choice but to get to Achiltibuie and wing it.

'It's not impossible, they were clearly exhausted and they weren't exactly ancient.'

He was being evasive. 'That's still a long way by sea,' I said.

'They said they'd island-hopped; gone from one to the other, in stages.'

It would have taken many hours even on a calm day. I didn't believe they'd done it, yet how could they possibly have arrived at Tanera More and then Achiltibuie, other than by sea? If by chance they'd hitched a lift, surely they would have gone directly to Ullapool, not landed on this sparsely populated coastline where strangers stood out like neon signs.

They would not have had enough fuel for the trip and the idea of them rowing here seemed preposterous. Even island hopping would have been grueling, a distance of at least eight miles.

One of them had been ill, said Danny but he could not remember which one. He'd driven them around Ullapool on many occasions and they'd always paid well. He was fuzzy on dates but, like Billy, he remembered them as generous. Years later Danny had also driven Eve and Duncan's two children on their school run. They would have sat on the same seats as Miller and Bellord.

I asked Danny about Mrs. Mackay.

'She ran a guest house with her husband in Moss Road but

one of them died some little while back. I can't remember which one,' he concluded.

Danny walked me to the front door. Our meeting was over.

Roselea Guest House, where Miller and Bellord were arrested in 1976, was not hard to find. It was a typical chalet bungalow that took in guests through the season.

There was no sign for Roselea outside and I'd not met Mrs. Mackay, but I had seen her being interviewed outside this very place on the BBC Everyman programme. She'd admitted to feeling very sad and shocked when Miller and Bellord were arrested. She'd cried and said they were the kindest of men and that she certainly wouldn't like to pass judgment on them, and added they would be welcome back into her home at any time.

I walked along the short path through the pretty flower-filled garden and knocked at the door. It wasn't Mrs. Mackay who answered but the new owner. She said that both the Mackays had died. She'd bought the business from Mrs. Mackay some years ago. Apparently Mrs. Mackay had left Ullapool to escape gossip following a protracted family crisis. She'd never got used to being away from her beloved Roselea and Ullapool and died soon after leaving.

We'd done everything we could: followed all leads, interviewed the casually involved, checked archives and trekked the Island. We'd left it too long before coming back to Ullapool and people's memories had either faded or the guardians of Miller and Bellord's Ullapool secrets had decided only to give me enough information to placate my nosiness.

There was a great deal missing, hulking gaps in accounts not helped by the locals' poor recall. Yet we had achieved much. We knew they'd made at least two trips to Ullapool from the mainland, that several innocent people helped them and that they must have been at Roselea for a considerable time for Mrs. Mackay to have formed such an attachment to them. And the time they rang me for money it was, most likely, not to be used for their stay on the Island but to prolong their stay in Ullapool. They really hadn't meant to come back at all. If they'd returned to face the music weeks after I'd dropped them on Priest, it would not have surprised me. What about three months later, when their food must have run out? Perhaps they had a new coterie of friends by then. Even Billy, Danny and Mrs. Mackay may have been in touch.

Ever since I'd known him Miller had kept in touch with people from way back. Sometimes people who'd disappeared off his radar would again turn up in his life, particularly those who'd had a sudden downturn in their lives. Don Cockell, the British and European champion boxer, had been psychologically coached by Jim Miller throughout momentous parts of his career, including the time leading up to his most famous fight against Rocky Marciano. The title fight had taken the stuffing out of Cockell's career and for a while he and Miller parted company. Things went really bad for Cockell, who tried a number of jobs before stepping back into Jim Miller's life. But Miller was unable to help. Cockell's last job was as a maintenance man and he died of cancer in 1983.

Miller and Bellord were out of my life but not out of my mind. And I'm not sure they ever would be. Not a problem, but one day we would have to meet. It was fated, you might say. We all live three lives: public, private and secret but the truth for me was I preferred to have less of a secret life and more of a private one.

Over the next ten years Carol and I finished our courses. We bought a house as we struggled out of the past decade. It had taken ten years to sort out the Southern Organs affair, settle the legal bills, fight the finance companies, square my apologies with old friends and family and rebuild up my decimated credit rating.

Thoughts of Miller and Bellord came in waves, crashing on the shores of my mind one minute only to ease back into a calm and untroubled sea the next. Another ten years gone. Margaret was still stoically running the House and we'd meet once a year on her birthday for lunch. It was always such a delight to see her. She was eighty or thereabouts but still the attractive tall blonde she always was. Matron Joan was ninety and still bright as a new pin. I guess things would have gone along for the rest of my life without my ever having another chance to meet Miller, but fate decided on another wake up call.

# 24

# Finding Jim Miller

Cineflix, the film company who contacted Margaret about Jim Miller and John Bellord, pressed her for an interview. She declined. They asked her about me, hoping to get my story. The proposed documentary was to be distributed world-wide. Margaret, always loyal, refused to give them my name without clearing it with me first. I was intrigued and said yes but needed to be careful. Margaret and the House had been through enough without the affair being dragged back into the limelight.

Cineflix didn't need permission to make the documentary, but promised to be as sensitive as they could to my concerns. They pointed out that it would be in my best interests to say my piece on camera and not leave the story totally in the hands of creative producers.

Amanda Sealy, a Cineflix Producer, rang and we arranged to meet at my home. She had a breathless enthusiasm for my side of the story, but when she explained what angle the programme would take, it was not quite what I expected. The Southern Organ's story was to be part of a series titled, Psychic Detectives. Six or eight programmes built around psychics who help police solve crimes. Our episode would be pitched around

Bob Cracknell's story and how he helped 'solve' the Southern Organ's Fraud in 1976. I couldn't recall there being enough proof for this claim.

The producer was persuasive but I needed a guarantee that the House would not be mentioned or filmed. Cineflix needed a location with the gravitas of the original House and grounds. I knew Sussex fairly well and suggested I check out potential sites, talk to hoteliers and get permission for filming. Once Amanda agreed, I felt happy about the arrangement because it gave me control over this important aspect of the tale and avoided unnecessary publicity for Margaret and the House.

Amanda was a delight. She arrived at my home in Steyning, thanked me for agreeing to do the interview, brought chocolates and even offered to wash up after lunch. Being a programme and film maker was quite another career for her, she'd been a nurse. That was probably why she was so good at the caring bit and, I have to say, totally disarming.

After a good trek round Sussex by foot, car and internet, I came across Ghyll Manor, a hotel and restaurant in the Sussex countryside. It was perfect. From certain angles it looked like the impressive country house we were looking for.

Cineflix had already made several attempts to trace Miller and Bellord but without success. Had they managed to disappear again? 'Did I know where they were?' Of course not.

I think Jim Miller might have blown a gasket at the thought of a psychic meddling with his tale and the making of such a film. He would have insisted on meeting Bob Cracknell before deciding on any participation, if any, and would have had none of it unless he had editorial control.

Weeks later I met Amanda for lunch, just around the corner from London Victoria in a busy Italian restaurant. She was excited, not just about the Psychic Detective series. Someone in the movie and TV business, who'd read the early draft of my book, wanted to make a film of the story. Halfway through the meal our conversation veered off into a dialogue about the unpredictability of relationships, including hers. From there our discussion regarding a proposed film went nowhere, but it had shaken things up. The whole Cineflix affair brought back clear images of the hunt for Jim Miller and once again I could feel him breathing down my neck.

I contacted my nephew, David Green, in Los Angeles. David is a freelance writer contracted to, amongst others, the Disney Corporation. If there was a film in the pipeline he wanted first crack at the screenplay and stressed the importance of completing an early draft quickly, while things were still bubbling. I put him in touch with Amanda and for a while things looked promising as emails and phone calls flew back and forth across the pond.

I made an appointment to see the manager of the Ghyll Manor Hotel. He agreed to the estate being used for the TV series and was excited at the prospect of having a film crew there. He might even get some publicity, and location fees would be discussed. The Cineflix team, once they'd finished the exterior shots, would only need to use the large banqueting room for interviews. It wouldn't disrupt the hotel's business too much, just a few heavy cables, a film crew and technicians walking in and out and vehicles parked discreetly in the grounds. Amanda secured the deal and we arranged a day for my on-screen interview.

Shooting time for film or TV is expensive. Apart from financing the production team and equipment on location and in the studio, there are the daunting economics of a tight time scale, including a travel budget and fees and expenses for the interviewees, some of who believed they should be getting a slice of the cake.

Others involved with the Southern Organ's fraud case were

due to be at Ghyll Manor on the same day: Norman Luck, crime reporter from the Daily Express, who in the final edit referred to the bishop's *various dalliances:* Detective Constable Dave Fickweiler from the Sussex Fraud Squad, who spoke about the blackmailed bishop and his relationship with *a number of ladies of the night.* Such old fashioned words. I'd liked to have met Dave Fickweiler, Bob Cracknell and Norman Luck at Ghyll, but we were kept apart.

On reflection, Norman Luck's pursuit of my story had been good professional reporting. He'd been courteous but dogged, sensitive but direct and never pretended to be anything other than chief crime reporter for the Daily Express. The day he'd brought Bob Cracknell along, although unsettling for me, was a clever but not unethical move. In this computer age with phone hacking, secret filming, reporters pretending to be friends, or offering bribes, and YouTube, Facebook and Twitter all shovelling coals on fires, Miller and the Southern Organs scam wouldn't have stood a chance. Someone would have reported the dodgy agreements with a leaked email, text or tweet. A helicopter would have zig-zagged across Ullapool and the Summer Isles with heat-seeking cameras. They would have located two human-shaped hot spots in a tent on Priest and it would have been over in days.

Waiting for the interview I should have felt pressured but instead I sat relaxed and ready in the banqueting hall of Ghyll Manor. The director, briefed by Amanda, certainly knew his stuff. He fired pertinent and searching questions across the room, encouraging me to take my time, answer the questions and interrupt him if I needed to correct irregularities. The camera, set some distance from where I sat, moved on a 'dolly', a small track enabling the operator to travel across the room and pan shots. The camera kept crossing the room. The effect was one of me flicking in and out of shot, alternating with the blurred perspective of a strategically placed candelabra.

I was on camera for an hour. The final edit would be about three minutes long. The film crew were friendly, hardworking, interested in what they were doing and asked me to join them for bacon sarnies and coffee.

Amanda caught a rotten cold and couldn't accompany the film crew to Ullapool. They only had a couple of days to shoot the scenes in Scotland but said they'd managed some great footage. The weather was so rough, they couldn't land on Priest Island so settled on shots taken from the mainland out toward the Minch, hoping the finished edit would look as if it was shot from the Island. Bob Cracknell did part of his interview bobbing up and down on choppy seas around the Summer Isles. The 'bothy scene' was filmed in makeshift ruins they'd found not far from Ullapool, not the bothy on Priest.

Delays are a way of life in the entertainment industry, so my nephew David tells me. I was experiencing that at first hand. The relationship between Amanda and David seemed to lose steam as David got bogged down with work in Los Angeles. As post-production of the Psychic Detective series dragged on, I felt the book or the film would never happen.

Eventually they completed the Cineflix documentary. Pete Harrison, the leader of my old band in the sixties and now living in Ohio, sent me a copy of the American version. It went on to be released in Australia, Canada and India but not here in the UK. I ran the DVD through again. They'd got some photos mixed up. They'd assumed the shots of Formula 5000 racing drive Clive Baker were of Geoff Green. If the programme went out in the UK no doubt Clive would sue. He was being depicted as the guy who'd helped the fraudsters. To be fair, the black and white photos, when compared, showed a remarkable likeness. But he was in full motor racing gear! Production on the UK programme had to be stopped.

There followed a frantic exchange of international phone calls, emails, express delivery packages and substitute photographs. It was too late to do anything about the American, Canadian and Australian versions, they'd already been aired. Cineflix had to pray that Clive Baker didn't get to see the international version. He may not have minded the shots being confused, but in our litigious society, especially after being duped by Miller, he might be understandably angry.

In the end ITV held off releasing the UK version of the Psychic Detective programme. Years on it is still languishing on an ITV shelf. It was well done on the whole and Bob Cracknell was a convincing psychic, but certain inaccuracies diminished his story. He always claimed that they'd lived in a cave and described the bothy in the film as being like a cave. To me, a bothy is more like a house and a house is where most people would hide out, given the chance.

I have no complaints. I was treated well by Cineflix. I didn't ask for payment for my help or interview. I thought that might seem mercenary under the circumstances. I found them thorough, courteous and grateful. Amanda kept in close touch throughout and when it looked as if the proposed showing of the series in the UK looked uncertain, Ian Taylor, Head of Development at Cineflix, made sure I received a copy of the UK episode, 'The Southern Organs Fraud'.

The international version of the programme, accessible on Bob Cracknell's website, still shows Clive Baker as Geoff Green. To add insult to injury, Bob credited me with the title, 'a prominent racing driver'. Clive would not be happy. I guess Bob could not show the UK version as it had never been released and would probably be branded illegal.

*

In 2009, thirty four years after the event, I dreamt frequently of finding Miller again. The urge to seek him out and meet was so strong, I could no longer deny it. I started a computer search and enquiry using a couple of people search sites. The idea that names and current addresses pop up automatically seemed too good to be true, and it was.

These search companies, presumably, have access to census, electoral rolls and maybe stuff we don't even know about, but there are blind spots in the system. The site boasted of having access to over three hundred and fifty million records. It took time to discover that Miller and Bellord lived in 1 Masson Road, Matlock Bath, Derbyshire. At least they had done until 2002 when they became 'invisible' again. None of my searches came up with a current address. I wrote to the residents of Masson Road. They had no idea where Miller was now and believed that John Bellord had died of stomach cancer. I cannot tell you how sad I was at that revelation. Too late now, to face John at least. Well, thirty five years on would be too late, wouldn't it?

Here's an eerie bit. Around the time they were living at Masson Road, Carol and I were on our way to a friend's sixtieth birthday in Leicestershire. We stayed a few days in Matlock Bath and dined in The Balti, a local Indian restaurant. Unknown to us then and just around the corner a few hundred metres away was Miller and Bellord's home. They'd always had a love of Asian food and wouldn't that have been a turn up, if they'd decided that very night to go for an Indian meal. It was the most likely, of all the restaurants in Matlock Bath, to be their favourite eatery. The food was terrific and the walk from their home only minutes away. After I'd picked myself up from the floor we would have been compelled to talk, maybe deciding to eat together. I'd developed a few scripts over the years, 'what ifs', should we ever come face to face. I didn't think I'd missed out many potential scenarios. But all meeting in an Indian

Restaurant, two hundred miles from home? No, I hadn't considered that.

Jim would be knocking on now, around ninety I think, and may be in care. That would make him almost impossible to find on these search engines. I could only guess he was still in Derbyshire. I wrote to and emailed Derbyshire Social Services and phoned the call centre for High Peak and North Dales Social services. They wouldn't or couldn't help.

Finding out the names of all the care homes and nursing homes in Derbyshire was not difficult but it did take time. Ensuring I had the names of current managers was essential. I would only get one shot, so my letter needed careful thought and a touch of persuasive writing. I decided against phone calls, imagining an overworked staff nurse or carer picking up the phone, not having the time or inclination to search their register of patients, then giving me short shrift. It would only take one misplaced phone call, one hasty, careless reply, and my chance would be lost.

My plan was to work outward from the Matlock Bath area and write to the twenty-plus nursing and care homes. Of those, only one refused to check their books and help. Ironically it was a Cheshire Home, part of the group founded by Lord Cheshire and one to which Jim Miller, rather controversially I recall, delivered an unorthodox but robust lecture on 'mind medicine' so many years ago.

No luck. After a considerable amount of time I received answers from all but two. One in particular, the Meadows Care Home in Alfreton, with no idea of the impact their letter might have had, dealt me a blow some time later. I'd initially written to them in April 2009 but got no reply. I was thinking of giving them a ring to make sure they'd got the letter. While procrastinating about whether or not to call, because I now felt up against a brick wall regarding my search for Jim Miller, I received their answer.

*Meadows Care Home*

*4th June 2009*
*Dear Geoff*

    *I am sorry for the late reply to your letter but I have only just found it. I am sorry to inform you that Jim passed away on 7th May. He was extremely poorly and came for 'end of life' care'. He was only at the Meadows for six days.*
    *I apologise for any stress this may have caused you.*
    *Yours sincerely*
    *Julia Davies*

That was it I guess. Was it really all over? It was not the closure I'd hoped for.

So after years of being exposed to Miller's philosophy had we responded like Pavlov's dogs, all acting in a predictable way when a bell rang? Had Miller effectively rewired us over years, insidiously, like the passive smoking we were exposed to every time he lit his pipe: promising revelation, enlightenment and a better life? Would he be troubled by karma as we speak? Karma. Baggage. Nothing more than an accumulation of our past—beyond a single life if you can stretch to it, or many lives if you can stretch it even further. Anything is possible. We don't know, do we? Not a bad thing to believe in, though. At least we'd try to lead a decent life and not hurt our fellow man or creatures of the planet. We'd be our own strict but fair parent with responsibility for everything we do.

Now it's all over, I wonder what Eddie would have made of it?

'What do you think of your friends now?' he'd ask, with an

annoying grin.

I'd ignore the heavy emphasis on friends. 'They were full of good intentions, *but life got in the way of their plans,*' I'd reply.

Eddie would have remained uncharacteristically silent, started up the Norton, signalled for me to get on the back and headed off toward the Great West Road shouting, YEEHAW, with even more gusto than usual.

# 25

# The Final Chapter

My letter to Julia Davies would have been delivered to The Meadows in April. Anyone opening the letter would have known whether Jim Miller was there or not and hopefully replied soon after. Of course Julia's letter pointed out that Jim Miller was only there for six days before he died. Some twist of fate must have kept my letter in the 'in tray'. In a way I was truly grateful for that glitch because had it not happened, I would not have discovered how Jim Miller spent his final days. And I would never have been introduced to their old friend who told me about the last years in the life of Jim Miller and John Bellord.

Matlock Bath is a pretty village on the River Derwent. Its main street follows the river and at the eastern end of the village, rounds northward and leaves the river to continue on toward Matlock. Situated on that bend, on the opposite side of the road, is the Balti Restaurant where Carol and I ate last time we were there, with Masson Road off an uphill turning, a few yards from the eatery. Jim and John left there some time ago but friends who'd helped them lived close by.

From the care home where Jim Miller died, I was given the

name and contact number of the man who'd been looking after him for many years. To respect a delicate situation and his privacy, I will call him Mr. Brown. I told him I was an old friend of Jim Miller's who hadn't seen him since 1975 and heard that he'd died. To my surprise, Mr. Brown agreed to meet.

As far as I could gather, from the limited information imparted by Mr. Brown, Miller and Bellord had led quiet lives. They did not own a house or car and lived, at least since the Browns met and married, in rented accommodation. John Bellord continued learning to play the organ and Jim Miller spent his time writing a book on healing and philosophy, a project he'd started decades before but never finished. According to Mr. Brown, he'd lost heart altogether when John Bellord died.

# Author's note

I wasn't present at the court scene described in the first chapter. But the event did take place at exactly that time and John Bellord's words from the witness stand were reported verbatim by the press.

A few names have been changed to protect those who needed protecting.

The dialogue throughout the story is typical rather than verbatim: as close as it can be allowing for distortion through editing the lengthy, sometimes wandering, conversations.

The legal correspondence and reports are verbatim and printed in full, as are the headlines featured in the media.

Throughout the story I refer to Miller and Bellord sometimes by their surnames or full names and at other times by Christian names only. This was how it was throughout my association with them.

# Acknowledgements

My wife Carol, who had 'Paying for the Past' rattling the house for years in its various manifestations, deserves nothing but the highest praise. She has read, pencilled and ploughed her way through several drafts and never once doubted it would survive.

I can never express enough gratitude to Margaret Cutler for her support, before, during and after the crime, and to John Howell and Joan Sparrow, for their kindness during the aftermath of Miller and Bellord's arrest.

Thanks to those who stood by me at the time and my friends and readers, who looked at my story prior to publication and gave feedback through several drafts. Eve and Duncan of Ardvreck, who looked after us on our trips to Ullapool, provided us with a warm bed and arranged for Marius, a local fisherman, to take us back to Priest Island in 1996.

The people of Ullapool, mentioned in my book, who recalled, as first hand witnesses, the time Miller and Bellord spent in their community and their recollections of the manhunt and events of 1975 and 1976 as they unfolded.

I will always be grateful to my solicitor Robert Rogers who guided me through the tricky confrontation with the Sussex fraud squad and the following protracted negotiations that led to my exoneration.

Thanks to Dovecote Press, current publishers of Fraser

Darling's books and writings, for allowing me to quote passages from, Island Years.

I am grateful to Norman Luck, Chief Crime Reporter for the Daily Express in 1975, who agreed to meet me again, decades after the crime, and for his interest in getting my book published. Sadly Norman died of cancer in 2012.

Thanks also, to Eugene Costello who gave permission to quote from his book, 'White Gold'.

# Author Bio

Geoff Green wrote the first draft of Paying for the Past two decades ago. His true crime adventure has been life changing, taking a decade to go through the courts. A diary he kept at the time, along with media and public interest, inspired him to finish the book.

Geoff left school at fourteen and took a dozen jobs before heading back to education and a first class honours degree in osteopathic medicine. He brushed up his writing skills, published research and articles in peer reviewed journals and completed two novels, The Sand Hide and Cold Friends.

Geoff works as an osteopath and lives in the Sussex village of Steyning with his wife Carol, a sculptor. Together they have walked some of the greatest treks in the world including, the Inca Trail in Peru, jungle hikes in The Amazon basin, The Grand Canyon and the Great wall of China.

Geoff grew up with folk music, skiffle and rock and roll. The Dices, his first band, formed around 1957, entertained punters in pubs, clubs and dance halls. He sang with other bands at the Shepherds Bush and Chiswick Empires before joining pop group, Peter and the Wolves, in 1962.

Between working and writing, Geoff loves to paint, walk, read, eat out and watch a good film.